UNDERSTANDING
ADOLESCENCE

By the same author

Coping with Illness (Hodder and Stoughton)
Roots and Shoots (Hodder and Stoughton)
As Trees Walking (The Paternoster Press)
Restoring the Image (The Paternoster Press)

UNDERSTANDING ADOLESCENCE

Dr ROGER HURDING

HODDER AND STOUGHTON
LONDON SYDNEY AUCKLAND TORONTO

Bible quotations are taken from the New International Version, unless indicated otherwise.

British Library Cataloguing in Publication Data

Hurding, Roger F. (Roger Frederick), *1934–*
   Understanding adolescence
   1. Adolescence. Christian viewpoint
   I. Title   II. Series
   261.8'34235

   ISBN 0-340-42662 4

To Sarah, Simon and Rache,
loved and loving in adolescence
and beyond

CONTENTS

PREFACE

As the dedication of this book shows, Joy and I are profoundly grateful for the 'workshop on adolescence' our three offspring have engaged us in over the past dozen years or so. At times we have been slow learners, but, on the whole, the enterprise has been both enlightening and exhilarating. This is not to deny that there have been periods when this educational journey has been exhausting and infuriating. None the less, more than anyone, Sarah, Simon and Rache have been the mentors who have shaped the thinking (and feeling!) that is written into the pages of *Understanding Adolescence*.

There have, of course, been other influences – not least our recollections of our own teenage years, back in the post-war days when, unbelievably, there existed a state before the eruption of the world of pop, rock and the general newsworthiness of being young. My particular interest in adolescent patients within general practice in the 1960s was given a further boost by my work as a student health doctor throughout the 1970s. From the mid 1970s to the late 1980s our own three home-grown teenagers (together with 'The Cousins', my sister's much-loved quartet – Ruth, Jane, Peter and David) have kept us on our toes in all things adolescent.

In the daunting task of writing a book about the most complex and significant decade in anybody's life I am grateful to a wide range of resources. As well as to Christine Plunkett, my patient editor, I should like to express thanks to the staff at Bristol public library; to Su Brown, librarian at Trinity College; to Louise Baker of ECL Bookshop, Bristol; to John Smith, head of student services at Bristol Polytechnic, for some pointers in the area of race relations;

to Steve Butler for his encouragement over the chapter on 'Changing Lifestyles' and to Michael Healey for permission to share something of his story in the closing pages of this book. Let me finally declare my gratitude to the myriad of young people who have contributed incognito, including those from Christ Church, Clifton, who filled in question-naires. I have given innumerable cameo sketches of the stories of adolescents, culled from a variety of sources, including the experiences of many I have known person-ally. In two or three cases, I have compiled accounts from a mixture of actual situations and imagined detail. Names, places and other 'hard facts' have been obscured, where necessary, to protect identity and honour confidences.

This adolescence is an 'in-between' time. It is like a bridge spanning, on the one side, the world of make-believe and playtime, and, on the other, the world of bank accounts and trying to earn a living. Overall, the traffic is one-way; and yet many of the travellers seem to dart to and fro on the bridge, sometimes appearing to enter adulthood, sometimes returning to the ways of children. All 'grown-ups', by definition, have crossed over – even though many seem to have short memories for the delights and pains of the crossing. They grow fearful of and anxious about those who make the journey after them, appearing to notice only the ones who shout and do wild things on the way over. They seem not to see that the majority cross unscathed.

It is the aim of this book to help both teenagers and older people to realise the *normality* of the 'in-between' years. Adolescence is not an affliction: it is a natural transition on the road to maturity. It is to be understood rather than feared, celebrated rather than bemoaned. Brother Roger, of the Christian community in Taizé, France, seems to sound the right note when he declares:

> . . . I would go to the uttermost ends of the earth, to the world's farthest end, to tell over and over again that I trust the new generations, that I trust the young.[1]

Roger F. Hurding

1

CHANGING BODIES

Until I was 15 I was more familiar with Africa than my own body

Joe Orton

A friend of mine, contrasting his own two small daughters with a family of adolescent children, said with some apprehension, 'I don't know how we'll manage when they reach their teen years!' He preferred the present realities of nappy-changing, bath-time and nights up with an unwell baby to the prospect of boyfriend-changing, pub-time and nights up waiting for a footloose daughter. A similar concern is expressed in a letter from a housemaster to a teenager's mother: 'The affectionate small boy who has quite justifiably been your pride and joy is about to undergo such a transformation that you may well begin to wonder whether you have mothered a monster.'[1]

Views like these of the disruptive nature of pending adolescence are widespread – not least because of the fear that a much-loved child will change out of all recognition and will somehow become unmanageable. The anxiety may be of losing someone very precious. And yet, as the schoolmaster added in his letter: 'If you stand *firm as a rock* in the midst of his tempestuous life the small boy whom you thought you had lost will return to you as a charming young man . . . He will have been worth waiting for.' That is the point. The journey of adolescence may or may not be tempestuous, but its outcome will, more often than not, be worth waiting for.

Let us, then, seek to understand the nature of the

journey by first looking at some of the physical and emotional changes in the early years of the shift from childhood to adult life.

The Growing Body

The most obvious aspect of approaching adolescence is bodily change, a change designed to fit the developing young person for the demands and responsibilities of maturity. This physical transformation (known as 'puberty', from the Latin *pubertas*, 'the age of manhood') is stimulated and controlled by a complex interplay of the body's hormones. The secretion of these 'chemical messengers' into the bloodstream, besides prompting the development of the specifically sexual parts of the body, leads to general growth. The heart nearly doubles in size, the lungs expand, the muscles fill out and both stature and weight increase. The boy or girl begins to take on the strength and fertility of a man's or woman's body.

In Girls

Although there is a great variation in both the age of onset and the duration of the 'growth spurt', girls are averagely eighteen months to two years ahead of boys. In girls, the increase in height and weight usually begins between 11 and 13, though it may start as early as 7 or 8 or be as late as 14 or 15. There is variety, too, in the order of the appearance of sexual characteristics. Generally, though, the onset of puberty is shown by a rounding of the hips and a slight swelling of the breasts (the so-called 'bud' stage of development). Downy, non-pigmented hair begins to appear in the pubic region, while the womb, vagina, clitoris and labia (or 'lips') get bigger. The pubic hair takes on its natural colour while 'body' hair appears in the armpits. The breasts continue to swell, the nipples start to show pigmentation and the areola (the pinkish area around the nipple) widens.

Usually, it is not until the growth spurt has reached its peak that the periods begin (the menarche). It may take another year before the emerging young woman can conceive, by which time the breasts will have become fuller and the 'body' hair more luxuriant.

In Boys

The physical changes of puberty in boys take place on average between the ages of 13 and 15, although maturing may begin as early as 10 or as late as 16 or so. Again, there is a wide range in the sequence of events. Frequently, the first visible signs of hormonal activity are the enlargement of the testes and scrotum, and the appearance of pubic hair. As the growth spurt begins, the penis gets bigger and hair starts to appear in the moustache area and under the arms. Later, as the larynx (Adam's apple) grows, the voice begins to break; further, sperm production increases and emissions of semen occur during sleep. In time, the pubic hair becomes pigmented and facial hair grows in the beard region. The transformation of Shakespeare's 'whining school-boy, with his satchel, and shining morning face' into 'the lover, sighing like furnace' is well on its way.

The Body and the Emotions

I have described the physical aspects of puberty in matter-of-fact terms, but every adolescent, parent, teacher and youth leader knows that the emotional and psychological strain of these changes can be considerable. At any age, the person we feel we are is tied up with our view of our bodies. If we are 'at home' with our bodies, accepting their size and shape, all well and good, but life is not so easy when bodily proportions change from day to day with the rapidity of adolescent growth. Further, our idea of body-image is strongly affected by other people and the mass media. If everyone declares that beauty is pear-shaped then those with a lean and hungry look may feel out of sorts. If

the slimmest of figures is widely acclaimed then those who
are broad in the beam are, literally, out of shape. Pressures
like these are especially acute in the early teen years and
can show themselves in anxiety about the growth spurt and
the accompanying sexual changes.

Similarly, there may be stress about the body's racial
characteristics – often aggravated by the prejudices of
others. One boy, from a family which had immigrated
shortly before, was told by other pupils, 'We're not going to
play with you because you're coloured.' This youngster did
not wash for many days and then said to the same group,
'I'm not coloured . . . I'm just dirty.' This denial of who one
is, as expressed through the body, is a sad reflection of the
racism in many parts of our society. Fortunately, many
young people from ethnic minorities are able to declare
that 'black is beautiful' and hold their heads high.

Worry about Growth

There are two elements in the rapid change in height and
weight that can bother young people: the timing and the
nature of the spurt.

The timing of change I still have a vivid memory of
standing in a bus with a school-friend when we were both
aged about 13. We felt we were in our prime: full of zest,
reasonably bright, good at sport. We positively glowed
when an elderly woman, eyeing our bare legs and grazed
footballers' knees, turned to her companions and said
something to the effect of, 'Look at those two; they're like
young gods!' That was my peak of physical glory for, within
the next year or so, my friend outstripped me with his
growth spurt – and I never caught up! One of the tallest in
the class before puberty, I was reduced to 'average height'
by the time we reached the fifth form. Feelings of inferiority, as in my case, may arise when the growth of puberty is
delayed – particularly among boys, where the competitive
spirit of being bigger, if not better, is strong. Conversely, an

early growth spurt can give a sense of superiority. One young man, when asked how he had felt about his increased stature, replied, 'How did I feel about it at the time? I wasn't really too bothered. I towered above everybody else. I quite enjoyed it actually – I don't think it hindered me in any way.'[2]

The nature of change   Whereas the timing of the growth spurt can be a problem to both girls and boys, the nature of that change can also lead to a great deal of embarrassment and awkwardness. The growth in different parts of the body varies in rate. The head, hands and feet are the first to reach adult proportions, while arms and legs grow faster than the torso. As a result, a girl may feel her prematurely large hands are ugly and be unhappy about wearing rings and bracelets. Another may complain that her feet have been too big for ages and now she is 'all legs'.

One paediatrician has commented, 'A boy stops growing out of his trousers (at least in length) a year before he stops growing out of his jackets.'[3] There is a particular type of agony for many boys at this stage in that, when most of the girls in their class have developed obvious sexual attractiveness, they are battling with long, gangling limbs, trousers that are too short, voices that go up and down and crops of facial pimples. It is a time of acute inner pain when kerbs are tripped up, doors are banged into, cups of coffee are knocked over and long hours spent in front of mirrors fail to reassure.

Worry about Sexual Changes

The difficulties of accommodating an unfamiliarly large body are made worse by the sexual changes of puberty. As with the growth spurt, there can be concern about both the timing and quality of development. Among 12-year-old girls, early maturing is seen as a disadvantage because they are still at the age when other children, of either sex, are simply companions. However, by the age of 14 or 15, girls value evidence of their emerging sexuality.

Whereas girls can be uneasy with early signs of sexual change, boys are often anxious when puberty is delayed. Research has suggested that male 'late developers' tend to be less popular, more talkative and restless, and more inclined to low self-esteem and feelings of rejection.[4] This sounds to me like a classic vicious circle in which adolescent boys, already feeling inferior among their deep-voiced, bigger contemporaries, are made to feel worse by the favouritism shown towards the more mature 'copers'.

In girls   Even where the rate of development is average, there can be a great deal of anxiety about the quality of change. Girls may be concerned, for example, about the size of their breasts – often in relation to the ideal figure of advertisements. When a girl feels that her bust is too big, she may become round-shouldered and wear large, loose-fitting clothes to hide her shape. On the other hand, breasts that are smaller than average may lead to feelings of sexual inferiority that can persist into adult life.

During my years working as a doctor among students, I saw many women in their late teens and early twenties who were worried about their small breasts; others in their thirties and forties seen in counselling situations still lacked assurance of their femininity for the same reason. One wonders how much such women are the victims of male-dominated advertising. It is essential to realise that, just as all bodily proportions vary from one person to another, so there is considerable range in the size of the bust. Small breasts do not mean that a girl or woman is less arousable or desirable sexually – or, for that matter, that one day she will not be able to breast-feed her baby.

Although the late onset of periods may be viewed anxiously by the adolescent girl (and, perhaps, even more by her mother), it is extremely rare for there to be any serious medical reason for the delay. The body's cycle is, of course, sensitive to all physical factors and so, for example, poor nutrition and long-term illness can slow down the arrival of the menarche. However, in cultures where the standard of living is adequate for everyday needs, it is emotional and mental stress that are the commonest causes of delay. Anxiety over a change of school, moving house or leaving home, the strain of trying to find a job or starting employment, the loss of a valued friendship, the break-up of the parents' marriage, the death of someone close, worry about being accepted by others or finding a boyfriend, can all hold up the start of menstruation.

Where a 17-year-old, say, is still waiting for her first period, it is reasonable to consult the family doctor. However, if she is of average height for her age, shows signs of normal sexual development (the growth of breasts, pubic hair, etc.) and particularly if her mother and her mother's mother also have a history of late menarche, then there is no need for concern. It is only on the rare occasion when a girl of 15 or 16 not only has delayed periods but is of short stature, shows no evidence of breast development and has a different pattern from her mother's and maternal grandmother's cycle that medical investigations are needed.

Another source of worry about periods is in their frequency. The fact is that the adolescent menstrual rhythm is *not* usually the 'textbook' one of a span of 28 days from the beginning of one period to the start of the next. The variation can be anything from 18 to 45 days during the first few years of having periods – and each period may last for 3 to 8 days.

Apart from pregnancy and anorexia nervosa (which will be discussed in Chapters 7 and 8 respectively), it is quite common for whole periods to be missed for months or even a year or two. As with the delayed menarche this is usually due to stress. Many young women find, for example, their periods vanish during the run-up to an important exam or interview. Others lose them on leaving home and setting up in a new place of work or study. I remember one student whose periods stopped just before her first term at university and did not start again until her finals were over.

Besides understanding the variation in the onset and frequency of periods, it is important for both the teenager and those around her to try to avoid a generally negative view of menstruation. Commonly called 'the curse', it is easy for periods to be regarded with dread as a great disrupter of engagements. It is not unusual for there to be accompanying headache, backache, dizziness, abdominal cramp and bloated feelings – particularly with the initial periods. When a girl is encouraged to take these in her stride, such symptoms usually become more manageable. Where they persist to an unpleasant degree, and are not relieved by simple pain relief, then medical advice can be sought.

In boys There are, of course, parallel anxieties which can preoccupy the adolescent boy. Generally these concerns relate either to whether physical development is normal or to the coping with unfamiliar sexual urges. In the first category, boys in their early teens may be worried if their hips are more rounded than those of their male friends. The fear that their masculinity is in doubt may be made worse if, at mid-adolescence, they notice certain breast changes. In fact all teenage boys experience an enlargement of the pinkish area around the nipple and up to 20 or 30 per cent also have a visible swelling of the breast tissues, sometimes with local tenderness. Such young men can be reassured: they are not changing into girls! After the start of the growth spurt, the balance in the body's hormones adjusts so that normal male contours develop.

School changing-rooms are the scene of anxious comparison. As well as fears about looking like a girl, adolescent boys may be concerned that their maleness is not male enough. In particular, a teenager may be worried that his penis is too small and he may need a great deal of assurance that the size of the organ has nothing to do with his virility or, eventually, his ability to give sexual satisfaction.

More generally, the awakening sexual urges of puberty can lead to much anxiety about being normal. Erections of the penis, for instance, may be a focus of concern. Sometimes the teenager is puzzled because he often wakes in the morning with an erect penis, fearing (or hoping!) that he is 'oversexed'. He needs to learn that a full bladder can stimulate the penis as much as sexual desire. At other times he may be embarrassed rather than puzzled, feeling that his ready erections show a lack of self-control. This embarrassment may be specially strong when wearing tight jeans, standing in a bus or train, or in female company.

I recall one young patient who suffered greatly because of his acute awareness of his erections, seeing these as the mark of being sinful rather than manful. It is sad that a natural response to everyday stimuli can be viewed *in itself* as morally wrong rather than as a mark of normal maturing. The teenager who can learn to relax – and even rejoice – in his sexual development will find, in turn, that his erections are a less pressing issue.

The adolescent boy may also be troubled by his first 'wet dreams', when he may wake from sleep to find himself sticky with freshly discharged semen. These nocturnal emissions may or may not be accompanied by dreams of an erotic nature. The first ejaculation – whether during a wet dream or from masturbating – may be a source of worry to the unprepared teenager. Before puberty, it is common for boys – even as early as infancy – to receive some pleasure from stimulating the penis to erection. Even so, in adolescence, the first experience of sudden emission of seminal fluid can be overwhelming. (Masturbation, in turn, can itself become a focus of anxiety and will be dealt with more fully in Chapter 6). There is often a tendency for wet dreams to be more problematic when masturbation is not practised – and vice versa. In one day recently I had conversations with two men who looked back on their early adolescence. One had never masturbated but had been greatly perplexed by ejaculating in his sleep; the other had not experienced wet dreams but had become a compulsive masturbator. There is great variety in normality.

The Body's Dilemma

We have seen something of the profound, and sometimes bewildering, changes that take place in the bodies of young men and women during the early years of adolescence. The strains and stresses of coming to terms with a growing and changing body are, in our modern society, made more acute by the realities of early puberty and late marriages.

Early Puberty

There is strong evidence that the physical growth of children and teenagers has speeded up over the last 100 years so that the changes of puberty occur faster and earlier today.[5] As a result, full adult height is now reached at 16–18 and both stature and height are greater in contemporary young adults than in former generations. One writer has pointed out that the original seats in La Scala opera house in Milan (built in the 1770s) are 13 inches wide, whereas new seats need to be 24 inches across to be comfortable. In 1962, Dr James Tanner reported that 16½-year-old English boys at Marlborough College averaged just over 4 inches taller in the 1950s than in the 1870s. In 1970, it was observed that the feet of the American male had been increasing by ⅓ inch in length (one shoe size) in each succeeding generation.

Most of us who are in our middle years or older have the impression that the peak of growth in adolescence comes earlier and results in taller products than in our own teenage years. I was reminded of this quite forcibly the other day when in discussion with the musical director of a Bristol church. A number of the church's choir vestments had been 'borrowed' by girls from a local school who had not yet reached their adolescent growth spurt. It was the shorter robes of the more ancient choir members that were taken: none of the garments belonging to the tall younger men and women of the choir was suitable.

Another clear marker of the speeding up of adolescent

development is found in the earlier average age for the onset of periods. It is established that the menarche has come sooner by about four months every ten years since 1850. A young woman in the early years of the Victorian era was likely to start her periods between the ages of 16 and 17 rather than in the 12 to 14-year-old range that is common today. It seems that there has been a flattening out of this rate of change since the early 1970s. Perhaps this is just as well in terms of human sexuality and fertility for, at the former rate, it has been estimated that by the year 2240 girls of 4 would be having periods! Although there is a great deal of evidence to indicate that an earlier menarche relates to improved nutrition, health care and housing conditions, it is suggested that there is a natural, or biological, lower limit at just over an average age of 12.

Later Marriage

Along with the trend towards earlier maturing there has been an opposite movement towards later marriage. In former civilisations and in primitive societies throughout history, marriages have been arranged or encouraged for offspring of a much younger age. In ancient Rome, for example, girls of 12–14 married boys of 16–20 and a young woman who was still unmarried at 19 was regarded as an old maid. Similarly, among Jews at the time of Christ it was the custom to marry early. This sometimes seemed to depend more on parental decision than on the young person's sexual maturity as girls under the age of 12 (and therefore minors by Jewish law) could be married off by the father. More generally, it was the father who chose a wife for his son and, in turn, it was the girl's father who said 'yes' or 'no' to the prospective son-in-law.

We see an earlier example of this pattern in Genesis 24 in the story of Abraham's servant who was sent to the area of his master's family roots to look for a wife for Isaac. Fortunately for Isaac (for Rebekah was not only resource-ful but 'very beautiful'), her father, Bethuel, backed by brother Laban, agreed on the match. The existence of these 'Biblical marriage bureaux' meant that young men could expect to marry at the age of 16 or 17 while, as we have seen, the women were often married off much younger.

Parallel patterns to the early marriages of the past still exist in certain cultures today. For example, among tribal peoples, such as the Arapesh of the Pacific, a girl's first period is celebrated as the beginning of fertility and the immediate gateway to sexual union.[6] In all these examples the majority of young men and women consummate their marriages once sexual maturity is reached.

In marked contrast to early and primitive societies, there has been a trend towards later marriages in Western civilisation over the last 400 years or so. In the late sixteenth century women usually married at about 20, at 22 during the eighteenth century and at an average of 25 years during the first half of the twentieth century. Since the Second World War there has been a tendency to marry a little earlier. The mean age for men to marry is usually a couple of years older than for women.[7]

In Rome, 2,000 years ago, a 12-year-old girl who was marrying shed the symbols of childhood one day – her toys and simple tunic – to take up the emblems of womanhood the next – spindle, distaff and, following the wedding night, a long dress, or stola. There were no 'in-between' years. Today, in the West, earlier puberty and later marriage leads to the prolonged period of change we call adolescence. It is the adjustment to the more drawn-out changes in attitudes, identity, relationships and allegiance among contemporary teenagers that is the theme of the rest of this book.

2

CHANGING IDENTITIES

*Don't laugh at youth for his affectations; he is only
trying on one face after another to find his own*
                                    Logan Pearsall Smith

Alison West is typical of many in their mid-teen years. The
middle of three sisters, she always missed out on the
responsibility given to the eldest, Mary, and the favouritism showered on the youngest, Paula. Leaving school at the
age of 16 with four CSEs, she felt acutely the gulf between
herself and her bright older sister, now at university and
studying to be a lawyer. She was aware, too, that now that
Mary was away from home she lived in the shadow of Paula
who, at the age of 14, shamed her with her various enthusiasms and successes. Paula was winning prizes at interschool swimming matches and was generally praised as a
most promising cello player. Alison sensed keenly her own
overweight ineptness in all things sporting and the music
teacher's censure that she was tone-deaf!

It was during the long summer months between leaving
school and the vague prospect of taking up with a YTS job
that Alison came to the conclusion that she must make her
mark on the dismissive world around her. It was not that
she wanted to hurt her parents: she simply wanted some
sort of reaction from them. Mary was hiking round Europe
and, to Alison's annoyance, sending beautifully-written
postcards home every week or so, while Paula was impress-
ing everyone by attending a music workshop in Devon – for
which, so their parents kept announcing, she had saved up

from her own pocket-money. And so Alison, lost for ideas as it were, simply left home.

She had put money by from baby-sitting and a weekly paper-round and so was able to buy a single ticket for a northern city where an old school-friend of hers now lived. Her mother had said goodbye to her that morning when Alison boarded the bus for the local town – ostensibly for a day looking round the shops, but in reality to catch the train North. Her unease grew to anxious concern when Alison was not home for their evening meal. Following two frantic hours of contacting as many of Alison's friends as they could, without success, Mr and Mrs West were relieved to hear the phone ring and receive a 'reverse charges' call from Merseyside. Alison loved her parents and, having reached her friend's house, felt she must phone home and explain.

Explain? Explain what? She did her best to answer the fusillade of questions but, amid her mother's tears and her father's angry accusations, she felt strangely exonerated. She already knew, in her head at least, that her parents cared for her, but somehow the strength of their reaction reassured her. She, Alison West, overweight, not very bright nor specially talented, did matter after all.

In today's jargon, Alison was having an 'identity crisis' and was suffering from 'role confusion'. In other words, she did not know who she was, deep down inside, nor quite what sort of person she should be. Her story is just one example of the innumerable ways that crises of identity can show themselves. Let us, then, look more closely at why a changing sense of the self is so crucial in the journey from childhood to adulthood.

Personal Identity

Most people in their more mature years have some sense of who they are and it can be instructive to sit down with pen and paper and make a list of, say, twenty statements, completing the sentence, 'I am . . .' I might declare that I am a human being, a man, a Christian, a husband, a father, a son, a brother, an uncle, a nephew, a friend, a doctor, a counsellor, a lecturer, a writer, a reader, a church leader, and so on. Such admissions are, on the whole, safe and really rather respectable. They are simple statements of fact which can be verified by others through observation, the perusal of marriage and birth certificates and the assessment of other documents.

To say, for example, 'I am a lecturer' is a straight confession of a particular role I have at specific times of the year at a certain theological college in Bristol. But as I continue with my list, I find that I have written down first the safe 'roles' of everyday life and I am beginning to wrestle with words that test my awareness of what I am like as a person: 'I am interesting (or am I?)', 'I am humorous (who says?)', and so on.

These uncertainties remind me that even in adult life we can have our 'identity crises'. I vividly recall, not so many years ago, an occasion when I was suddenly thrown as to just who I really was. Joy and I had willingly agreed that our home could be the base from which a very good friend, Carol, would be married. Circumstances were such that it was impractical for her father to give her away and so an uncle of hers, who was a member of the diplomatic service overseas, had been asked to do the honours. As I understood it, there had been comparatively little recent contact within the family and the uncle and his wife had met neither the bridegroom nor ourselves previously.

In the midst of the feverish round of last-minute activities before the drive to church, Carol's uncle and aunt, both of whom were titled, arrived in a sports car. I, still dressed in jersey and cords, opened the car door to Carol's elegantly attired aunt. She fixed me with her aristocratic eye and asked, 'And *who* are you?' My identikit checklist was of no avail. I was 'caught without a wedding garment'. I was neither the bridegroom nor a member of the bride's family and my declared status as 'simply a friend', from whose house Carol was getting married, seemed not to impress.

Fortunately, such occasions of acute uncertainty are relatively rare in most people's adult years. And yet for many in their mid or late adolescence there can be times of real crisis when the question, 'And who are you?' is impossible to cope with – simply because the inner query 'Who am I?' is still unanswered.

Dick Keyes has written helpfully about this quest for a sense of 'I am me' in his book, *Beyond Identity*. He points out that the word 'identity' has the same root as 'identical' and implies the idea of 'sameness'. He argues that when it is used psychologically 'a true and positive sense of identity' has two sides: an awareness of 'self-sameness' and the presence of 'self-respect'.[1] In other words, a sense of identity is found where we see ourselves as reasonably 'together' as people and where, on the whole, we are at peace with what we see.

Ogden Nash's rhyme 'The Octopus' gives an example of a spot of difficulty over a sense of identity:

> Tell me, oh octopus, I begs
> Is those things arms, or is they legs?
> I marvel at thee, octopus
> If I were thou, I'd call me us.[2]

In this ditty, the observer cannot imagine a creature with so many parts having any sense of 'self-sameness', let alone experiencing self-respect!

Personal Identity in Childhood

However, our view of who we are does not suddenly take shape in our teen years. From the cradle to the grave our assessment of ourselves is being continually moulded and modified. One particularly important time before adolescence, in which the child begins to develop a clear sense of who she or he is, is between the ages of 2½ and 4 years. If the age of 2 is the 'age of self-will' in which the child tests parents and the environment to their limits, the following couple of years can be called the 'age of identification'.[3]

Within this period a process takes place in which the child first of all *imitates* what the parents do. In fact, this copying of adult action starts even earlier, between the ages of 1 and 2: if there is gardening to be done then little John or Jane will be there also, perhaps using a toothbrush to copy Mum's or Dad's digging movements; if peas are to be shelled in the kitchen then the 2-year-old is there as well, up on a stool, with his or her own bowl and accumulation of scattered peas. In time, this mimicking becomes more sophisticated because the 2½ to 3-year-old is also *suggestible* and readily picks up how Mum and Dad are feeling. If a parent is basically courageous, the child will be too; where a mother or father is riddled with anxiety then a son or daughter may become anxious as well.

Thirdly, and by the age of 3 to 4, the child passes through a time of *identifying* with his or her parents. In effect the boy or girl has moved on from saying 'I act like Mum or Dad' through 'I feel like Mum or Dad' to 'I *am* Mum or Dad'! These identifications are crucial as, to some extent, they may last throughout life. The daughter who identifies with a caring, neighbourly mother may well grow up to be a concerned and helpful member of the community. A son who says 'I'm Dad' and struts around the house as if he owned it may develop into a young man as pompous as his father.

As I have suggested, this fashioning into a parent's likeness may be for good or ill. Imitating, being suggestible and identifying can be the means of picking up both positive and negative patterns of behaviour, feeling and simply being. However, by the age of 4 or so the child usually (and most parents will be glad of this!) moves beyond identifying too closely with Mum or Dad. At this stage, a child can, in effect, say 'I'm Jane' or 'I'm John'. He or she has a sense of 'I'm *me*', an awareness of identity that is then lived out in the 'age of individuality' (4 to 7) and the 'age of socialisation' (7 to 12).

Where parents, in spite of all their faults, have been loving and caring, these later years of childhood will see the emergence of a boy or girl who is reasonably self-assured, has a conscience shaped by parental values and is encouraged in the building up of both personality and relating to others in shared activity.[4] Most of us can remember something of that period in our own lives before the bodily changes of puberty set in – very good years for many, when appetites were strong, there was a lot of energy and imagination, and friends were special without being too sensitive or clinging. Parents, too, may look back at that time with gratitude (the difficult, worrying bits are easily forgotten) for it was often a time for their own education when they saw the world afresh through their children's eyes. As Martha, the young housemaid in Frances Hodgson Burnett's *The Secret Garden*, said of her own mother, 'It's like she says: "A woman as brings up twelve children learns something besides her ABC. Children's as good as 'rithmetic to set you findin' out things." '[5]

Personal Identity in Adolescence

I have spent some time emphasising the emergence of a sense of identity during childhood because that feeling of 'I am me' in the 6- or 8-year-old is the raw material which will be freshly mixed within the teen years. For many this mixing is a reasonably smooth blending; for some, like Alison West whom we thought about at the beginning of the chapter, it is a severe shake-up.

It was with such as Alison in mind that Erik Erikson, the American psychologist, first coined the term 'identity crisis'. In fact, during the 1960s and 1970s, this phrase became an essential part of everyday language in university halls and on college campuses both sides of the Atlantic. Erikson once saw a notice at Harvard university which announced: 'Identity crisis. 6.00 p.m. Friday, Room B128. All welcome.'[6] Having an identity crisis became an obligatory part of tertiary education!

However, the idea that every adolescent needs to go through such an experience is dated. More recent research seems to establish that only 25 to 35 per cent of the total population of teenagers at any particular age suffers the sort of disturbances that Erikson once described as 'normative' for young people. John C. Coleman, in his comprehensive *The Nature of Adolescence*, concludes:

> It seems probable . . . that for the majority of adolescents the most viable course will be to avoid any sudden identity crisis, adapting very gradually over a period of years to the changes in identity experienced by them.[7]

This 'gradual adaptation' has many aspects, including the bodily changes we considered in chapter 1, as well as transformations in ways of thinking, adjustments to emotional independence and new understandings of the roles to be lived out day by day. In the coming chapters we shall pick up with some of the more relational and social perspectives of these changes, but, for the moment, let us look briefly at the more individual facets of teenage identity: *body-image*, *thought-world* and *identity achievement*.

Body-image   How we view our own bodies is an integral part of our idea of just who we are and the question of 'body-image' can preoccupy the adolescent mind enormously. We have already seen how such matters as the growth spurt and the size of a girl's breasts or a boy's penis can become a daily worry to the self-conscious teenager. In a survey I carried out among young people at a church youth club concern over various aspects of physical appearance, especially in early to mid-adolescence, was marked. In reply to the question 'What do you like most about yourself?' one girl of 14 said, 'From my knees down to my ankles'. Her shapely legs were a source of reassurance to her. However, in answer to 'What do you like least about yourself?' she wrote, 'My face [!]'.

In the more racist areas of society, the sensitivity with which teenagers often view themselves is heightened by the bigoted attitudes of others. Sometimes these malevolent influences are resisted as when adolescents proclaim that 'black is beautiful'; at other times cruel comments can lead to a longing to be different, as when one British girl from the Caribbean would scrub herself daily to get rid of the dark hue of her skin. Those from mixed parentage, as we shall see later, may feel particularly at a loss. Although many adjust well, and indeed seem especially gifted and attractive, others face great inner conflict as to which race and culture they really belong.

We shall return again and again to the matter of body-image since how the young person sees himself or herself physically (or imagines others regard his or her appearance) is a key ingredient in the adjustments of the teen years.

Thought-world   Part and parcel of this sometimes obsessive interest in the body is the nature of adolescent reasoning. There is much that could be said here, but the work of David Elkind has helped to condense the discussion.[8] He uses the phrase 'adolescent egocentrism' to underline the teenager's essential fixation on the self. Unlike children before puberty, who tend to think very factually ('Mum has bought me a new coat for Christmas and so I now have two'), adolescents are inclined to reflect on wider possibilities ('Mum bought me a new coat for Christmas – I bet she's ashamed of me in that old one!').

The young person now has acute self-consciousness to contend with and part of this is to know not only what he or she thinks but to be aware of what others are, or might be, thinking. This leads to Elkind's idea of the 'imaginary audience' where the teenager, because she is preoccupied with, say, her rounded shoulders, believes that everyone else is centring their thoughts on them. This persistent concern about appearance can lead to one adolescent's conviction that her figure is admired by all around her and to another's that his spotty skin is the source of endless criticism.

Another characteristic of teenage thinking is the 'personal fable', in which the young person's imagination is kindled to see himself or herself as very special indeed, as experiencing unique suffering or misery, or as possessing great powers over circumstances and other people. The stories, either factual or fictional, that an adolescent recounts within may be poured out on to the pages of a diary. These are very private documents and woe to the parent who yields to the temptation to pry! Apart from the invasion of privacy, the mother or father who gives way to curiosity may chance upon a flight of fancy which will disturb their dreams: 'Grandma is clearly a witch and eats little children for breakfast – I'll see if she'll eat Susie on Sunday' – or 'Last night's bank raid was my best yet – I'll go for the "big one" tomorrow!'

Two diaries which illustrate the rich variety of adolescent reflection and which any of us can enter are those of Anne Frank and Adrian Mole. In *The Diary of Anne Frank* we meet the beautifully written musings of a Jewish Dutch girl in her early teens, hiding away from the Germans during the Second World War, along with family and friends. Soon after she had experienced her first few periods, her awareness of her changing identity and its link with her body-image come through in this entry for January 5th, 1944:

> Sis Heyster also writes that girls of this age don't feel quite certain of themselves, and discover that they themselves are individuals with ideas, thoughts, and habits. After I came here, when I was just fourteen, I began to think about myself sooner than most girls, and to know that I am a 'person'. Sometimes, when I lie in bed at night, I have a terrible desire to feel my breasts and to listen to the quiet rhythmic beat of my heart.[9]

In contrast, Sue Townsend's *The Secret Diary of Adrian Mole* is fictitious and is a masterpiece of adolescent 'personal fable'. Adrian Mole, troubled by acne and his deep longings for Pandora and convinced that he is both an intellectual and a poet, fantasises just before his fourteenth birthday on what he would do with £30,000. He writes of the prospects of his return from travelling the globe:

> When I came back from the world I would be tall, brown and full of ironical experiences and Pandora would cry into her pillow at night because of the chance she missed to be Mrs Pandora Mole. I would qualify to be a vet in record time then I would buy a farmhouse. I would convert one room into a study so that I could have somewhere quiet to be intellectual in.
>
> I wouldn't waste thirty thousand pounds on buying a semi-detached house![10]

Identity achieved Somehow or other, often in fits and starts, the young person gradually comes through the adjustments to body-image and changed ways of thinking to the achievement of a sense of 'I am me'. Sometimes this quest is drawn out and the journey is full of uncertainties as to who he or she really is. Mark, at the age of 18, brings in some money by painting signboards and hopes, one day, to be an instructor in physical education. He met his 16-year-old girlfriend, Katy, at an athletics club where they both run.

When interviewed with her, he declared, 'I wanted to be the best sportsman. I'm not very bright . . . I wanted to impress the girls.'

On being asked, 'Do you have a true self, then?' he replied, 'No, I don't think so. I change, like Jekyll and Hyde.' He later spoke of his father's strong reaction to some misdemeanour he, Mark, had committed: 'Dad was overpowering. Dad really scared me . . . I took up running . . . I got a bit more freedom through running.'[11]

Sometimes, though, the realisation of a clear-cut identity comes suddenly, often after many more limited awakenings. This was true for Emily. She had had strange feelings about the fragility of her very being on a number of occasions during her mid-teens. In the kitchen on her father's birthday, when she was 18, and following a candle-lit celebration meal with her parents, she said to him, 'If you and Mum hadn't met and married, I wouldn't exist.' This was said with the appreciation of life's precarious nature and yet matter-of-factly, with a new and certain knowledge of personal value and individuality.

Sexual Identity

As has already been implied, the movement towards the achievement of a general sense of identity includes the adolescent's awareness of his maleness or her femaleness. In other words, the teenager is able, in time, to say not only 'I am me' but 'I am a man', or 'I am a woman'. It is here that the issues are often confused because we need to talk about both *gender* (society's ideas on masculinity and femininity) and *sex* (the biological distinctions between male and female). Elaine Storkey clarifies this discussion, with a particular emphasis on womanhood:

> To be female is simply to have a certain anatomy. To be a woman is to be surrounded by a whole set of gender assumptions: ideas of femininity, appropriate roles and behaviour. The problem is that most people do not recognise the difference between sex and gender. They see all their attitudes about being a woman as part of the natural order of things. They are 'givens'.[12]

Today, when the debates about feminism and sexism are increasingly out in the open, the distinctions between sex and gender have become pressingly important. The traditional assumptions that if one is male one should be 'masculine' (that is to say, a dominant, 'up-front', aggressive, decisive and forthright 'go-getter') or, if female, one should be 'feminine' (that is to say, a self-effacing, 'back seat', compliant, passive, conforming 'stay-at-home') are challenged by many of us who seek to stress the common humanity of men and women, without denying essential biological differences.[13]

Let us look briefly then at how these concepts of sex and gender affect the developing adolescent. First of all, we need to look back to childhood once more to get our bearings.

Sexual Identity in Childhood

In spite of parental voices to the contrary, it is virtually impossible for a stranger to distinguish a fully-clothed baby girl or boy by simply looking at the child. (No! the pink or blue wrappings may *not* be the precise clue they used to be!) And yet most parents tend to talk to and handle their infant differently depending on the child's sex. In one experiment, at the University of Sussex, mothers were invited into a laboratory to play with babies they had never met before, and the results were filmed. At various times, and with a range of mothers, the same baby was presented as either a girl or a boy.

This research established some very different ways of handling the children in relation to which sex they were believed to be. For example, 'boys' were given a toy hammer and 'girls' a doll to play with, but, perhaps more significant, a restless 'boy' was responded to by further attempts to play with 'him', while a 'girl' who kept fidgeting was seen to need a good cuddle.[14]

Whatever any intrinsic distinctions there might be between the sexes in the first year of life, there is no doubt that the majority of parents – at least traditionally – have brought up their growing children according to certain stereotypes. It has been pointed out that fathers, in particular, have often shown more concern that their sons turn out to be 'masculine' (graduating, say, from rough-and-tumbles on the floor with Dad through warlike computer games to playing football for the local team) and that their daughters should develop as unquestionably 'feminine' (for instance, moving from playing with Cindy dolls to helping Mum with the cooking to training as a nurse).

Although children, on the whole, accept the everyday realities of their sex and gender, they can also receive a fair degree of latitude from the adult world over their patterns of behaviour before puberty. In many families a girl who loves to climb trees and kick a ball around with the lads will be acceptable – for the time being, anyway – as a 'tomboy'. Similarly, a son's disposition to solitude, reflection and study may, generally speaking, be tolerated at the age of 8 or 10. In both cases, a lot of parents will be less than at ease with a rugby-playing daughter of 16 or a son who writes poetry and shuns team games at the same age.

Sexual Identity in Adolescence

It is small wonder, then, that adolescents quite often find adjustments to sex and gender difficult. As well as trying to cope with their own inner turmoil, teenagers frequently experience pressures from teachers and friends, as well as parents, to conform to the expected rules of conduct. As a result, it is not unusual for those in the less secure days of their early teens to fit in readily with the accepted stereotypes. One 14-year-old girl reacted strongly to the idea of a man wearing a woman's clothes: 'I wouldn't go near him, ugh! . . . They must have something wrong with them, maybe they were brought up that way, because they shouldn't act feminine, that is our identity, that is our position, not theirs. They should be masculine.'[15]

On the other hand, young people in later adolescence seem more at home with their sexual identity. Mark, the 18-year-old runner mentioned earlier, though macho in many ways, was able to say in front of his girlfriend, Katy: 'I feel I'm quite feminine . . . I feel that's a compliment.'

Many older people may still have a great deal of difficulty in accepting the validity of such statements as Mark's about sex and gender. Prejudice about the roles of men and women run very deep – not least in certain Christian circles. Many traditional believers' families cultivate views on 'sex stereotypes' which owe more to the prevailing climate of the cultures they live in than to Biblical norms: boys that rush around in warring gangs, male adolescents who captain football teams and grown men who are ambitious, and even pushy, are acclaimed as 'normal'; girls who rock their dolls to sleep, female adolescents who acquire good shorthand speeds and adult women who are domestic and 'know their place' in a male world, are commended. Men who take up nursing or women who join the police force are not condemned openly, but are somehow felt to be not quite fitting in as they should.

Responses like these are perfectly understandable for we are all subject to some extent to the world we live in. Sadly though, there is sometimes a vigorous defence of male and female stereotypes on the grounds of the Scriptures' apparent teaching. This is not the place to explore this vital matter fully, but such views often neglect the harmony, mutuality and equality of men and women found both in the Creation narratives and in Paul's declaration in Galatians 3:28, which has been called 'The Magna Carta of Humanity'[16]:

There is neither Jew nor Greek, slave nor free, male nor female, for you are all one in Christ Jesus.

Whatever beliefs we hold on the place of women and men in the family, the Church and in the wider society, let us be prepared to learn from many young people who, in seeking to come to terms with their sexual identity, are often remarkably free from the sort of prejudice, that, however subtly, elevates men and demotes women. Mark is not the consistent figure of the macho male athlete: at times he actually feels it a 'compliment' to be in touch with his gentler, so-called 'feminine' side.

Sometimes adult unease about adolescent 'sex and gender' relates to fears of homosexuality. Here there can be the mistaken opinion that the quieter, more receptive qualities of certain men, and the dominant, more head-strong aspects of some women, *automatically* indicate a sexual attraction for the same sex. This is yet another stereotypical view which grossly oversimplifies the issues. We shall look more fully at this area in chapter 6.

God and Identity

As we have seen throughout this chapter, the key to the journey from childhood to adult life is the building of a new sense of identity – both as an individual ('I am me') and as a sexual being ('I am a young man', 'I am a young woman'). In many ways, this process inevitably involves 'adolescent egocentrism' in which the teenager is caught up with the need to be heard. Alison West, whose story opened this chapter, felt she had to step out of line into a bid for some sort of freedom before her family would acknowledge her. We have the essence of this inner pressure, to be recognised as a person in one's own right, in the opening lines of the song which rallied so many young adolescents in the early 1980s: Toyah Wilcox's 'I Wanna Be Free':

> I don't wanna go to school, don't wanna be
> nobody's fool, I wanna be me.

Apart from the catchy tune and Toyah's aggressive deliv-ery, the popularity of this piece was guaranteed by its appeal to the age-old teenagers' longing 'to be left alone' by those who want to run their lives for them. The search for identity was seen in the largely negative terms of what the singer did *not* want to be ('I don't wanna be sweet 'n' neat', and so on) in order to be herself ('I wanna be me . . . I wanna be free').

With respect to this legitimate quest for a sense of 'I am me', which can preoccupy many years in an adolescent's life, let us ask where God fits in. Is the whole enterprise

simply and solely a psychological and emotional realign-
ment that is untouched by anything the Bible might have to
say? In a later chapter, on 'changing loyalties', we shall
assess more fully the response of young people to higher
commitments, especially to the call of Christ. But here it
might be helpful to address ourselves to the perspective
of 'God and identity' in the teenager's growth towards
maturity.

Before looking at some relevant Scriptural principles it is
worth saying that the issue of personal identity dogs the
footsteps of most of us throughout our lives – in particular
during adolescence and in mid-life. Jules Feiffer, the
cartoonist, once made the point well:

> At sixteen I was stupid, confused, insecure and in-
> decisive. At twenty-five I was wise, self-confident,
> prepossessing and assertive. At forty-five I am stupid,
> confused, insecure and indecisive. Who would have
> supposed that maturity is only a short break in
> adolescence?[17]

Perhaps one of the abiding themes of both the teen years
and the middle years (incidentally, times when unemployment and retirement loom respectively) is the question of
wherein does my identity lie? Traditionally, the answer
given by many has been, 'Why, in my work of course!' It
can be especially aggravating for an out-of-work young
person of 19 or a newly redundant man or woman of 50 to
be asked by a stranger as an opening gambit, 'What do you
do?' Even worse, for many women, are the queries, 'What
does your father do?' or 'What does your husband do?',
with the implication that one's importance as a woman
must lie in the paid occupation of a male relative. However
much the adult world of full employment may look askance
at 'those mixed-up teenagers' it is the emphasis of many
young people on 'who I am', rather than 'what I do', that is
so refreshing. And this fits well, I believe, with Biblical
perspectives.

Erik Erikson, in his *Childhood and Society*, said this of adolescents: 'They are ever ready to install lasting idols and ideals as guardians of a final identity.'[18] And it is with reference to the 'idols and ideals' of youth that we can see the teenager's attempt to achieve that sense of 'self-sameness' and 'self-respect' which Dick Keyes describes as the essence of 'identity'. The Bible, of course, has much to say about idols (those people, things or causes that we worship) and ideals (those principles by which we live) and the part they play in the integration, or disintegration, of the personality. Erikson, though as far as I know never declaring a Christian commitment as such, has written elsewhere:

> How did man's need for individual identity evolve? Before Darwin, the answer was clear: because God created Adam in His own image, as a counterplayer of His Identity, and thus bequeathed to all man the glory and the despair of individuation and faith. I admit to not having come up with any better explanation.[19]

As we turn to the Scriptures we find that who we are depends on who God is. To use Erikson's phrase, we are 'counterplayers of His Identity' living out our lives in 'glory and despair'. Broadly speaking, men and women in the Bible either acknowledged that they were created by God, counterplayers who knew their need of forgiveness and help, or they resisted him with varying degrees of enthusiasm, setting themselves up as in control of their own destinies.

Job, for example, eventually declared to the Lord, 'I am unworthy – how can I reply to you?' (Job 40:4); the psalmist cried out, 'This poor man called, and the Lord heard him' (Ps. 34:6); Jeremiah, summoned to serve God while a youth, replied, 'Ah, Sovereign Lord . . . I do not know how to speak; I am only a child' (Jer. 1:6) and Peter, astounded by the miraculous catch of fish, fell at Jesus's knees and said, 'Go away from me, Lord; I am a sinful man!' (Luke 5:8).

In contrast, others fought tooth-and-nail against the claims of the Lord God, often, in so doing, virtually making themselves into gods. Biblical characters who thus met their judgment include: Jezebel, who plotted ruthlessly to further her husband's chaotic rule (2 Kings 9:30–7); Belshazzar, who set himself up 'against the Lord of heaven' (Dan. 5:22–31) and Herod Agrippa I, of whose oration the people shouted, 'This is the voice of a god, not of a man' (Acts 12:21–2).

In all the above examples, men and women stood or fell in their relating to the Lord. As Nikolai Berdyaev, the Russian writer, once put it, 'Where there is no God, there is no man': where God's existence is denied or where his relevance is dismissed, our very humanness can crumble to pieces. Conversely, our humanity only exists because God made us – and sustains us, if we will allow him. On our need to find out just who we are in relationship to the Lord God, including the requirement of a firm, psychological sense of identity, Dick Keyes writes:

> God is not a theological means to a higher psychological end. God is not a means to any other end. God is the Alpha and the Omega, the beginning and the end. Our true identity is found in accepting our status as creatures of this infinite Creator God and in rooting our sense of identity in his. Our identity is an identity derived.[20]

Both Moses and David found their identity as 'an identity derived'. When, on 'the mountain of God', the shepherd Moses stumbled across the bush that flamed and yet did not burn up, his reply to the one who called him by name was simple: 'Here I am' (Exod. 3:4). This statement, so straightforward as a declaration of one man's existence and availability before a holy God, soon gave way to doubts and questions. For Jehovah was suddenly asking too much of Moses. It was all very well for God to burn not only in the bush, as it were, but in anger. He had heard the cry of his people under the Egyptians' whiplash and was now ordering Moses to go to the despotic and unpredictable Pharaoh to ask for the release of the king's entire workforce! Moses was no Rambo-like, trigger-happy war veteran, prepared to shoot his way out of any tight corner. He said to God, not surprisingly, 'Who am I that I should go?'

It is here that Moses had to learn a profound lesson – a lesson which lays down the reality of an 'identity derived' for us all. When God assured him with the words, 'I will be with you', Moses found the whole proposition not only nerve-racking but vague. He needed to know the name of this God who confronted him, for it was only in the name that the true nature of a deity was revealed. This information would be his passport before the cross-questioning of his fellow Israelites. God's reply was devastating in its awesome simplicity: 'I AM WHO I AM. This is what you are to say to the Israelites: "I AM has sent me to you."' (Exod. 3:14).

Scholars have written much on the 'I am' statements of Jehovah, and the 'I am' sayings of Jesus recorded in John's gospel.[21] Whatever other shades of meaning they might have they are clearly declarations that God is God and he will brook no rivals. You or I can make 'I am' sentences, but they always emphasise our creatureliness and interdependence: 'I am a woman', 'I am a man', 'I am a bricklayer', 'I am a secretary', 'I am a student', 'I am a citizen' or, most fundamentally, 'I am a human being'. It is only God who can truly say, 'I AM WHO I AM' because it is only he who does not depend on anyone or anything else for his existence: he is the only one who does not have an 'identity derived'.

Among the Bible's teenagers, David stands out as a young man who, alone in the wilderness fending for his sheep and trusting the one above for help in despatching marauding beasts, saw that his sense of 'self-sameness' and 'self-respect' lay in his relationship with the 'Great I Am'. The youngest of the eight sons of Jesse, he could easily have been eaten up with 'adolescent egocentrism' for we read, 'He was ruddy, with a fine appearance and handsome features' (1 Sam. 16:12).

This lithe, sunburnt youth was not only a treat for the girls of Israel to gaze upon, he was highly gifted in other ways: his exploits in defending his father's flock, killing the fearsome Goliath and, in later years, 'leaping and dancing before the Lord' (2 Sam. 6:16) show his ability and athleticism; his earlier abilities as shepherd and boy-soldier paved the way for a man who knew how to survive on the run; and these somewhat macho traits were balanced by his musicianship on the harp and the flowering of a fine poetic style in the psalms.

And yet this highly talented young man was no strutting pop star, war-crazy hero or ambitious 'yuppie' on an ego trip. His sense of who he was did not rest in the conquests of battlefield, boardroom or bedroom (though in all these areas he was far from exemplary!), but in an 'identity derived'. In spite of all his gifts and all his faults, David's destiny was 'on target' for one reason only: he was 'a man after [the Lord's] own heart' (1 Sam. 13:14). Unlike Saul, whose giftedness went to his head, David trod the difficult path of fame in the only way any man or woman can – and keep their integrity. We read, 'In everything he did he had great success, because the Lord was with him' (1 Sam. 18:14).

Erikson is right. Somehow or other all young people (and adults for that matter) need to 'install lasting idols and ideals as guardians of a final identity'. The question is, which idols and ideals? Literally anything or anyone can become the centre of our lives: a friendship, a job, a sport, study, television, music, an admired leader, marriage, a career and, eventually, plans for that 'perfect' retirement.

Sometimes another person becomes the key to self-discovery. In the late 1960s and early 1970s the writings of R. D. Laing, the 'antipsychiatrist', became the path to personal insight for many in the student world. This guru-like figure explored the feelings of alienation which were specially prevalent among the adolescents of 'flower power', student sit-ins and marches against the bomb. One young man, who had seen me on a number of occasions, finally came to my consulting room with the smile of a new awakening and declared, 'I've been reading Laing, and I now understand myself!'

Sometimes it is a particular object or pursuit which becomes so all-absorbing that one's very existence is bound up with it and I can think of no better example of such an obsession than that of Toad's for motor-cars. Kenneth Grahame's *The Wind in the Willows* is brimful with perceptions about human, rather than animal, nature. His account of Badger's difficulty in dislodging Toad from his dangerous exploits on the highway is a prime instance of the tenacity with which we can cling to our 'idols and ideals'.

After giving the culprit a lengthy dressing down in the smoking-room of Toad Hall, Badger emerges with a limp, but suitably penitent, Toad. The senior animal explains to his friends that 'Toad has at last seen the error of his ways' and 'has undertaken to give up motor-cars entirely and for ever'. Rat is less convinced about the strength of Toad's contrition and 'could not help thinking he perceived something vaguely resembling a twinkle in that animal's still sorrowful eye'. Badger, though, sure of his counselling technique, persists, asking Toad to repeat before the others his full admissions of guilt and remorse which he had made earlier. Grahame continues:

> There was a long, long pause. Toad looked desperately this way and that, while the other animals waited in grave silence. At last he spoke.
>
> 'No!' he said a little sullenly, but stoutly; 'I'm *not* sorry. And it wasn't folly at all! It was simply glorious!'[22]

Treasures in Heaven

Whether the personal search for significance leads to a fixation on other people or on other things, the words of

Jesus on life's fundamental priorities are searchingly relevant. In the Sermon on the Mount he says this to his followers:

> Do not store up for yourselves treasures on earth, where moth and rust destroy, and where thieves break in and steal. But store up for yourselves treasures in heaven, where moth and rust do not destroy, and where thieves do not break in and steal. For where your treasure is, there your heart will be also (Matt 6:19–21).

The Greek word *thesauros* used here indicates a storeroom overflowing with oriental riches and garments and gives us a picture of all a person might desire in the here and now.[23] Jesus contrasts the folly of material greed with the call to store up 'treasures in heaven', that is to commit ourselves to putting God first. And this right choice is all-embracing, for the rest of Matthew 6 shows that storing up 'heavenly treasure' means a trusting obedience in the everyday realities of money, clothing, food and drink.

Jesus's punch line, 'For where your treasure is, there your heart will be also' has a lot to say about the 'idols and ideals' which lead the adolescent in search for identity. We can paraphrase our Lord's words as 'For where what you most desire in life is, there will your inner commitment and motivation be.' Dick Keyes brings out the challenge of this saying of Christ's well:

> Everyone has some kind of treasure. Everyone also has a heart – the inmost core of the self, your psychological and spiritual centre of gravity. Jesus says that your heart will move to reside wherever your treasure is. In other words, you make a symbolic extension of yourself outside yourself. If your treasure is a new suit, or car, that is where your heart is. If the boundaries of your self encompass that suit or car, your sense of identity is at stake when they are damaged. Hence

your disproportionate rage if soup gets spilled on your suit or your car is scratched.[24]

The good old-fashioned word for placing our treasure anywhere other than in God is *idolatry*. It is an uncompromising word, summoning up pictures of mindless people bowing low before mindless gods carved in wood or stone. And yet, as we have seen, both from the Scriptures and from everyday life that anyone or anything can become the object of our veneration. As G. K. Chesterton put it, 'When a man ceases to worship God he does not worship nothing, he worships anything.'[25] Some idolatries are easy to recognise – at least in other people! Others, because they weave their way in through the back door while we are busy proclaiming God's kingdom from the rooftop, may be hard to spot. Jim Wallis, founder of the Sojourners community in the black slums of Washington DC, gives a salutary warning:

> We were tempted to make an idol out of our simple lifestyle. Our identification with the poor threatened to become an idol. We were tempted to idolatry in our actions of public protest. Our principle of nonviolence became an inviting idol . . . Having exposed our idols in the larger culture, we came face-to-face with other idols closer to home. Being closer to home, they were harder to recognize.[26]

Adolescence is a time of 'changing identities' – of a search for personal, sexual and, as we shall see in the coming chapters, social identity. In this journey of exploration 'idols and ideals' are often experimented with, given temporary honour and then discarded. In time, though, choices have to be made and the course for adult life set. None of us is completely free of idolatry because our 'identity derived' readily looks this way and that to find someone or something to worship. When we run out of ideas, we can always worship ourselves!

And yet, Jesus's challenge remains: we are not to store up earthly treasures, living materialistically, but are called to hoard heavenly treasures, seeking first God's kingdom and righteousness (Matt. 6:33). Each of us, whether we are 18, 48 or 78, need to allow our 'idols and ideals' to give way to God's rightful sovereignty so that our identity can be secure in Christ. We, made in God's likeness, discover just who we really are in our relationship with the Son, who is 'the image of the invisible God' (Col. 1:15). We can come to him daily in confidence for the riches we seek – because, as Paul writes, in Christ 'are hidden all the treasures of wisdom and knowledge' (Col. 2:3).

3

CHANGING IMAGES

Young people are looking for a formula for putting on the universe

> Marshall McLuhan

Tom at 15 felt he was 'one of the lads'. He tolerated school most of the time, but he really lived for the weekends when he could spend many long hours with his mates. During the week, in term-time, he sweated his way through each day in blazer and tie, though he did his best to get his blazer as muddy as possible and found his tie more useful as a weapon than a garment. But at weekends he was Tom 'Morrissey' Collins, one of a gang of six 15- and 16-year-olds who stalked the local high street and park to impress the girls. Tom envied some of the older boys in his gang who were the proud possessors of lovingly polished 2-stroke scooters and small motor-bikes, and yet felt it worth keeping in with them as the bikers gave the gatherings of Tom and his friends, at street corners and outside pubs, 'a bit more class'.

Tom was typical of his age (mid-teens) and the age he lived in (the mid-1980s). During the week it was television, video, computer games, pop records and rock-music magazines that helped him survive school and a modicum of homework. Though he was always criticising the singers and groups, his favourite programmes were *Top of the Pops* and *The Tube*. He had watched much more telly when younger but he still made sure he saw *EastEnders*, *Brookside* and *Dallas* with the rest of the family. Sometimes he would persuade his mum to let him watch, along with his dad, *Hill Street Blues* and *The A-Team*. He could never understand why his mother was so bothered by the violence in these two programmes. He felt the beatings and killings were 'chicken feed' compared with the video 'nasty' he had seen with his mates the year before.

The previous Christmas, his father had appeared with a microcomputer and a mass of intriguing software so some evenings Tom, and occasionally one of his friends, would settle down to *Space Invaders* or *Hammurabi*. When there was no worthwhile television, Dad had not hired an exciting enough video film or when he was fed up with the computer games, he would curl up on his bed and listen to a record of his favourite band, The Smiths, or browse through the latest edition of *New Musical Express*.

The great thing about the end of some weeks though, apart from the routine chance to be seen in action in the nearby town, was the opportunity to take the bus to the city on Saturday or Sunday night for a rock concert. Tom and his mates always groomed themselves most thoroughly for this delight and appeared at the bus stop as six 'look alikes'. The year was 1985 and so they all had the 'flat-top' hairstyle – shaved close at the back and sides, but longer on top and held upright by generous lashings of gel (*en brosse*, like a brush, the French teacher at school called it).

Each of them wore baggy trousers, turned up at the ankles, and well-scuffed suede 'desert' boots. Depending on the weather, they either wore once-white T-shirts or looser, open-necked shirts and long-sleeved outsize Aran sweaters or cardigans. Tom though – and this is how he earned his nickname – looked the most like The Smiths' lead singer Morrissey, displaying a particularly good spike of hair at the front and wearing a fine pair of thick tortoiseshell-rimmed spectacles. On weekend nights Tom walked tall and stood at his rightful place at the head of the bus queue – for, to all intents and purposes, he *was* Morrissey.

We have cited Tom as just one teenager in a particular year. Equally, we could have taken any other 15-year-old, in any of the years between the mid-1950s and the advent of the 1990s, and produced a composite picture of a young person whose whole lifestyle was shot through with what is loosely called the 'pop culture'. The details would have varied with changes in the mass media: the waning influence of the cinema in the post-war years; the ascendancy of television over both the radio and the local cinema; the increasing success of video and computerisation; the bewildering kaleidoscope of pop and rock music reflected in the fads and fashions of the young.

However, behind the diversity we see, to quote Marshall McLuhan, young people who 'are looking for a formula for putting on the universe'.[1] They are seeking to participate in the world around in ways that give them, on the one hand, a sense of belonging to their particular set and, on the other hand, ways of shocking, rebelling against, or being simply different from the established order of things.

The 'formula' any particular Tom, or Thomasina, finds in any special year of their adolescence may be different from what they discovered the year before, or will hit upon a year later, but it will help them to 'put on the universe' for the time being. Putting it another way, and recalling Erikson from our last chapter, young people are always ready to incorporate 'idols and ideals' in their search for a sense of identity. And the fact is that the majority of teenagers today, who have access to the urbanised world, seek out idols and ideals, for at least part of their adolescent years, in some aspect or other of the pop culture.

There will always be youngsters, from homes without television, video recorders and computer games, who shun teenage magazines and are absorbed throughout by, say, classical music and fine literature. None-the-less, it is increasingly difficult in the West to survive from the age of 12 to 20 without some little outburst of contemporary fashion or some unguarded moment of foot-tapping to the beat of rock music, however distantly played.

Whether we like it or not, the pop scene, in all its diverse manifestations, shapes the lives of most of us in one way or another. Sociologists, as we shall see later, now talk of the 'teenagerisation' of the adult world. It is the adolescent supremely, though, who finds a sense of belonging, of *social* identity, in and through the changing images and lifestyles of our 'wired society'. Let us look now at some of the main aspects of the 'age of communication' and their relevance to the everyday lives of the young.

Television

In William Nicholson's film *The Vision*, an American-sponsored network, the People's Channel, is depicted as a monolith whose sole aim is to take over the airways of Europe in order to mastermind the Western world in opposition to the supposed Soviet threat.[2] In preparation for this takeover by satellite television each home is offered a free receiver dish. Behind-the-scenes research reveals that the targeted audience is 'soft at 8.30 p.m., Mondays'. The public face of the People's Channel has many of the trappings of a 'moral majority' Christianity: the general atmosphere of back-slapping goodwill brings the director to comment, 'Other networks are cold – we're warm'; and the entire production team closes its eyes in rapt silence before going on the air as they 'turn to God on the hour'.

In one scene, Grace Gardner (Lee Remick), the channel's American controller, takes the new presenter, James Marriner (Dirk Bogarde), into her private chapel within the network's complex. Standing before a crucifix with her crusading zeal shining forth, she declares, 'I'm a missionary. I've given up my life to serve others.'

'What's it all for, Grace?' asks James.

'We're going to rebuild the will of a continent.'

'With television?'

'Yes, with television,' she replies.

This view of television's all-pervasive nature, controlling the destinies of nations, is not far from the truth in the reckoning of many. And yet, in these days of BBC 1, BBC

2, ITV and Channel 4, along with the widespread prospect of cable TV, there need be little fear of the sort of mass brainwashing towards a particular political stance that a monopoly like the People's Channel might bring. Nevertheless, there are prophets of doom who hail the advent of 'the box' in declamatory terms: Professor Urie Bronfenbrenner has declared, 'Turning on the television set can turn off the process that transforms children into people'; Jerry Mander has written, 'Television is sensory deprivation'; and Roald Dahl has given the advice, 'just don't install the idiotic thing at all'.[3]

There is no doubt there are negative conclusions which can be drawn about the impact of television on the so-called 'television generation'. Martin Large's *Who's Bringing Them Up?*, for example, charts some of the research of the 1970s which describes a range of adverse effects in children who develop 'square eyes' on into early adolescence. Among these studies, the simple act of watching television repeatedly is criticised. It is pointed out that this habit often takes place in a darkened area where the child's entire attention is commanded by the patterns of coloured light at the far end of the room. The typical 'telly stare' is a gaze which is held with virtually no head movement and with eyes that are slightly unfocused. Assessment of brainwaves during watching reveals a general slowing down of their activity and the predominance of alpha waves – a pattern which also operates when the eyes are closed.

Herbert Krugmen of Florida has contrasted the 'spaced out' state of mind that arises with long stretches of viewing with the more actively engaged picture which emerges with reading.[4] The brain's electrical responses to the printed page show 'a picture of relaxed attention, interest and mental activity' whereas exposure to television reveals 'elements of both drowsiness and alertness' together with evidence of boredom.

In fairness though, there are books as well as visual programmes which can bore many of us to tears. Conversely, television can be arrestingly involving in what it presents and can thus (in spite of the different brain-waves!) at times rival a good book. The main contention in Martin Large's book is the 'great time robbery' in the lives of developing children where play, imagination and relating to others can all be undermined by the instant entertainment of the cathode-ray tube. He urges practical steps in order to create a 'more lively family culture', including carefully planned viewing and the priorities of bedtime stories, meals together without television and 'regular outings on Sundays instead of viewing'.[5]

Social surveys confirm what is a common observation in families with teenagers: that many young people begin to watch less television in early to mid-adolescence. Shared activities with teenage friends – whether disco-dancing or choir practice, a couple of hours in the pub or a couple of days' camping – begin to take precedence over the television. We have seen in the first two chapters some of the reasons for this switch of emphasis. As puberty arrives both bodily changes and the quest for a sense of personal and sexual identity drive youngsters together more and more. This coming together is the anvil on which feelings of belonging to one another are forged. Being with friends begins to have priority over watching the silver screen.

Even so, the pull of television is a very powerful one in any age group. By 1985, the world's TV audience was 2.5 billion people in 162 countries. In the same year, 98 per cent of British households had a television while nearly 50 per cent had the use of two or more sets. The number of man or woman hours spent in front of the box is staggering: averagely 4–5 hours a day in the United Kingdom; 6 hours in the United States; and 8 hours in Japan. After sleeping and working, viewing is the commonest way of spending time in our urbanised societies.[6] And, although the most extensive watching occurs in pre-school children and the elderly, many adolescents can still spend an average of three or more hours a day in front of the television.[7] In terms of leisure priorities, in one survey of six hundred young people (aged 14 to 19) from around Britain, 52 per cent said that they were more likely to be curled up in front of television than out on the sports field or drinking at the local pub.[8]

And what will our imaginary teenager be glued to over the twenty-three hours a week that he or she may be watching? As with the adult audience, the answer is probably anything and everything – and yet there are bound to be favourite programmes. As we saw with Tom 'Morrissey' Collins it is likely that soap operas, such as *EastEnders*, will include many young people among their fans. Slots like *Top of the Pops* (which about ten million watch), *The Tube*, *Soul Train*, *Whistle Test* and *The Chart Show*, with their strong appeals to the worlds of pop and rock music, will often be essential viewing. Documentaries which focus on the perennial subjects associated with adolescence – drug addiction, delinquency, anorexia and abortion – may be more riveting to worried parents than their sons or daughters.

The particular attractions of 'soap' and 'pop' in teenage viewing are expressions of two different, but important, aspects of adolescent life. The compulsiveness of many 'soaps' lies in their universal appeal to every age group. Grandparents, parents, other adults and youngsters can each identify primarily with their own generation, while being amused, intrigued or disgusted by the antics on the screen of those older or younger. Here there is a 'fly-on-the-wall' privilege which gives adult and teenager alike the opportunity 'to see what will happen next' to any one of a number of key characters – some loved, some hated, most tolerated. In the 'soap' there is, in effect, a continuous 'slice of life' which can be entered into, for half an hour or so twice a week, without having to take on board all the complexity and heartache of the saga. Sometimes, a series attracts by its depictions of the unattainable, dangling before the viewer visions of unbelievable wealth and power (as in *Dallas* and *Dynasty*); at other times, a sequence draws because of memories evoked or because the personalities shown are everyday, ordinary, accessible (as in *Brookside*, *EastEnders* and *Coronation Street*).

Whereas 'soap'-watching can be something of a family affair for the adolescent, the lure of 'pop' programmes lies in their very differentness from the adult world. Although the late 1980s have seen a new trend where the appeal of pop and rock has been carried into the lives of those in their twenties and thirties, slots like *Top of the Pops* and *The Chart Show* still have the capacity to make parents wince and react. As we shall argue more fully in the next chapter, each generation of teenagers seeks to find its own series of social identities, often expressed in the fads, fashions and music of the prevailing pop and rock cultures. Where Radio 1, discs and tape may provide the continuity of sound, television, along with teenage magazines and video, helps foster a sense of belonging in terms of the visual impact of hairstyle, teenage dress and overall 'image'.

Video

In the winter of 1982–3 the British tabloid press, which tends to see TV as a rival, celebrated the drop in the graph for the numbers watching television. The figures had risen for some years, but at last they had peaked and were now dipping – or so the popular papers thought. It was some time before this temporary lapse in viewing was seen to relate to the increasing success of the video recorder (VCR).[9] By 1985 nearly a third of British households (representing about twenty million people) possessed a VCR.[10] The advent of video has, of course, increased the choice of viewing greatly and this choice is opened even wider by the easy availability of films for hire through video libraries and shops.

Whatever research may say about the nature of brain-waves and the trancelike state that can be engendered through simply *watching* material on the television screen, it is here that we need to say more about the *content* of what is seen. The reality is that, through the hiring of 'adult' films (those classified by the British Board of Film Classification, or BBFC, as suitable for viewing by those 18 or over) from video shops and clubs, many children and teenagers under 18 are able to watch unsuitable material in the home. These category '18' and 'R 18' films often contain strong elements of horror, violence, the occult or explicit sex. One survey, carried out during the winter of 1983–4, revealed that over 57 per cent of those interviewed, aged 7 to 16, had seen at least one such film and nearly 30 per cent had seen four or more.[11]

Further, it is not unexpected that this same study discovered close links between parental attitudes and activities and the degree to which children and young adolescents find ready access to 'shock-horror' movies. Nearly 80 per cent of parents owning or renting VCRs were found to be members of video clubs and so, by implication, 'adult' films might be readily available in their homes. Further, the offspring of families which were lenient about viewing habits had seen significantly more 'video nasties' than those in families where there was greater circumspection and control over what was watched.

The choice of 'shock-horror' films that today's young people can make is depressingly wide. Although, in July 1984, restrictions were placed by Parliament on High Street rental shops, private video clubs have been able to side-step the law through mail order. Thus the subversive material known as 'video nasties' has continued in availability. These have been defined as those feature films that contain scenes 'of such violence and sadism involving either human beings or animals' that they would not be granted a BBFC certificate for general release.[12] Movies of this nature focus lingeringly on rape, torture, dismemberment, cannibalism and other obscenities, exhibiting titles like *The Living Dead*, *I Spit on Your Grave*, *Driller Killer* and *Zombie Flesh-Eaters*. The content of such films makes the street violence of *Starsky and Hutch* and the ribaldries of the *Benny Hill Show* look like a vicarage tea-party.

What effect does the watching of, say, *I Spit on Your Grave* have on a band of 13- or 16-year-olds crowded eagerly into a darkened room, while the household's parents are down at the pub or out for a meal?

Sociologists, public pressure groups and the purveyors of mass communication have argued to and fro for decades on the links, if any, between 'sex and violence', in what are loosely called 'the visual arts', and human behaviour. David Barrat in *Media Sociology* gives the example of paternalistic concern expressed in the *Edinburgh Review* in 1851!

> One powerful agent for the depraving of the boyish classes of our towns and cities is to be found in the cheap shows and theatres, which are so specially chosen and arranged for the attraction and ensnaring of the young. When for three-pence a boy can procure some hours of vivid enjoyment from exciting scenery, music and acting . . . it is not to be wondered at that the boy who is led on to haunt them becomes rapidly corrupted and demoralised, and seeks to be the doer of the infamies which have interested him as a spectator.[13]

The debate on the corruption of 'the boyish (and girlish) classes' has waxed and waned ever since. Barrat points out that from 1900 to the late 1930s the media were seen to have an essentially adverse effect, being blamed for both the rise of Nazism in Germany and the degradation of cultural standards throughout Western society. From about 1940 till the early 1960s various studies, especially in the United States, concluded that the former fears of mass manipulation had been ill-founded and that cinema and television were generally benign in their influence. Since the mid-1960s research has concentrated more on the *content* of programmes, acknowledging the great complexity of evaluating *effects*.[14]

Even so, Graham Melville-Thomas, the child psychiatrist, in a survey of work which has looked at the relationship between violent programmes and the lives of young viewers, draws important, though tentative, conclusions. For example, he notes a report in 1979 which reviewed over two hundred studies that indicated an increase of aggressive activity following the witnessing of violence. He adds:

> The accumulative effects on all types of young personality can still only be conjectured, but research to date strongly indicates associations between . . . aggressive behaviour and viewing violent material on television.[15]

He notes too that in 1982 the report on a comprehensive study by the National Institute for Mental Health established beyond all reasonable doubt that 'violence on the screen does have negative effects on children'.

When we turn our attention to the unbounded levels of sado-masochism and explicit sex in 'adult' films and the video nasties it would take an individual of extraordinarily cast-iron constitution, and possessing the dullest of imaginations, to deny links between viewing obscenities of such grossness and, at the very least, a contaminated thought-world. Sceptics have pointed out that there have always been brutality and cruelty within the fantasy world of the young – whether amid the evil step-parents, witches, wizards and giants of Hans Christian Andersen and the Brothers Grimm or the wargs, orcs, trolls, black riders and balrogs of Tolkien.

And yet there are key differences between the violence portrayed within the traditions of folklore and the worlds of the video nasty. The former, whatever its moments of terror (and I can still recall my childhood fright at the very *greenness* of the witch's skin in the film *The Wizard of Oz*), depicts the perennial battle between good and evil and, almost invariably, offers some resolution of the tale in favour of the just, diligent, oppressed or misunderstood. In contrast, the 'shock-horror' tactics of today's 'nasties' work hard simply to terrify and, it seems, corrupt. The settings are often the everyday ones of home or neighbourhood. Effort is made to give every sordid detail of degradation with clinical exactitude: 'No, you are not watching *Panorama* or *Arena*. But what you see is just as factual and could happen in *this* house *tonight* . . .'

And the videos are made particularly harrowing by filming them as if the viewer is either the perpetrator or the victim of whichever obscenity is on offer: 'It is *me* doing the torturing' or 'It is *me* being hacked to pieces!' The matter-of-factness of an 11-year-old girl, who said she had seen seven video nasties and five '18' rated adult films, indicates how these horrors can desensitise a young mind. She declared that her most remembered sequence was from *Halloween* 'where the boy chops his mum up' and added, '*Halloween* stayed in my mind for a week.'[16]

In 1985 Christina Preston, an English and drama teacher, investigated the imaginative world of 240 13-year-olds who attended a mixed comprehensive school in the Croydon area.[17] She asked them to complete a piece on 'the contents of a garden shed belonging to an elderly man who kept himself to himself'. Although there were amusing and thoughtful passages among the essays, generally she found them 'full of gratuitous violence, unemotional killing, scenes of blood and gore, and [a] lack of common humanity'. Unimpressed by classroom cries of 'They aren't scary, Miss', 'They make you laugh, Miss' and 'They don't worry me', she concluded that the watching of video nasties was relevant to the corrupted imaginations of these early adolescents. In her report on her findings she urged parents and teachers to be 'honest with our children over our complacency' about their viewing habits and argued for the need to open up discussion and critical evaluation among young people in the area of film watching.

In his well-documented book, *Children at Risk*, David Porter, in the related context of 'fantasy role-playing' games (particularly games like *Call of Cthulhu, Man, Myth and Magic*, *Dungeons and Dragons* and *Advanced Dungeons and Dragons*, which invite the young into worlds of horror, violence, explicit sex and the occult) warns:

> Human evil is not like mumps and chicken pox. It's not something to be got over early by deliberately expos-ing children to infection. Protection can, and should, mean preparation. It should mean that parents use the limited, priceless years of childhood and early adolesc-ence to equip their children to live in a world where not many will give them the same consideration.[18]

Responsible people like Christina Preston and David Porter point out the need for parents and teachers to prepare the young for the realities of life – without exposing them to the shock-horror of 'adult' films, video nasties, certain fantasy role-playing games, horror comics and, as we shall see, the sick end of the pop and rock music scene. Where children and adolescents have experience of such obscenities (and we have already mentioned the large numbers who have) they desperately need the chance to talk about what they have seen in order to come to terms with its dehumanising nature. The masks of glamour and suspense can thus be stripped off to reveal the true nature of the malicious matter viewed or played with.

Evil, of the flagrant variety we are discussing, has in fact a limited repertoire, tending to gravitate towards the lowest common denominator of banality and sordidness. 'Ex-teriorising the rottenness', to use the term of William James, the psychologist, can help the child or teenager not only to resist further temptation but find a diminution of the nightmare quality of the memory. Above all, where a young person is looking to Christ as the 'idol and ideal' of life, then a sense of cleansing and new beginnings can be found through confessing and sharing such bad encounters by talking to the Lord or a Christian friend.

Teenage Magazines

Along with the film world of cinema, television and video, the phenomenon of the 'teenage magazine' is a key influence in mediating pop culture to the young and in forming their identities. We can examine the content and style of such magazines by looking at a few examples in the market for those in early adolescence and then for the mid- to late teens. The ones considered are particularly aimed at girls and young women. Here, I am excluding the horror comics and pop and rock music magazines which, generally, appeal more to male readers. The former (for example, *Scream!*) tend to explore the same sinister territory as some of the fantasy role-playing games and video nasties[19] – and the latter will be referred to from time to time in the next chapter.

For Early Teens

A number of magazines, which include *Jackie*, *Patches*, *Nikki*, *Oh Boy* and *Blue Jeans*, are designed for and widely read by girls as they pass through puberty into their early teens. *Blue Jeans*, for example, in a survey in 1985 found that the average age of its readership was 14 – though the spread was from 9 to 24 years of age.

Generally, these magazines are well worked out for the preoccupations of their age-range: an increased awareness of physical appearance; an emphasis on beauty treatment and clothes; coping with the novelty of menstruation; handling relationships with boys; and an avid interest in the stars of TV, Radio 1 and pop music world. In an average edition, a girl might linger over the latest fashions in casual wear, receive advice on dealing with acne, bad breath and period pains, learn how to improve her posture and join a club for vegetarians, follow what happened to Pam when her parents burst into her party, tackle a crossword on the pop scene and pull out a full-sized colour picture of a 'hunky' rock star – and all this for the price of two second-class stamps!

Apart from the stories in photo-strip style, quizzes, brief chatty articles and ads, two regular features are the horoscopes and the answers page. Although the former can lead to fatalistic views about destiny and a superstitious attitude to life, the predictive comments in this set of magazines are not world-shattering. For example, 'Starspot' in *Nikki* (January 11th, 1986) urges its Leo readers: 'Stop being such a lazy lump, and get up and do something' and 'Stars' in *Blue Jeans* (January 2nd, 1988) offers those born under Aries: 'Boys mean trouble this week so stick with your girl friends.' Vagueness, and an occasional burst of common sense, seem to be the order of the day.

In *Nikki*, for the younger end of early adolescence, the answers page tends to deal with questions on such subjects as a lack of school friends, which parent to live with following a divorce, whether it is right to wear dangly earrings at school, how to give up nail-biting and the wherewithal of joining a fan club. Magazines like *Oh Boy*, *Blue Jeans* and *Jackie*, for a slightly older market, are likely to receive more letters on the ups and downs of relating to boys. Even though there may be few strictly moral guidelines given in the area of sexual involvement, counsel is usually a straight, 'no nonsense' affair. For example *Jackie* (January 9th, 1988) gives, in answer to a letter, advice which correctly argues the value of speaking and living truthfully, acknowledges the sexual fantasy-world of the mid-teens, stresses the illegality of underage sex but stops short of the moral issues of genital intimacy outside married commitment. We will pick up with this question of sexual morality among young people later in this chapter and again in chapter 6.

For Mid- to Late Teens

Answers to letters in magazines for the younger teenager, in pointing out the illegality of sex under 16, are one of the keys to the focus of many of the glossies for the older adolescent: that is to say, once a girl is 'of age' then sexual intercourse is seen as an integral part of normality – as well as legality. Having said that, there is no reason to believe that the more adult publications are not read eagerly by thousands of younger readers. As someone put it, '*Just Seventeen* is called that so that it'll be read by 13- to 14-year-olds!'[20] Thus, the early adolescent is prepared for 'life after 16' by the mammoth presuppositions on sex of editorial boards belonging to magazines for the older teenager. Glossy magazines for teenage girls have cashed in on adolescent sexual awareness, and consumerism, since the early 1970s and have, rightly, been the subject of a number of reports by The Responsible Society (now Family and Youth Concern).[21] Broadly, these magazines, though two or three times dearer, continue with the same 'recipe' as those for younger teenagers: the 'body beautiful' – its nurturing with skin cleansers, moisturisers and deodorants and its adornment with clothes, cosmetics and 'accessories'; the world of pop and film stardom; and questions about sex and sexuality. The gradation of interest and emphasis is carefully calibrated for the desired readership.

Like the magazines for younger teenagers, these glossies for late adolescent and young adult women have the horoscope and the answers page as regular features. The vague and humdrum predictions of *Jackie* and *Blue Jeans* give way to the more precise, yet equally humdrum, star-gazings of *Just Seventeen* and *19*. The more specific element is seen, for instance, in *Just Seventeen* (November 17th, 1983), which offers Aries readers, 'The 29th is a good day to put things into action – you'll have plenty of energy then'. Banality, and the pervasive mentality of a trust in fate, is suggested in *19* (July 1987) which puts forward 'The tide of luck flowing in your favour will continue . . .' for those born under the sign of Cancer, and 'Lady luck continues to smile on you . . .' for those under Gemini.

It is seemingly innocent enough to talk of 'the tide of luck' or 'Lady luck' as the source of favourable days ahead, but, when reflected on, such a view may be seen for the travesty of reality it is. Here the glossies, along with the wider press, feed a delusion that everyday life is all a matter of patterns laid down by the day of an individual's birth. The belief that human existence is governed by the stars is a far cry from the Biblical perspectives of the sovereignty of God, the subversive activity of the enemy and the day-to-day repercussions of people's choices. It is a clever ruse by the powers of darkness to keep young and old star-gazing while 'the devil prowls around like a roaring lion looking for someone to devour' (1 Pet. 5:8). The Book of Isaiah points to the folly of relying on the constellations as the key to preventing calamity:

> All the counsel you have received has only worn you
> out!
> Let your astrologers come forward,
> those stargazers who make predictions month by
> month,
> let them save you from what is coming upon you.
> Surely they are like stubble;
> the fire will burn them up.
> They cannot even save themselves
> from the power of the flame . . .
> Each of them goes on in his error;
> there is not one that can save you (Isa. 47:13–15).

The purveyors of horoscopes offer no warmth and comfort in life, let alone rescue from pending judgment. Isaiah, and indeed the whole of the Bible, declares again and again that the Lord God is the *only* origin of true counsel and an assured destiny:

> Turn to me and be saved,
> all you ends of the earth;
> for I am God, and there is no other (Isa. 45:22).

As well as in an easy-going acceptance of astrology and the ready marketing of consumerism, it is in the area of sexual mores that a Christian reader will have reservations about the glossies' ethos. Family and Youth Concern has singled out *Honey* as an example of a magazine with a permissive view on sex and sexuality. In their 1986 report they acknowledged some improvement in recent years, though they still found attitudes expressed with scarcely a nod towards any ethical consideration. For example, the report cites a feature in February 1986 which made out to discuss either side of the 'Should we live together or not?' debate. The woman *opposed* to moving in with a man friend declared herself to be 'the survivor of one failed marriage and several live-in arrangements' and 'did not discuss the moral implications of the debate at all'.[22]

The magazine *One to One*, launched in January 1988, has taken off the gloves to reveal an exceedingly frank approach to all matters sexual. Although broadly aimed at the young adult woman it seems open to the probability of a late adolescent readership, too: an initial questionnaire includes *Look Now* and *19* among the alternative monthlies that the new reader of *One to One* might buy; and the beautifully photographed women in its pages include several who could be either side of 20. The first edition is the beginning of a series which will amount to a sex manual of great explicitness and includes features on 'Staying in Love', 'The Pill', 'Sensual Massage', the problems of sexual involvement with a married man (sometimes called adultery!), a factual piece on sperm and a short story under the general title of 'Women Write Erotica'.

There is no doubt that one of the foundation-stones of teenage magazines is the reality of adolescent sexuality. Those written for younger readers are often sensitive to the awakening body awareness of girls in their early teens. Those glossies which seek to reach the minds and purses of older teenagers sell their wares with varying degrees of candour on sexual matters. The main articles and the answers page provide the touchstone which reveals the huge assumption, as we have earlier noted, that sexual intercourse, once a girl is 16, is simply part of the fabric of everyday life – to be protected by contraception, but *not* to be intruded upon by moral scruples.

Before completing this section, I must mention the refreshing attempt by one Christian organisation, Scripture Union, to launch a teenage magazine 'with a difference'. *Jam*, or 'Jesus and me', is aimed at the whole adolescent age-range and brings a down-to-earth Biblical perspective to the everyday concerns of young people. For example, the edition of September 1987 has an article on one 21-year-old's ordeal of being raped and the forgiveness she found towards those who violated her; a piece on wise spending and budgeting; an interview with Dr Veronica Moss of the Mildmay Mission hospital and the prejudice she encounters towards AIDS sufferers – even among the young; and a five-page spread on 'Sex 'n' That' which offers practical advice – on, for instance, the pressing question of 'How far can I go?' – without either prudishness or giving way on God's blueprint for sexual intimacy.

At this stage of a discussion on the pop culture we have, as it were, left Tom 'Morrissey' Collins standing tall at the head of the bus queue, his mind and heart full of the sight and sound of The Smiths in concert. Even though he would continue to have his fill of *The Tube* and *Hill Street Blues* on TV, enjoy the latest computer games, watch the occasional 'adult' video film with his dad, and drown out any potential silence with Radio 1 while in his room and with his Sony Walkman while out on his own, he would hardly ever see a copy of *Jackie* or *Just Seventeen*. Apart from the interruption of school-books his staple reading diet would still be made up of *Melody Maker*, *New Musical Express* and the comic magazine *Escape*. But it was the world of pop music which filled his mind and ears – through radio, TV, his steadily growing collection of records, the musical weeklies, school discos, gigs in the city's pubs, and, supremely, in the rock concerts he and his mates went to from time to time.

That was in 1985. In the next chapter we shall look at the wider story of pop and rock music in order to develop some sort of understanding of its complexity and thus tease out some guidelines for evaluating the whole pop scene – music, TV, video, magazines, fashion – in all its strengths and weaknesses. My desire is that our thinking and feeling will be more attuned to the excitement and boredom, hope and despair that mark the waxing and waning of pop culture.

4

CHANGING LIFESTYLES

*Pop, rather like politics, is something everyone has
an opinion on*

John Street

The monolithic world of pop and rock music impregnates
every part of the mass media with its language of the body
and the emotions. That voice has many tones – sometimes
soothing, sometimes strident – and cannot be ignored. Its
sounds and sights are found in the beat and chat of Radio 1,
in the exuberance and frenzy of *Top of the Pops*, *The Tube*
and *The Chart Show* on TV, in the extravaganza of such
video films as David Bowie's *Let's Dance* and Michael
Jackson's *Thriller* and in the singles and albums, cassettes
and compact discs of the ephemeral pop-record industry.
For the dedicated there are the live performances, whether
through gigs in pubs and night-clubs or in fully-fledged
concerts of well-known bands on tour. For those with
slenderer means (and, perhaps, anxious parents) there are
the discos, at school or in youth clubs, where the lack of live
music is forgotten in the pulsating crush.

But, as we have seen in the last chapter, it is not just the
music. Wherever the leisured young are the trappings of
pop and rock are not far away: in music mags like *NME*,
Melody Maker and *Smash Hits*; in the adulatory articles
and pull-out photos of *Blue Jeans* and *Just Seventeen*; in the
T-shirts, posters and mailings of fan clubs; in the chitchat of
school playgrounds and street corners; and, most of all, in
the hairstyles and clothes which trace a dozen and one

distinctions between one group of fans and another. For countless young people since the 1950s, for at least some of their adolescent years, pop and rock have become life itself.

Before taking a closer look at the strengths and weaknesses of the complex phenomenon of the pop world let us attempt some clarification of what is meant by the terms 'pop' and 'rock'. My own suspicion is that, like 'counselling' and 'psychotherapy', the concepts behind pop and rock are especially difficult to disentangle, because the words are rarely defined and are used interchangeably. Nevertheless, John Street makes the effort in his book *Rebel Rock*. He emphasises, on the one hand, the huge commercialisation of pop, which is 'mass-produced for mass sales to the young'. On the other hand, in rock, there is 'the ethos of self-expression which draws an intimate tie between the personal and the performance'. He cites, by way of an example, pop's freedom from needing to make political statements, whereas in rock 'the opportunity to speak out remains'.[1] Pop may sing about falling in love and having fun, rock about fighting the authorities and banning the bomb. Street sums up these overlapping definitions as follows:

> Chart-oriented pop can be distinguished from rock, for example, by the emphasis on live performance and by the character of its audience. Rock's following tends to be male; pop fans tend to be younger and female. Pop's essence is captured on record, rock's in concert.[2]

The world of music within the wider culture of pop and rock is no simple organism: it incorporates, for example, the commercialism of showbiz, the question of artistic endeavour and the communication of ideas, comments and beliefs. The production of one hit record or one rock concert rests on a whole mini-society of people and issues: funding, management, the relationship between the 'star' and the rest of the group, publicity, the image projected, the personality and lifestyle of the lead singer, lyrics, quality of music, amplification, the use of video, the sub-culture encouraged, and so on. So any attempt to evaluate the essence and extras of pop and rock must seek discern-ment amid the complexity of what is under scrutiny. Bland dismissals ('It's all of the devil') or naïve adulation ('What a marvellous world for the young') just will not do. John Street points to both the influence of pop and the need for discrimination when he writes:

> Pop's better moments are always matched by moments of crass commercialism or sickly sentimentality. And if pop's successes matter, then so do its failures. The guardians of public morality see only a series of bad moments. But in this they share the view that pop matters, that it affects the way people act and think. Whether pop is banal or brilliant, it is political because it affects or reflects the way people behave.[3]

It is, in fact, largely true that 'The guardians of public morality see only a series of bad moments.' Media outrage at the goings-on of Presley, the Beatles, the Stones, The Who, the Sex Pistols, Frankie Goes to Hollywood, Madonna, and the Beastie Boys, always makes good reading, listening or viewing. However, behind public notoriety can lie a strange mix of bad morals and good music – or, on the other hand, behind public acclaim we can discover a doubtful blend of good morals and bad music! How are we to get it right? Or, to put it another way, how are we to see pop culture in terms of the kingdom of God? Do we argue, as some do, that it is entirely enemy territory and is beyond redemption? Or do we recognise that every cultural enterprise not only can be, but must be open to the lordship of Christ? Can we begin to see, therefore, how God's mandate in Romans 12:1–2 might be applied in the changing lifestyles of the young, and not so young, who are exposed to or caught up in the pop world:

Therefore, I urge you, brothers, in view of God's mercy, to offer your bodies as living sacrifices, holy and pleasing to God – this is your spiritual act of worship. Do not conform any longer to the pattern of this world, but be transformed by the renewing of your mind. Then you will be able to test and approve what God's will is – his good, pleasing and perfect will.

With these verses in mind, I should like to look at the exciting, mercurial world of pop and rock under four headings: *pop as fun*; *pop as art*; *pop as message*; and *pop as identity*. In doing this, I hope to show that there are two sides to the discussion: pop, as well as being fun, art, message and identity, can also mean decadence, kitsch, nonsense and lostness. We shall keep this darker side in our thinking, too, as we continue with our enquiry.

Pop as Fun

The other day, while Joy was reading out the familiar story of the Prodigal Son, I was struck by a phrase which leapt out of the text at me: '. . . he heard music and dancing. So he called one of the servants and asked him what was going on' (Luke 15:25–6). As we know, the older brother felt his nose put out of joint by the generosity of the father on the return of his ne'er-do-well son. And, like the older brother, many of us hear the sounds of 'music and dancing' – perhaps from a teenager's bedroom – and, stuffily, we want to know what is going on. It may be that, along with the elder son, we fail to see that popular music and the culture behind it can be fun.

The word 'fun', though occasionally surfacing nowadays, as in the name of the pop group Fun Boy Three, is rather antiquated, smacking of prewar 'fun fairs' and the 'fun and games' of earlier generations in holiday mood. In our family, the phrase 'What fun!' is almost always used ironically and the caption 'Fun for all the family', meant to entice to some Christian conference or weekend away, will simply lead to groans of dismay. And yet the dictionary definitions of 'diversion', 'mirth', 'delight' and 'boisterous gaiety' are about right for much of the appeal of pop.

Johan Huizinga, the historian, in his book *Homo Ludens*, talks about humanity at play. He points out the uniqueness of the English word 'fun' and shows that it is an essential part of play. He declares the mystery of play in the order of things. Nature, he writes, could easily have given us more 'mechanical' ways of relaxing or discharging energy. Instead, 'she gave us play, with its tension, its mirth, and its fun.'[4] We see something of this delight within the richness of God's creativity in the Scriptures. The translations in the Jerusalem Bible bring this out, for example, in Psalm 104:33–4:

> I mean to sing to Yahweh all my life,
> I mean to play for my God as long as I live.
> May my musings be pleasing to him,
> For Yahweh gives me joy.

and in Proverbs 3:17:

> [Wisdom's] ways are filled with delight,
> her paths all lead to contentment.

Although parents, and the adult world generally, may find little delight in the colourful music and kaleidoscopic clothes and hair-dos of the younger generation, it is healthy to see that such styles often represent play as much as outrage, fun as much as rebellion. Adolescent years can be worth celebrating, and the 'diversions' and 'boisterous gaiety' of dressing up and feeling the rhythm and beat of the music can be simply enjoyable. The fun, of course, can be increased if parental eyebrows and voices are raised.

Our younger daughter, Rache, who once, I seem to remember, had brown hair would, during her mid-teens, use a range of rinses and dyes. Over a couple of years or so she produced a fine auburn tint which became the envy of many of her contemporaries. Twinkling-eyed, she would explain to me, 'The rinses simply bring out the natural redness of my hair.' The effectiveness of her point was demonstrated when new friends, seeing Rache with her brother Simon, whose hair is naturally red, would comment, 'Rache, we can see by your hair that you're brother and sister!' Currently, she is bringing out the 'natural blackness' of her hair.

In the pop world, as in all other aspects of life, anything can be taken to an excess – whether it is fashion, style, buying records, or following a particular band. Fun and play can turn into selfish pleasure-seeking. Such hedonism can be readily modelled on the lives and attitudes of admired groups and pop stars. Examples abound throughout the story of pop and rock – not least because outrageous behaviour that cocks a snook at the Establishment is infectious among the young. The cavorting antics of Elvis Presley, condemned by some churches, made girls swoon and cash-tills ring. The Rolling Stones were marketed as the 'bad guys' in contrast to the clean image of the Beatles: their every obscenity, real and imagined, intended and unintended, was made public property. In the late 1960s, where the Stones had been loud, brash and vulgar, that quintessential 'mod' group, The Who, were louder, brasher and more vulgar.

Although there is a limited vocabulary to vulgarity it was the emergence of punk rock, a decade later, that pushed that vocabulary to its limits in a most throughgoing way. The most notorious of these bands to reach the limelight was the Sex Pistols, launched by Malcolm McLaren in the autumn of 1975. The aggressive and loud-mouthed behaviour of this group became a byword as they were dropped by one major record company after another and banned by both television and radio. From 1975 to 1978 or so, punk rockers spat at one another at gigs, smashed up concert halls, scuffled with a new generation of Teds in the King's Road, ran high on amphetamines and 'pogo-ed' themselves silly, as they leapt up and down in the football stadium atmosphere of performances by the Clash, the Buzzcocks, the Damned and X-Ray Spex. It was Johnny Rotten, the Sex Pistols' lead singer, who summed up the uglier side of 'pop as fun' when he declared, 'We're doing exactly what we want to do – what we've always done.'[5]

The 'Lord of the Dance', to use Sidney Carter's phrase, is no killjoy and yet this same Lord calls us all to say 'no' to self-centredness and 'yes' to him. The challenge comes through clearly in Paul's call for us to offer our lives to God and his service, turning our backs on whatever opposes the coming of the kingdom. J. B. Phillips' version of Romans 12:2 is well known and is exactly right in relation to the huge pressures on young people to conform to the idols and ideals of the latest pop subculture: 'Don't let the world around you squeeze you into its own mould'. In 1 John 2:16, the worldly forces that cold-shoulder the Father of the universe comprise: 'The cravings of sinful man, the lust of his eyes and the boasting of what he has and does.' Here, the unbridled desires which can be fostered by the seamier and brasher faces of the pop industry are condemned. The insatiable quest for money, possessions, sexual favours, drug-induced 'highs' – whether indulged in by the 'stars' or their frenetic followers – are ruled out of court.

And yet, pop can be fun. The elements of play, relaxation and festivity, all legitimate parts of our human existence, are at their most life-enhancing where the lordship of Christ is owned. As in all other aspects of everyday life, the note of gratitude to a loving father is the right one:

> For everything God created is good, and nothing is to be rejected if it is received with thanksgiving, because it is consecrated by the word of God and prayer (1 Tim. 4:4–5).

Pop as Art

The idea of pop as art may sound pretentious – but it is important to say that, artistically speaking, as in all musical forms, there is good, bad and indifferent pop and rock. The criteria for assessing any art form are, of course, highly subjective. One person's 'rave' band is another person's 'trash' music. Who is to say, for example, that the Beatles were better than Buck's Fizz or The Who than Wham!? If the parameters of commercial success are taken then they have all done well, albeit for different audiences. If the durability of their musical output is looked at then other conclusions are drawn.

Leland Ryken, looking at literature from a Christian perspective, outlines the main ingredients of artistic achievement as form, progression, rhythm, variety in unity, contrast and balance, and style.[6] In examining these elements within the music of pop and rock in the last thirty years, most observers would have very different enthusiasms for this or that soloist, group or style. Although it is invidious for me to single out any particular band or individual for the final accolade, I should like nevertheless to consider briefly the rise of U2 as an example of genuine artistic endeavour within the world of rock and pop.

In March 1985 the *Rolling Stone* magazine hailed U2 with the cover headline, 'Our Choice: Band of the 80s'. Two years later, their album *The Joshua Tree* sold seven million copies in six weeks and the *New Musical Express* declared, 'To cross U2's path in 1987 is to look into rock and roll at its most potent.' How is it that four teenagers – Paul 'Bono' Hewson, Adam Clayton, Larry Mullen and Dave 'The Edge' Evans – from a multidenominational school in Dublin in the mid- and late 1970s, came to dominate the worldwide rock scene ten years later? No simple theories of string-pulling, financial backing, showbiz gimmickry or the chemistry of outrage seem to fit. Whatever the group's corporate and individual faults might be, there is no doubt that their music has the form, progression, rhythm, variety, contrast, balance and style of Ryken's hallmarks of artistry. Millions of young, and not so young, people are grateful that such talent has somehow been discovered and made widely available.

This is not the place to analyse fully the band's formidable musicianship and the impact of their stage performances both sides of the Atlantic – and so one or two anecdotal points will have to suffice. A comment in *Melody Maker* in 1982, when the group was just beginning to become big news in the rock world, indicates something of U2's rich creativity:

> U2 don't just ignore the conventions of a 25-year-old rock 'n' roll tradition, they deliberately push them aside and breathe their own new life into the body. It's nothing weird or radical – just voice, bass, guitar, drums – but it's the belief and imagination that counts. And U2's music can't help being influenced by the Irish tradition – it's laced with a lyricism and melodic sense that's missing from so much English rock.[7]

Success, of course, can go to the head so that what was once art becomes sullied as a means to an end – the goal of self-aggrandisement. In spite of the hyperboles of the media in the late 1980s, U2 have battled to keep their artistic integrity. Bono, the lead singer, in the face of a press that is adulatory about the 'U2 phenomenon', has tried, on a number of occasions, to focus attention on their music *as music*. For example, in an interview recorded in *Time Out* in the summer of 1987, he said, 'Some of the recent pieces on us have . . . forgotten that above all we're a rock band . . . The music is articulate in a way that I'm not.'[8]

And yet it remains to be said that an integral aspect of art is *content* and it is here that the lyrics of U2's music offer reflection and insight that have a truly Biblical perspective as their mainspring. Steve Turner, in his *Hungry for Heaven*, puts it like this:

. . . the band that has consolidated the redemptive theme in a most glorious way is Ireland's U2. With a backbone of Christian belief, and going completely against the orthodoxy of the day, they've managed to combine a restless frustration with the way things are alongside hope and celebration.[9]

Pop as Message

Many Christians, though, seem to see art as simply a vehicle for conceptual truth. Poetry and fictional prose are acceptable as long as the message is clear; painting and sculpture must be representative of sharply defined Biblical statements; theatre has to tell the story straight in Gospel terms; dance should be sanitised into forms heavy with a symbolism which speaks uncompromisingly; and music must mediate the good news. It would be an interesting exercise to apply the same criterion to other key areas of life – say the scientific, business and technological worlds: all chemical reactions must symbolise specific Scriptural truth; all annual meetings of commercial companies must declare clear Gospel messages on their shareholders' handouts; computer hardware and software must carry visible Biblical captions to be acceptable.

Surely, such views stand God's way with people on its head. He has called us, in creation, to be good stewards of every aspect of life – and that must include the cultural and artistic. There is no evidence that the mandate for faithful dominion was set aside by the Fall. Admittedly, in the here and now there is an uphill struggle ('By the sweat of your brow' – Gen 3:19), but we are reminded that *all* belongs to Christ ('He is before all things, and in him all things hold together' – Col. 1:17) and that God still has a redemptive plan for his created order ('the creation itself will be liberated from its bondage to decay and brought into the glorious freedom of the children of God' – Rom. 8:21).

A common danger is to play down the creative and

upgrade the redemptive in a way that threatens a split between these two interwoven themes of God's dealings with us. Thus, there is a tendency to *use*, for instance, music as purely a convenient medium 'for getting the message across': 'Just get the guitar chords right, turn up the amps and let 'em have the Gospel – right between the ears!' Instead of allowing Christ's lordship to influence every facet of the art rather than just the words, which are often sung *at* the audience, music and musicianship are debased. This is not to deny that there *are* messages in the pop culture – messages of outrage, rebellion, hedonism, nihilism, despair, goodwill, hope, and so on. The point is that the value of pop and rock as creativity is downgraded where a few chords are thrown together and wrapped around a sloganised 'message' – whether projected by thoroughgoing pagans, believers or whomever.

Many Christians in the world of pop and rock have wrestled with these issues. In the mid-1960s, Cliff Richard, following his conversion, experienced a great deal of uncertainty about God's calling. Already a ballad singer of great renown, he eventually decided against the carefully considered alternative of a career in teaching. He said of this dilemma, 'I admit I was foolish in considering teaching now. I thought it was not possible to remain a Christian and stay in show business. I now know it is. I shall continue my religious studies, but I shall not become a teacher until show business gives me up.'[10] Cliff's life of stardom now spans thirty years or so. He admits he is part of the world of 'showbiz' pop and yet, within the musical rules of that genre, he has always shown great integrity in the name of Christ – and that integrity carries its own 'message'.

From a quite different tradition – that of folk and rock – Bruce Cockburn is a Christian who has allowed the Lord's sovereignty to challenge the whole enterprise of his music-making. Dubbed a 'bearded mystic' in the early 1970s, this Canadian folk songwriter became a Christian in 1974 through reading C. S. Lewis and the Bible. Influenced later by jazz and reggae, and then, in turn, by more aggressive rock 'n' roll styles, he has produced a series of bestselling albums – including, for example, *Dancing in the Dragon's Jaws* – which demonstrate his personal pilgrimage and his wonder at the Lord of all. Interviewed at the Greenbelt Arts Festival in 1984, he put his finger on the links between an individual's faith and his or her artistic efforts: 'If you're going to celebrate Christ in your art then your art has to be of top quality or the best you can do.'[11] During the 1980s, Cockburn's faithfulness to the God of the Bible has led him to songs of great power and poignancy – songs which inveigh against political and social injustice in words that echo the holy rage of Isaiah and Amos.

There is, of course, a long history of protest in the saga of popular music, especially in the traditions of folk and rock, with roots running back to the blues and Gospel music of black America and to the folk-songs of the agricultural and industrial revolutions in Britain. Bob Dylan, of course, was one of the key folk/rock figures in the United States of the 1960s who led disillusioned young people in a 'basic contempt for the whole American life style, for its greed and smugness and stupidities, its war and its ghettoes, its heroes and villains.'[12]

Following his turning to Christ in the mid-1970s, Dylan's story of protest was freshly expressed in his albums, *Slow Train Coming*, *Saved* and *Shot of Love*, in which he declared the primacy of the Lord in his life and urged his listeners to repent. Many Christians rejoiced in the beauty and poetry of these songs, as well as in their uncompromising words. However, it can be argued that a greater maturity surfaces in the later album *Infidels*, of which David Porter has written:

> In the sixties and seventies Dylan's gift was to express on our behalf the pain of being human in an inhuman world. As a Christian, he has given us anthems, hymns, and battle-cries. Now in *Infidels* he has portrayed on our behalf the perplexity of the Christian who knows the reality of the old man still active in his

heart. It's a profoundly disturbing album, expressing for us the pain of knowing that perfection is within us – but not yet. Too obscure for a confession, it's at least his prayer-letter. I hope it gets well-read.[13]

Perhaps it is thus that Bob Dylan is moving closer to other Christian musicians like members of U2 and Bruce Cockburn who, to quote Martin Wroe, 'use their faith as a lens with which to bring the world and all its mystery and misery into focus.'[14]

Pop can be 'message', though, not only in right words set to good or bad music, or in good music performed in the name of Christ, but also in the context and purpose of music-making. Examples abound, including the tours of Cliff Richard for Tear Fund, Bruce Cockburn for Oxfam and U2 for Amnesty International.

Perhaps most outstanding, because of their vast popular appeal and the enormity of the suffering they sought to alleviate, were the combined efforts of Band Aid and Live Aid under the fund-raising genius of Bob Geldof. The success of Band Aid's *Do They Know it's Christmas?* in 1984, along with the equivalent from the United States, *We are the World*, was superseded by the great pop spectacle of Live Aid at Wembley in July 1985. The impact of the television presentation, revealing huge crowds of ardent young people mesmerised by the juxtaposition of leading rock and pop stars and haunting film sequences of starving Africa, unzipped the purses of the West. And somehow it was the gaunt figure of Bob Geldof, like some latter-day prophet, brooding over the proceedings, which stirred the sleeping consciences of millions. Eamon Dunphy put it like this:

Presiding over this spectacular collage of entertainment, darkened by death, stood Geldof, the archetypal rock 'n' roll hustler turned conscience of the Western world. Scruffy, in blue jeans and T-shirt, designer stubble lending menace to his anger, Geldof symbolised the difference between compassion which could be dirty and bitter, and complacency with its grey suits and collars and ties.[15]

The 'message' of pop can, of course, come in many ways and in many guises – whether in the raw, aggressive voice of the young unemployed in punk or Oi! music; the alliance between black reggae and white punk in 'Rock Against Racism'; the feminist perspectives of all-women bands like the Raincoats, the Slits and the Mistakes; the reflective challenges of a Bruce Springsteen or a Bruce Cockburn; the invitation to think and act politically in the songs of Billy Bragg; the impassioned harmonies of the black women's group Sweet Honey in the Rock with their exposure of all forms of oppression; the hopes of a better way evoked at a U2 concert; in the celebrations at a Greenbelt Arts Festival; or in the massive impact for a needy world in Band Aid, Live Aid or, joining forces with the full panoply of showbiz, in 1988's Comic Relief.

The voice of concern is not, of course, pop's only voice. In the middle of the fun and the artistry there are decadent lifestyles and bad music. And yet, let those with 'ears to hear' discern, amid the sounds of Babel, the prophetic voice – for we have a God who spoke through the pagan king Cyrus[16] – which challenges us all today through the likes of Geldof and, indeed, speaks in and through every aspect of humanity's culture. At times, even the world of pop and rock, in spite of its follies and excesses, can pick up with the message of the Lord God to his wayward people:

If you do away with the yoke of oppression,
with the pointing finger and malicious talk,
and if you spend yourselves on behalf of the hungry
and satisfy the needs of the oppressed,
then your light will rise in the darkness,
and your night will become like the noonday.

(Isa. 58:9–10).

Pop as Identity

Throughout these last two chapters we have seen how pop culture, in all its aspects, is the medium in which countless adolescents, for at least part of their teenage lives, develop an increasing sense of social identity. This feeling of belonging, as with the sense of personal identity we looked at in chapter 2, has within it the twin facets of 'sameness' and 'acceptance'. Here there is the need to identify with (be the same as) a wider group which, in turn, welcomes and accepts the individual within its ranks.

An integral part of this social cohesion is the fact that other clusters of people exist – both contemporaries and younger and older generations – who are seen as different, and therefore *not* belonging to the group in question. Teenagers need, for their growth in corporate identity, to be able to look askance at other teenagers 'who are not getting it quite right' as well as at younger siblings, who are to be pitied for their limited horizons, and at the adult world for its apparent dullness and pomposity. In other words, young people need to be able to say, 'This is *us*. *We* are different. Allow us to be that way . . .' And it is pop and rock music that often provide the rallying-points for this distinctiveness.

In the next two chapters, we shall look more fully at the socialisation of adolescents, but for the moment I want to consider just two aspects of social identity in relation to pop culture. These are, to use the sociologists' terms, *tribalism* and *teenagerisation*.

Tribalism

Trying to establish your identity in the earlier years of pop and rock was, in some ways, simpler than it is today: in the 1950s you were either a Teddy boy or not (in those particularly sexist days to be a Teddy girl was to be an appendage of the male species) and in the early and mid-1960s you could be a mod or a rocker. However, by the end of the

1960s and the beginning of the 1970s the range of subcultures was growing and teenagers had the choice of
joining the greasers, Hell's Angels, hippies or skinheads,
besides having the option still of residual mods, rockers
and even the occasional regrouping of Teds.

Penny, reflecting recently on her early adolescence back
in the early 1970s, recalls the clearly-defined tribalism
which her contemporaries adhered to. She was, at the ages
of 12 and 13, a devoted fan of the Osmond Brothers.
Wearing purple, brushed cotton flared jeans, a brown
corduroy, peaked cap and with 'I love Donny' written on
her trainers, she felt secure within her set. Those outside
her clique of teenyboppers belonged to strange and threatening tribes. These alien groupings comprised: the 'tarty'
ones – girls who worshipped David Bowie as Ziggy Star-
dust, painted their nails with dark varnish, wore high
platform heels and bedecked their faces with glitter and
star-shaped sequins; the 'hard' ones, mostly her female
peers' older brothers, who were followers of T Rex and
Slade and dressed up in thin cotton shirts, opened to the
waist, wide, short trousers, striped socks and high platform
boots; and the 'very hard' ones, fans of heavy rock bands
like Genesis, Uriah Heep and Jethro Tull, who grew their
hair long, wore leather jackets and included, for example,
14-year-olds that Penny knew dabbled in the occult.

This identification with specific lifestyles continued,
through the rise of punk and Oi! music, into the 1980s when
the post-punk era saw a fragmentation of the world of pop
and rock into innumerable splinterings. Megan, whose
story we will pick up again in the next chapter, was representative of the heavy tribalism of the early 1980s. Wearing
black eyeliner, black lipstick and black clothes, her hair
bleached and back-combed, this 15-year-old felt secure in
the night life of the 'Gothic' subculture. Looking back on
this period of her life five or six years later, she still
distinguished the particular magnetism of her 'tribe' against
that of punk aggression and the posturings of glam-rock.

Penny and Megan are just two examples, from the early

1970s and early 1980s respectively, of individuals who found a strong social identity in being part of their particular tribe. This principle of belonging, with all its trappings of clothes, music, image and lifestyle, is further complicated by exactly what it is that the teenager belongs to. Being part of a group can never be a neutral affair: a 'tribe' stands for something – whether for good or ill. In reality, there are good and bad aspects in most groupings. Just as with individuals, collections of people can be destructive or constructive, mean or generous, outrageous or conforming, in turn.

There are many instances of tribalism that we could take: the mods, self-regarding and fashion-conscious, riders of scooters and takers of pep pills; the rockers, descendants of the original Teds, hair plastered in grease and clad in black leather, riding motor-bikes and high on alcohol; the hippies, long-haired, bearded, beaded, unwashed and spaced out on pot and acid; the skinheads, wearing Doc Marten boots and 'bomber' jackets, addicted to drink and violence against minority groups; the glam-rockers, besequinned purveyors of sexual ambiguity; the proponents of heavy metal, macho image-makers who celebrate fast cars and fast women and, at times, use the symbols of Nazism and satanism; and the followers of Gothic rock, dressed in black and flirting with the sado-masochistic imagery of Middle European tales of horror.

Such 'one-liners' on each subculture can appear judgmental and tend to the stereotypical. They do not do justice to the complexity of the lifestyles hinted at nor to the good, bad, or indifferent qualities of the music that spurs on the members of each tribe and subtribe. I want, therefore, to deal a little more fully with two particular tribal groupings: punk rockers and Rastafarians.

The badges of punk tribalism are well known. In the mid-1970s a 'let's be disgusting' style was set for punk fashion: hair was cut close to the scalp and dyed in lurid colours ('Mohican' styles came later); both sexes wore make-up such as green eye-shadow, blue lipstick and white foundation; body tattoo, including the head and neck, became the rage; girls wore see-through fishnet vests or tops with zips across their breasts, Lurex drainpipes and high stiletto heels; boys wore shirts with the arms ripped out or T-shirts slashed as if by knife attacks; noses were pierced and adorned with safety pins, ears sported rings shaped like scissors, necks were encircled by pendants of razor blades and limbs displayed the marks of 'bondage' – a veritable ragbag of chains and leather straps.

As Peter Everett puts it in his *You'll Never Be 16 Again*: 'The overall impression is of Clockwork Orange meets New York sado-masochism with just a hint of Weimar.'[17] At the same time, the music of punk erupted with a 'do-it-yourself' drive. Self-appointed bands picked up their untuned guitars and exploded their rough-edged lyrics with untutored voices in pubs up and down the land. Out of these groups a few emerged to blast their way into public recognition, if not acceptance. It is important to realise that both punk fashion and music, though in time highly commercialised, had their roots in the drab lives of working-class youngsters in settings that were high in unemployment. In effect, they said, 'If society doesn't need us . . . we don't need society; if they deny us employment, respect and rewards, we shall make ourselves as unemployable and unrespectable as we can . . .'[18]

Punk rockers, like the Stones and The Who of ten years earlier, were out to offend but, unlike their sixties' counterparts, they were specific about who and what they wanted to offend. Although there was a broad anarchistic streak in their posture against just about everything – monarchy, government, law and order, education, family life, religion – followers of punk music did make important links with black musicians in the fight against racism which marked the rock scene of the late 1970s.

A rebirth of Rastafarianism, in particular, had grown, like punk, out of urban deprivation – though in this case within the black community. Growing their hair long in 'dreadlocks' and gathered into woollen hats in red, black, gold and green (the colours of Ethiopia, seen as the promised land), Rastas followed an upsurge in reggae music whose origins run back to African beat via its West Indian variations. E. Ellis Cashmore, the sociologist, commends this combined protest of black and white tribalism in these terms:

> They, more than any other youth movement, reflected the transformation of youth from young people prospering in partially real but largely illusory affluence, proclaiming their collective identity and revelling in their lack of responsibilities and abundance of time and resources. The punk-rasta allegiance showed young people to be disapproving critics of society not youthful representations of it.[19]

Teenagerisation

In July 1978 the *Sunday Times* published an article which declared:

> 'Teenagers' were born in 1942, marketed in 1947, discovered in small flocks in Britain in 1956, cosseted and comforted during the 1960s, began to weaken as the cruel graph of youth unemployment climbed in the 1970s and can now, officially, be pronounced extinct.[20]

In retrospect, this final burial of 'teenagers' and their attendant pop culture seems premature. Even so, it is now received wisdom that the pop revolution of the 1950s and 1960s, with its heavy commitment to the adolescent market, has lost a great deal of its original fire. Despite the fresh fervour of punk and reggae music in the late 1970s the momentum of pop, as an essentially *teenage* phenomenon, seems to have been largely dissipated during the 1980s. The attempts to revive former successes in the post-punk period of 'new wave' appear to have gradually run out of steam.

The strands within this decline are complex and they

include the process of 'teenagerisation', in which a somewhat reluctant adult world has been wooed and won by the
same commercial forces which have enticed adolescents
since the mid-1950s. This tendency was seen, for instance,
in 1977 when the dress designer Zandra Rhodes took the
anarchistic imagery of punk rock and glamorised it into
the fashion of 'pretty punk'. Angela Carter, writing at that
time on 'up-market' punk, said:

> . . . the rich . . . are prepared to pay through the nose
> for gold plastic wrap mini-skirts, plastic raincoats,
> safety pins (sequinned specially for them) and bon-
> dage jackets made up, now, in specifically middle-class
> fabrics, like good tweed.[21]

This trend has continued through the 1980s so that Toby
Young, commenting in *New Society* in 1985, could write
of the way in which 'teenage subcultures are elevated to the
former status of wider, adult society and wider, adult
society is reduced to the status of a subculture.'[22] He points
out that 'as pop musicians get older, so does their audience'
and gives the examples of the way people of 25 and over
listen to Dire Straits, the Rolling Stones, Bruce Springsteen
and David Bowie, while those over 35 are more committed
to the 'Soap Rock' of Richard Clayderman, Cliff Richard
and Barry Manilow. Young declares that Manilow can send
50-year-old housewives into the screams, hair-tearing and
faints which used to be the preserve of 15-year-olds in the
days of Presley and the Beatles.

As did the monied adolescents of the 1960s, the up-and-
coming young adults of the 1980s are responding to the lure
of 'image' in a wider context than the music they enjoy.
Subcultures include, to follow Young: Sloane Rangers –
aged about 24, educated at public school, followers of *The
Archers* and owners of cottages in the country; Yuppies –
aged 28 or so, newly married, driving 'medium-to-good'
cars and watchers of *Miami Vice*; and the Brogues –
middle-aged, Irish and speaking in soft tones.

All this could be quite depressing for teenagers seeking to establish their own significance and feelings of belonging – particularly in the face of unemployment or racial discrimination and the success stories of those who, though not much older, seem to have everything. And yet, in the late 1980s, adolescents still have their pop culture within which they can seek a sense of social identity. Although it is said that there is no 'next big thing' anticipated in pop and rock, there are 'many next little things' where young people are getting together to make or listen to music and support relatively minor artists in their endeavours. Peter Everett concludes his book *You'll Never Be 16 Again* by commending these fresh efforts to break new ground:

> When something radically new emerges from this creative stew, my wish for it is that it may be a long time before anyone over twenty-five finds out about it.[23]

Ultimately, of course, both young and old, as we argued earlier, find their truest *personal* identity in their relationship with God through Christ. Similarly, the richest *social* identity is found within the Church, the body of Christ. But, sadly, for many teenagers, that discovery is frustrated by the attitudes and actions of the adult Christian world. On the one hand, adolescent idealism can be turned aside by the complacency and cynicism of older Christians and, on the other hand, the vibrancy and excitement of the changing lifestyles of the young are often met by the blank wall of traditionalism and a frank lack of imagination among church leaders. We shall return to these dilemmas in the coming chapters but, for the moment, let me close this section with the challenge posed by Andrew Thornton, youth adviser for the Church of Scotland in Glasgow and also a rock musician of some repute:

> In short, we have to realise deep down that because of their youthful vitality, their intolerance of pretence

and their integral part in our wholeness as a family, the church *needs* young people. Question the paternalistic attitude that says 'young people need the church', and change it to 'let God incline the hearts of fathers to their children' (Luke 1:17). That movement is as costly as the call to discipleship always has been – but it's there in black and white as one of the signs of the Kingdom of God and it is part of the Gospel in today's church – more than ever before.[24]

5

CHANGING RELATIONSHIPS: WITH PARENTS

*The relationship between parents and teenagers is
often a greater problem for the former than the latter*
                                        Martin Herbert

Parents have always found the prospect of their children's
adolescence nerve-racking. More widely, the adult generation has often blamed the young for just about every
disruption in society. Despite our exposure of the comparatively recent 'teenage revolution' in the last two chapters,
these feelings of aversion are not new. Look, for example,
at the following:

> This youth is rotten from the very bottom of their
> hearts; the young people are malicious and lazy; they
> will never be as youth happened to be before; our
> today's youth will not be able to maintain our culture.[1]

And these words of despair were not written about the
punks of the 1970s or the football hooligans of the 1980s,
but about the young people of ancient Babylon, living more
than three thousand years ago.

Why is it that teenagers have been on the receiving end of
such a bad press throughout history? Putting it differently,
why is it that the idea of the 'generation gap' has taken root
deeply in the thinking of so many?

To explore questions like these let us examine the changing relationships of the young with, firstly, their parents and

other adults, and then, in the next chapter, with their contemporaries.

During their journey from childhood to maturity, adolescents experience a range of crucial relationships with the older generations. Most fundamentally and far-reaching, it is the ties between teenagers and their parents that are the vehicle of greatest change. This is not to deny that for many young people the circle of influence may be wider or, indeed, centred elsewhere. Aunts, uncles, grandparents, parents' friends, schoolteachers, youth workers, clergy and other Christian leaders may all play their part, alongside the parents.

In other situations – where a young person has been adopted, is orphaned, is in a 'one parent' family, has been turned out of home or where parents are divorced – the 'significant' adults may well not include mother or father. In any case, the essential thing is that the teenager can relate to the adult world in some way or other – preferably, as we shall see, to at least one older man and woman. We shall keep this basic need in mind as we consider *types of parenthood, the Bible and parenthood* and *parents (and other adults) as models*, before returning to the so-called *generation gap*.

Types of Parenthood

I suspect that just about every parent of teenagers reading this book will feel that they are not getting their parenting right in one way or another. At times they will feel they are doing rather well and begin to rest on their laurels – only to find their complacency shaken by some new crisis. At other times they may be racked by self-questioning: 'Are we too strict – or not strict enough?' 'Why do we always seem to put our foot in it?' 'How is it we usually end up with a flaming row?' or, most pressingly, 'Where did we go wrong?'

There are, of course, two sides to every relationship, and both parents and teenagers can be cussed and reasonable in turns. Let us, for the moment though, focus on the parental side as we explore the various types of parenthood.[2]

Autocratic

Here there is a tendency for one or both parents to rule the roost in a powerful and dictatorial way. Often such parents have been tight disciplinarians while their offspring were children and, now they have teenagers on their hands, they continue resolutely with the same formula. Parental monopoly on all decision-making pre-empts discussion and is commonly reinforced by physical punishment. Where a short, sharp smack might have been right for a disobedient child, the autocratic parent demeans the adolescent by side-stepping the need for reason and explanation, and resorting to corporal punishment. What, if administered with love and firmness, was simple retribution at 5 or 8 can become assault at 15 or 18.

The author of one study on styles of parenthood points out that the authoritarian parent 'attempts to shape, control and evaluate the behaviour of the child in accordance with a set standard of conduct'.[3] Within such a family the child, and later the adolescent, is moulded in his or her parents' image. Understandably, because of a resolute belief in a 'set standard of conduct', many parents from the traditional faiths adopt rigid ways of relating to their teenagers. Christians, Jews, Muslims, Hindus and Sikhs may, in effect, say to their young people: 'Don't you argue with us. *We* know what's best in every way. You just do as you're told.'

Here there is indoctrination rather than education, and the adolescent may discover a great deal of security in conforming to the parental pattern. Such young people may be trapped into becoming dull, dependent adults who never seem to have an original thought or take a creative step. Their parents have succeeded in producing passive 'look-alikes', who either join the ranks of 'stay-at-homes' or find life partners that fit the parental mould and offer a continued haven of safe tedium.

Others may be undermined by autocratic parents and react inwardly with low self-esteem. One adolescent wrote to me in these terms:

> I am a teenage male living in a Christian home. My father is very domineering and most conversations (if there are any) end in arguments. This makes home life unbearable and stifles my personality when my father is around.

Yet others can deal with the parental heavy hand only through a rebellion that is often displaced on to the world generally. Josef, at the age of 17, is of Polish stock and comes from a Roman Catholic family. Growing up in one of the poorer districts of London, he is probably responding to more than just his parents' traditionalism. He sees little value in working, feels that 'the Bible and the church are quite irrelevant for life today' and concludes that 'his parents do not really understand his needs'. In particular, he declares 'that it is a waste of time trying to talk about his problems with his father'.[4]

Permissive

Whereas autocratic parents make the decisions and leave their teenagers out of any discussion, permissive ones tend to allow their adolescent offspring to have the last word. Broadly speaking, such parents are either *overprotective* or *lax*.

The overprotective parent tends to dominate and submit to the adolescent in turns. The world is felt to be a fearful place and anxiety becomes the parental hallmark: 'Oh dear, she's ten minutes late – I'm sure she's been raped!' 'It's raining and I know he'll have an accident on that new motor-bike.' 'I'm convinced we can't trust that new boyfriend of Mary's – did you see the look in his eyes when they went out?' 'Honestly, John's gone to another of those noisy concerts; he knows how I worry about his hearing!' In such examples young people are permitted to do what they want, but their enterprises are cocooned by parental apprehension. These are the adolescents who may be embarrassed because it is always *their* parents who arrive too early after discos or parties to pick them up. Offspring who are shielded too readily often grow up into shy, awkward or nervous adults.

Overprotectiveness towards teenagers has many origins. It may arise from a family disposition: fussy parents can be the product of fussy parents. It may also be the result of some near-tragedy when, for instance, a much-loved son or daughter has recovered from a supposedly fatal illness or been rescued from serious danger. For other parents, personal insecurity may lead to too much emotional investment in the lives of youngsters. One mother admitted that she was 'too excited' by her family's achievements and 'too depressed' by their failures. She summed up her and her husband's feelings in these words: 'I didn't realise how dependent I was on my children . . . how we relied on them bolstering our self-esteem.'[5]

Where the overprotective parent may be permissive and loving, the *lax* parent is often permissive and rejecting. In essence, the teenager is told, 'Look, I don't mind what you do, but just keep out of my way!' Parental hostility may be subtle, and felt only by the adolescent, or obvious to all. Either way, the young person feels disowned and is likely to suffer from a poor self-regard for years. One student of 18 or 19, who came to see me about her general difficulty in relating to male friends, told me of the effect her mother's permissive and dismissive attitude had had on her. Referring back to her earlier teens, she said, 'When I went out of an evening, Mother would say, "I don't care when you come home." In time, I realised she not only didn't care what time I came in, she just didn't care!'

Democratic

Whereas autocratic parents monopolise all decisions and permissive ones often give their teenagers the last word, in democratic families there is participation. In a paper on parental control, one researcher describes the latter type of family as *authoritative* rather than authoritarian.[6] She argues that the democratic unit encourages 'autonomy and responsibility' – unlike the permissive model, which leads to a 'free-for-all' autonomy without responsibility, and the autocratic one, which fosters a rather grim-faced sense of responsibility, but with no real freedom.

It is democratic parents who seem to have the clearest idea as to what adolescence is all about. The fact is that young people, from the age of 12 onwards, show a sharp rise in the ability to think abstractly. During their early teens they can suddenly begin to take on board a more adult discussion which weighs up the pros and cons of this or that line of action. As I describe in *As Trees Walking*,[7] when I went blind for a year or so in the late 1970s, our son, Simon, then aged 13, promptly thought ahead and built himself a makeshift work-bench in the garage. With an incapacitated father, he could see that someone had to be on hand to tackle DIY jobs.

As the mid- and late teens are approached this facility to debate issues and plan for the future continues to expand, on into the early twenties. Both autocratic and permissive parents shortchange adolescents in their natural growth of adulthood: the one stunts the development of teenage reasoning and the other robs that reasoning of either responsibility or relevance.

In contrast, parents who are democratic allow their teenagers a voice that is heard. The young are encouraged to speak their minds and, at the same time, to listen to parental points of view. Democratic families are able to cope with disagreement without relapsing into authoritarianism or losing their love for one another.

Take one of the classic sources of conflict between parents and late adolescents: the desire of a son to buy a motor-cycle.[8] Discussion may be virtually non-existent in autocratic ('No, certainly not!') and permissive ('Of course, dear. No problem.') families. But democratic parents will seek to wrestle with the issues. They need to ask themselves what it is that they fear ('That he might have an accident and be injured or, worse, be killed; that he can't really afford a motor-bike . . .') and then they should ask their son exactly how his thinking is shaping, make sure they listen carefully and take his reasoning seriously. This is a difficult enough process, whatever the outcome, but it is one that encourages the teenager towards maturity.

Martin Herbert, in his *Living with Teenagers*, argues that home needs to be a 'launching centre' for adolescents.[9] He points out a piece of research, by the American psychologist J. Youniss, in which a series of students were questioned in their last year at school and then in their first year at college, where some lived in and others commuted from home. It seems that the boarders were better 'launched' – not only circumstantially but emotionally – for they, and their parents, 'showed more affection after the separation' and were more independent than the commuters.

Sometimes, however fair parents try to be, their teenagers may be slow to emerge with their own ways of thinking and being. Debby, for example, had to enter college before she could, first, reject parental perspectives and then reassimilate what was of value to her personally. She put it this way:

. . . in college . . . I rejected everything and said to myself, 'Okay, now I'm going to make a new Debby which has nothing to do with Mother and Father . . .' and what I started to put on were all new ideas. These ideas were opposite to what my parents believed. But slowly, what's happening is that I'm adding on a lot of things which they told me and I'm taking them as my own and I'm coming together with them.[10]

The Bible and Parenthood

As we turn to our Bibles for models of parenting we see, on the one hand, fallen patterns of behaviour and, on the other hand, key principles for families that seek to obey the Lord. Generally, throughout Biblical times, God's people lived within patriarchal societies and fathers had an autocratic role within their families. Authoritarianism can always engender rebellion and, within the Mosaic law, a persistently stubborn and disobedient son could meet with death by stoning at the hands of 'the elders at the gate of his town' (Deut. 21:18–21).

Conversely, a more permissive style of parenthood can be seen, for instance, in the story of Isaac and Rebekah. In Genesis 25, we read how Isaac prayed to the Lord for his infertile wife, Rebekah. In time she became pregnant and carried particularly restless twins. Perhaps encouraged by the prophecy that 'the older will serve the younger', she favoured the second-born child, Jacob, over the elder, Esau. As the children developed into adolescence and early manhood, we read:

> The boys grew up, and Esau became a skilful hunter, a man of the open country, while Jacob was a quiet man, staying among the tents. Isaac, who had a taste for wild game, loved Esau, but Rebekah loved Jacob (Gen. 25:27–8).

Here we see the seeds of favouritism, a certain form of permissiveness, which were to grow and bear ugly fruit in the years ahead. Jacob, smooth-skinned, reflective and a stay-at-home, was a 'lady's man' and cherished by his mother; Esau, hairy, active and venturesome, was a 'man's man' and celebrated by his father. With divided parents, each indulging their pet son, it is small wonder that the brothers grew up at loggerheads: deceit, hatred and near murder became the hallmarks of their sibling rivalry.

It is not surprising, too, that Jacob, in turn, eventually became an overprotective father. He had sired a huge family by his first wife, Leah, and, in sequence, by his two wives' servants, Bilhah and Zilpah. But it was upon the first-born of his beloved second wife, Rachel, that Jacob lavished all his attention. We read: 'Now Israel [Jacob's new name] loved Joseph more than any of his other sons' (Gen. 37:3). The familiar story of the 17-year-old Joseph's tale-bearing and arrogance, and the brothers' collective loathing of him, bears out once more the folly of discrimination and pandering in family life.

The pattern for parenting laid out in both Old and New Testaments indicates principles which are authoritative rather than authoritarian, democratic rather than permissive. In the Book of Proverbs, the wisdom of a direction-giving discipline, motivated by love, is clear in the bringing up of children: 'He who spares the rod hates his son, but he who loves him is careful to discipline him' (13:24); 'Train a child in the way he should go, and when he is old he will not turn from it' (22:6). Such caring instruction will lead, in time, to the sort of young person Proverbs was written for, 'giving . . . knowledge and discretion to the young' (1:4).

In Luke 2:41–52, we meet with the 12-year-old Jesus, visiting Jerusalem with his parents – possibly as a preparation for the bar mitzvah ('son of the commandment') of the next year, when he would 'come of age' as a young Jew. Here we see this incipient teenager demonstrating key principles for the right balance between parents and their growing offspring. It seems, in fact, that Mary and Joseph had it about right. They were not overprotective, feeling quite relaxed on the return journey that their boy would be among friends and relatives. They were not lax either, for when (after a clear day!) they realised he was not with the party, they acted swiftly. In all, it was three days before they tracked Jesus down in the temple courts. Autocratic parents would have reached rare heights of self-righteous fury by this time. But Mary and Joseph, presumably beside themselves with anxious concern, knew there must be some explanation. Their style was authoritative and democratic as they questioned Jesus and received his queries in return.

It is here we find the twin themes for the God-fearing family:

'Why were you searching for me?' he asked. 'Didn't you know I had to be in my Father's house?' But they did not understand what he was saying to them.

Then he went down to Nazareth with them and was obedient to them. But his mother treasured all these things in her heart. And Jesus grew in wisdom and stature, and in favour with God and men (Luke 2:49–52).

For the teenager to grow in wisdom, as well as stature, there needs to be the double commitment to the Father of all and to his or her parents. A wise mother, like Mary, will reflect on the conflicts and encouragements of this twofold discipline and 'treasure all these things in her heart'.

Parents (and Other Adults) as Models

As we saw in Chapter 2, from early childhood onwards, parents or parent-substitutes, are variously copied, felt with and identified with by their offspring (pp. 16–18). But it is during adolescence that the adult generation takes on a particularly strong influence for good or ill – especially in the broad areas of 'What should I do in life?' and 'What sort of man, or woman, do I want to be?' The resolution of such questions, during the teen years and early twenties, is referred to by sociologists as discovering one's 'work role' and 'sex role' respectively, and the parental example is seen as the 'model' for that discovery.

Perhaps the most crucial aspect of this modelling is the degree of *identification* that the adolescent has with his or her parents. John Coleman gives a helpful definition of this process as 'the extent to which the young person incorporates as his or her own the attitudes and characteristics belonging to another person'.[11] Clearly, the identifying can be very close as when, for example, a son appreciates his father's tough image as a coal-miner and aims to work down the same pit with the same manly vigour. Or the degree of incorporation of parental style may be virtually non-existent as when, for instance, a daughter rejects her mother's self-centred and unneighbourly ways and becomes an outgoing, warm-hearted social worker.

One particular group of young people who may face especially difficult times during adolescence are those of mixed parentage. With the increased fluidity of movement between one part of the world and another, the numbers of marriages between different nations and races have risen considerably. A teenager of, say, Anglo-Caribbean or Americo-Japanese stock may experience profound uncertainty as he or she puzzles over which cultural influences should have the greater say. David Stafford-Clark, the psychiatrist, points out that the offspring of mixed marriages are, in fact, often very gifted young people. Their identification with the rich, though complex, intermingling of their parents' backgrounds, may lead to personalities of great insight and ability. Stafford-Clark writes:

> Some of the finest people I have ever known were the product of mixed racial ancestry; a Scottish father and a Malayan mother produced one of the most distinguished, brave, charming and lovable airmen I ever met in the whole of World War II; and I met some fine ones; this man is one of my lifelong friends, and his children have the beauty of this kind of hybridization.[12]

Just as we have seen that in families which are well-adjusted there is usually a balance between parents and teenagers so such democratic units often display a symmetry of influence between mother and father. Bowerman and Bahr, for example, have shown that of the three possible family structures – patriarchal, matriarchal and 'equalitarian' – it is the last of these in which 'young people are most likely to look up to their parents'.[13] Further, where either mother or father is the more powerful figure, then the adolescent identifies less with *both* parents. And yet, it seems that mother's influence is more or less steady, regardless of her power-base, while identification with father is definitely poorer if he is seen as the weaker of the two. It appears as if the worst scenario for a young person's growth towards maturity is where the father is clearly the less powerful figure, and the best is where parents share their influence equally.

As we have already said, where parents are unavailable then other 'significant' adults need to be found. Paul Tournier, the Swiss doctor and writer, was orphaned of both parents by the age of 6. Following a lonely and unhappy childhood, he was rescued at the age of 16 by his classics master, who offered him genuine and caring friendship. Visiting the teacher's house weekly, Tournier wrote of this relationship, 'someone was listening to me . . . as a human being, a person'.[14] Identifying with the compassion of this older man, the young Tournier began to discover something of his role in life during the student days that followed: 'In this way there opened for me a period of social action and of intellectual and political debate, that was to last for a good number of years.'[15]

But Tournier, as with any other adolescent, needed to be able to incorporate 'attitudes and characteristics' from adults of *both* sexes. He deeply missed his much-loved mother and, when in his eighties, declared that the whole of his writings could be described as a 'long search for maternal tenderness'.[16] He married in his mid-twenties and his wife, Nelly, proved a close and loving companion; he said of her: '[she] became my partner in the search for God, my confidant and my confessor'.[17] Following her death in the 1970s he wrote that he felt 'orphaned for the third time'.[18]

Once again we see how research and everyday human experience confirm Biblical revelation. The Scriptures stress the importance of *both* mother and father in bringing up a family and imply the essential nature of parental example, or modelling. The Book of Proverbs, a compendium of wisdom for daily living, presents the value of paternal and maternal influence: 'Listen, my son, to your father's instruction and do not forsake your mother's teaching'(1:8) and proclaims the joy of parents when their loving concern bears fruit:

> The father of a righteous man has great joy;
> he who has a wise son delights in him.
> May your father and mother be glad;
> may she who gave you birth rejoice! (23:24–5).

In Ephesians 6:1–4, we meet the same level of a caring parenthood which is authoritative rather than authoritarian. Here, Paul gives instructions to the children first:

> Children, obey your parents in the Lord, for this is right. 'Honour your father and mother' – which is the first commandment with a promise – 'that it may go well with you and that you may enjoy long life on the earth.'

It is worth noting, in passing, that, in the Roman and Jewish worlds of the first century (as we saw in Chapter 1) most young people would be married by or during their teen years. For example, within Judaism a son would be expected to find a wife by the age of 16 or 17 and a father could marry off a daughter up to the age of 12 years and one day.[19] Be that as it may, the call in Ephesians 6 is for children and those in their early or mid-teens, while home-based, to obey their parents *in the Lord*. As we saw in the account of the 12-year-old Jesus, there is to be a double commitment for offspring: obedience to parents, set in the context of dedication to God.

As Paul says, this vocation is 'right' – that is, is of the very order of things, is intrinsic to the way we have been made or, as the theologians put it, is an aspect of 'natural law'.[20] However, the call to young people is richer: they are not only to obey their parents but to honour them – and this latter obligation should be seen as lifelong.[21] Here the teenager is to respond to a 'commandment' – that is, to an essential part of God's blueprint given through Moses to humankind or, using the technical term again, to 'revealed law'.

Even so, as with all Paul's words to the Christian 'household', the directives are not one-sided. The young are not urged to a blind obedience regardless of any challenge to parental responsibility. Here is no charter for the tyrant, the sadist or the child-abuser. Paul continues:

> Fathers, do not exasperate your children; instead, bring them up in the training and instruction of the Lord (Eph. 6:4).

In a patriarchal society it is not surprising that it is 'fathers' who are addressed primarily – and yet, as we have seen elsewhere in the Scriptures, the context of the previous verses is plainly that of both parents. It is likely that the men in the early Church were commonly contaminated by the autocratic male attitudes of the culture they lived in. Paul, in effect, says, 'Fathers, no bully-boy tactics with your children. Do not provoke or annoy them with your harshness, vindictiveness, selfishness, cynicism or sarcasm. Instead . . .'

It is salutary that much modern research has pointed to the pernicious nature of the 'absent father' syndrome – domestic situations where there is either no father (one-parent families where there has been separation, divorce or bereavement), a father who is virtually always away or a father who, though present, is weak and ineffectual. The Bible is clear. Not only are both parents important in successful nurturing and rearing but the right quality of fathering – so commonly neglected and played down – is of the essence in a God-centred family. This is not to say that families without a father cannot survive. Indeed many mothers in 'one-parent' situations bring their children up with great care and compassion. Furthermore, as we pointed out earlier, it is often the other 'significant' adults who help offset the disadvantages of an absent mother or father. A grandparent, aunt, uncle, neighbour, family friend, teacher, church leader or youth worker can bring the support, encouragement and example which balance those given by the solitary parent.

And it is the calling to bring up young people 'in the training and instruction of the Lord' that is the heart of the Biblical order of things. An integral aspect of this style of parenting is that just as children and teenagers identify with and model their lives on father and mother, so parents are to identify with and model their lives on the relationship between Jesus the Son and his heavenly Father.

In reflecting on this analogy it is worth stating that our God is not a sexist God! Although we call him Father, as Jesus did, we are not to read into him our stereotypical views. His nature as our Creator encompasses and supersedes that of his creatures. Within the Godhead lie all those virtues that we tend to label as 'male' and 'female'. He is not only the one of whom the psalmist wrote, 'As a father has compassion on his children, so the Lord has compassion on those who fear him' (Ps. 103:13), but he is also the one who could say to his people, 'Can a mother forget the baby at her breast and have no compassion on the child she has borne? Though she may forget, I will not forget you!' (Isa. 49:15).[22]

John White, in his *Parents in Pain*, summarises the point well:

> Some differences between male and female parents arise from culture and custom while others are innate, inborn. But God is the source of them all, innate or culture-bound. He is not father in the sense of not being mother. He can accurately be referred to as father-mother God. He is the source of all that is truly motherly and fatherly, and we are all, both fathers and mothers, called to be like him.[23]

The 'Generation Gap'

On an 'off' day, many parents of young children might hear themselves say, 'If they're like this now, what will they be like as teenagers?' Generally, as we have seen already, it is a commonly-held view among adults that adolescence is something nasty which happens to young people – and when it chances upon your own offspring you are in for big trouble. This image is, of course, newsworthy, and the mass media – when they are not milking teenagers for their money – thrive on portraying 'rebellious youth' with its drug-taking, promiscuity and hooliganism. To make matters worse, by the time a family reaches its teen years, with all the prospective pains of adjustment, parents are usually moving towards their own identity problems within their 'mid-life crises'.

In spite of all these fears, a great deal of recent research suggests that most families live through the teen years with harmony and, by implication, enjoyment. One study, for example, carried out in the late 1970s on the Isle of Wight, explored the extent of alienation between parents and their 14-year-olds. It was established that only 4 per cent of the adults felt an increase of strife at this stage of adolescence, while just 5 per cent of the young people reported any element of rejection towards their parents.[24]

And yet there is no doubt that there can be periods of considerable conflict between the two generations, peaking at the age of 15 among girls and tending to be at its most prominent at 17 and older with boys.[25] The areas of most frequent disagreement seem to be those of dress, hairstyle and the time of coming in at night – though in one survey of 16-year-olds only 10 per cent of parents said they often fell out with their teenagers over these matters. As we have already indicated, conflict seems more likely in autocratic and lax families than in democratic ones, where at least the attempt is made to come to a reasonable compromise on appearance and time-keeping.

At times, though, a real 'generation gap' surfaces where a deep rebellion is symptomatic of a particularly poor teenager/parent relationship. Megan, whom we mentioned among the Gothic rockers in the last chapter, lived out her reaction against her mother over three or four of her teen years. The first major showdown came when Megan, in her mid-teens, argued that the parental deadline of 11 p.m. one night should be extended to midnight. Once at a friend's flat she set to adorn herself for her evening out: bleached hair back-combed, black lipstick and eyeliner, very tight black jeans, untucked white shirt and a pair of stiletto-heeled ankle boots. The encounter between a bleary-eyed mother and a starry-eyed daughter at 1.30 a.m. did not do much for domestic harmony!

A year on, the production of scarlet hair, worn to the waist, and the elaborate painting of face, neck and shoulders in 'Gothic punk' style edged the declining relationship further down the line. Reflecting on the situation some years later, Megan said that she had been brought up with the maxim, 'You do what you want' and, when she had done just that, there had been 'a lot of friction'. She added that, in time, she had become a Christian and eventually found a true reconciliation with the mother she had resented for years.

Here, once more, we come back to the Biblical perspective: where both young people and their parents look to the lordship of Christ, there need be no 'gap' between the generations. Democratic, authoritative families which seek to put God first can live in ways where harmony and conflict, loving and being honest are part and parcel of everyday life.

It is perhaps not insignificant that among the last recorded words of Malachi, right at the end of the Old Testament, we read this prophecy about the Messiah's forerunner: 'He will turn the hearts of the fathers to their children, and the hearts of the children to their fathers' (4:6). This same promise of a healing of the 'generation gap' is picked up in the first pages of the Gospel story when the angel foretells the birth of John the Baptist and concludes:

> And he will go on before the Lord . . . to turn the hearts of the fathers to their children and the disobedient to the wisdom of the righteous – to make ready a people prepared for the Lord (Luke 1:17).

It is in commitment to that Lord that the changing relationships between young people and the older generation can be reshaped away from the idealism of early childhood to the give and take of the teen years. As Jean Vanier, the founder of the worldwide l'Arche communities, puts it:

> When a child experiences the absolute in relationship with God, then it discovers faithfulness, pardon, and the reality of a covenant relationship. Because of the covenant with God, covenant with parents and others becomes possible. Relationship is no longer based on compatibility, but on a covenant. Then the bonds between people are more profound than emotions, feelings and even capacities for love and hate. There, forgiveness is possible.[26]

6

CHANGING RELATIONSHIPS: WITH PEERS

In delay there lies no plenty;
Then come kiss me, sweet and twenty,
Youth's a stuff will not endure
William Shakespeare

As we have seen, at the age of 14 or so, Megan moved into open conflict with her mother. Feeling ill at ease in relating at home, she sought a sense of belonging elsewhere – and found her security in the night life of the Gothic subculture of the early 1980s. Looking back at this stage in her life, she admitted, 'Things were structured and definite as a "Goth", giving a way to run away from my parents. This gave me a definite boundary.' Through her mid- and late teens she found much of her social identity in the company of other uproarious young people.

Megan came in the 5 to 10 per cent of adolescents who experience serious confrontation with their parents and thus feel driven to seek solace somewhere else. However, the other side of the coin for all teenagers, within their changing relationships with their parents, reveals the various shifts in their relating to one another. Let us look at these changes in the domains of *family* and *friendship*. The third area considered, sex and sexuality, will be examined under the headings of *sexual awareness*, *sexual identity* and *sexual activity*.

Family

It was Alfred Adler, the Viennese psychologist, who first coined the phrase 'sibling rivalry', referring to the competition that can arise among brothers and sisters. As a generalisation, he postulated that the first-born tends to feel responsible, powerful and is inclined to live life by the rule-book; the second child, though a potential threat to the first, shapes up as a more forward-looking, outgoing young person who is less hidebound by regulations; while the youngest, because the smallest as a child, may become the most ambitious and combative of the bunch. Furthermore, the only child, living in the world of adults, may be precocious and overwise, seeing life outside the domestic circle as alien and rather threatening.[1]

Recent research has, on the whole, been less conclusive, though Adler's theories are borne out in many families. It is probably more correct to say that sibling position is just one of many variables, including types of parenting and the sex of the offspring, which affect an adolescent's relating. A careful study by Douvan and Adelson, however, did demonstrate that children from larger families are more independent and more involved socially with their contemporaries. Moreover, the youngest in a family is more likely to show a strong sense of loyalty to friends and a greater inclination to be influenced by peer pressures.[2]

The idea of sibling rivalry can be overplayed. Here is an extract of a letter from a 19-year-old, Josephine, to Abigail, her 14-year-old sister. In it we see a loving concern which identifies with the younger one's plight and tries to comfort:

How are things with your friends now, Abby? Remember what I said to you – just ignore them when they hurt you – they will grow up soon! Make as many friends as you can and don't be hurt if they seem to talk to each other more than to you. It's usually your imagination. Just join in with them and show them you don't mind!

Friendship

Josephine's letter to Abigail reveals something of the agony that many adolescents go through in their search for friends. Attending a local comprehensive school, and in a particular set which seemed to be bereft of potential soul mates, Abigail did her best to make and keep friends. One or two former companions were placed in other classes with virtually no overlap of their respective timetables. The middle years of her schooling were dominated by a certain gang of girls who made-up heavily and talked of nothing but boys, horses and the colour and quality of their nail varnish. Somehow, her more reflective nature and desire for a wider-ranging conversation were walked all over by what she called 'the fingernail brigade'. Ralph Waldo Emerson's dictum – 'The only way to have a friend is to be one'[3] – was not proving reliable for Abigail.

John Coleman, as an introduction to his survey of research on adolescent friendships, gives the following definition:

> Friendship may be taken to refer specifically to close relationships between two or perhaps more individuals, involving more self-disclosure and being of a more intimate nature than relationships among peer group members generally.[4]

Let us consider these changing relationships of 'self-disclosure', and a measure of intimacy, first among girls, then boys and finally from a Biblical perspective.

Girls

Analysis of friendship between girls by Douvan and Adelson shows three distinctive phases during the adolescent years.

In the *early stage* (11 to 13), friends are contemporaries with whom the young adolescent does things: swimming, bike rides in the country, window-shopping, collective visits to the chippy, swapping enthusiasms about this or that pop group. On the whole, feelings for one another do not run very deep and there is a fair degree of tolerance towards old contacts moving away and new ones entering the circle of friends.

In the *middle stage* (14 to 16) there is a profound bid for security in same-sex relationships. Here is a strong desire for loyalty and faithfulness on the one hand, and a propensity for jealousy and rivalry on the other. It is argued that the mid-teens are years when a girl desperately needs at least one other girl to identify with: someone with whom there can be give and take as each learns to adjust to changing emotions by testing out the other. This is a time when an awakening to the opposite sex can be both a threat and a thrill. Each girl needs a friend who will share in these uncertainties and not desert her for the company of boys.

This testing age of mid-adolescence is a period when there is a great need for privacy and the sharing of confidences among peers. Parents suddenly become an embarrassment and it is a wise adult who can accept the necessity of this temporary withdrawal. One mother, commenting on the re-emergence of her youngest daughter's availability, said: 'Last week it was OK to go shopping *together* – to be actually seen together. Jenny's now 16 and this was last OK when she was 13!' As we saw in the last chapter, teenage fads and fashions are often, at least partly, designed to effect this distancing. As one girl put it: 'And what was best about my haircut was that it made me look so awful. My mother wouldn't walk down the street with me. I think I liked that idea.'[5]

It is probably a relief all round when the *late stage* (17 and over) comes along – for friendship between young women then becomes a much more relaxed affair. In this phase, a friend's personality and interests are more central, and differences of style and belief are better understood and more acceptable. Where Abigail, at 14, was haunted by the 'fingernail brigade', at 18 and 19 she was able to build up a range of same-sex friendships which were rich in variety, without being too intense or exclusive.

The outline I have just given does of course vary from one section of the community to another. In West Indian and Asian families, for example, there are wider networks of friendship than among whites. This at least partly relates to the firmer ties of the extended family in the former groups. Moreover, there is a marked tendency for Asian girls, in particular, to form and keep strong same-sex friendships. One survey of 635 British 14- to 19-year-olds found 60 per cent of Asian girls with 'own gender' friends, compared with 21 per cent of the whites and 18 per cent of the West Indians. Here, Indian, Pakistani and Bangladeshi customs of arranged marriages may be highly relevant in protecting young women for their future partners.[6]

Boys

The pattern of same-sex relationships among adolescent boys is broadly similar to that among girls, except that there is a lower overall level of anxiety in friendships between male teenagers.

This discrepancy is most marked during the middle of the three stages. Research has found that, whereas mid-adolescent girls stress the importance of intimacy, sensitivity and trust in their relating, boys tend to major on achievement, action and self-sufficiency. Where girls are inclined to anxiety, conflict and envy in their relationships, boys seem to continue the collective, more outward-looking spirit of the early teens. One study, for example, has shown that, among 14- and 15-year-olds, boys were more welcoming of a newcomer to a small circle of friends than were girls.[7]

It is difficult to know how much these mid-teen differences between the sexes are part and parcel of inner needs or are largely imposed by social expectations. Douvan and Adelson, for instance, accentuate the way society expects 'a stronger interpersonal orientation' among girls and 'an orientation towards activity and autonomy' with male friendships. As with most generalisations about the sexes, there are many exceptions either way: girls in their mid-teens who revel in team games and a sense of outgoing camaraderie; boys of 15 or so who form close, finely-tuned relationships with one another.

Chaim Potok in *The Chosen* portrays a sensitive and caring relationship between two Jewish boys growing up in suburban New York. Both in their mid-teens, Reuven Malter has been brought up by a father aware of modern thinking while Danny Saunders is schooled in the precepts of the strict Hasidic sect. In the opening pages of the book, Reuven is concussed from a ball hit viciously by Danny in an interschool baseball match. Against the odds, the two boys are drawn to each other to form a friendship which binds them together in shared enthusiasms and mutual respect. But adolescent relationships often have an uphill struggle, particularly where parents disapprove of the associations. Danny's father, Reb Saunders, hearing of Reuven's father's Zionist leanings, strictly forbids further contact between the boys. Something of the agony of disrupted adolescent friendship comes through in Reuven's rage:

> For the rest of that semester, Danny and I ate in the same lunch-room, attended the same classes, studied in the same school synagogue, and often rode in the same trolley car – and never said a single word to each other. Our eyes met frequently, but our lips exchanged nothing. I lost all direct contact with him. It was an agony to sit in the same class with him, to pass him in the hallway, to see him in a trolley, to come in and out of the school building with him – and not say a word. I grew to hate Reb Saunders with a venomous passion that frightened me at times, and I consoled myself with wild fantasies of what I would do to him if he ever fell into my hands.[8]

The Bible and Friendship

Young people who value their friends are in good company, for the Bible rates friendship very highly – both in its teaching and by way of example.

The Book of Proverbs is a key text for every form of human relating, friendship included. Most adolescents would agree that relationships with friends (when they are working out) can be more rewarding than those within the family. Proverbs seems to bear this out when it declares, 'A friend loves at all times, and a brother is born for adversity' (17:17) and, '. . . there is a friend who sticks closer than a brother' (18:24).

Further, genuine friendship, essentially because it is loving and loyal, also has a tougher edge: 'Wounds from a friend can be trusted' (27:6) and 'As iron sharpens iron, so one man sharpens another' (27:17). Where a relationship means anything, there will be times when a friend will have to rebuke or criticise another. This 'wounding' is just one aspect of the way the mutuality of friendship can shape and hone character – 'iron sharpening iron'. Moreover, there is a call for a faithfulness in relating which can bridge the so-called 'generation gap': 'Do not forsake your friend and the friend of your father' (27:10).

Instructions like these – on the constancy, abrasiveness and reconciling qualities of true friendship – are mirrored in a number of exemplary relationships in the Scriptures: David and Jonathan; Ruth and Naomi; Paul and Timothy. Outstanding, though, is the imprimatur which Jesus gave to relating as friends. The Greek verb *phileo*, to show affection, love or give hospitality, is the root behind many of the New Testament words translated as 'friend' or 'friendship'. This caring and sharing was supremely demonstrated in the life of Jesus. The scope of his practical love was wide, for he was called 'a friend of tax collectors and "sinners"' (Matt. 11:19). More specifically, he addressed his followers as 'my friends' (Luke 12:4) and, in John 15:12–15, explained just why that was:

My command is this: love each other as I have loved you. Greater love has no-one than this, that he lay down his life for his friends. You are my friends if you do what I command. I no longer call you servants, because a servant does not know his master's business. Instead, I have called you friends, for everything that I learned from my Father I have made known to you.

Here, Jesus revealed that men and women could be friends of God – and that friendship should be marked by self-sacrifice and openness. The Lord showed his true humanity in his own need for friends – not only the full band of disciples but the closer grouping of Peter, James and John and the domestic circle of Mary, Martha and Lazarus.[9]

It was Jeremy Thorpe, speaking of Macmillan's Cabinet reshuffle in 1962, who turned round Jesus's words as follows: 'Greater love hath no man than this, that he lay down his friends for his life.'[10] Many adult relationships, sadly, follow Thorpe's maxim and sacrifice other people for selfish causes. Adolescent friendships can, of course, be equally sullied, but, from time to time, they show qualities of generosity and faithfulness that can shame many of us who are older. Such relating, at any age, is at its best when it is the outworking of a friendship with Jesus, the 'friend of sinners'.

Sexual Awareness

One way of viewing the whole of adolescence is to see it as a journey of sexual awakening. This new awareness was just round the corner for Frankie, the 12-year-old girl in Carson McCullers's *The Member of the Wedding*:

There was in the neighbourhood a clubhouse, and Frankie was not a member. The members of the club were girls who were thirteen and fourteen and even fifteen years old. They had parties with boys on Saturday night. Frankie knew all the club members, and until this summer she had been like a younger member of their crowd, but now they had this club and she was not a member. They had said she was too young and mean. On Saturday night she could hear the terrible music and see from far away their light. Sometimes she went around to the alley behind the clubhouse and stood near a honeysuckle fence. She stood in the alley and watched and listened. They were very long, those parties.[11]

As we saw in Chapter 1, there is a great range in the onset and completion of puberty and, by the same token, considerable variety as to exactly when a girl or boy becomes smitten by the opposite sex. For girls, the transition is frequently slower and their interest in boys, often rehearsed in the 'safety' of same-sex friendships, may be denied, diluted with other preoccupations or idealised in the shape of an adulated pop star. During these hormonal changes, fathers may become the object of mildly flirtatious behaviour from their daughters, while mothers look on with amusement or dismay.

In male adolescents, stirring sexual urges can be explosive. Quite suddenly, a reasonably straightforward, communicative and tolerably well-behaved boy can become a moody, truculent and monosyllabic young man. Sometimes the key is unpredictability, where sullenness and exuberance, cussedness and a desire to please come and go without apparent rhyme or reason. These uncertainties can be further embellished by periods when a son can become solicitous, and even amorous, towards his mother. At other times the switch in focus may be dramatic without, where parents are understanding, becoming too disruptive.

Stephen, throughout much of his later childhood, had been a keen and systematic bird-watcher. At the age of 15, much to the disbelief of everyone around him, his ornithological enthusiasms dramatically gave way to a different fervour: he had discovered girls. Overnight, binoculars, lunch-boxes and anoraks gave way to carefully groomed hair, well-chosen clothes and an impeccable attendance at the church youth club.

Two particular aspects of the earlier stages of sexual awakening are worth considering and they are *falling in love* and *masturbation*.

Falling in Love

Someone has said that averagely men fall in love seven times in a lifetime. This seems a rather chauvinistic statement and, I suspect, could be used to defend a whole range of doubtful enterprises. My first love was a contemporary called Jacqueline, when I was 6 or thereabouts. Starry-eyed, I walked great distances (or so they seemed at the time) to be with her. The highlight of ecstasy (and an acute embarrassment in retrospect) was when she and I sang solo in alternate verses of some nationalistic ballad to a piano accompaniment at one of her parties. I did not 'fall in love' again till puberty struck.

What do we mean by the phrase 'falling in love'? Roger Scruton, in *Sexual Desire*, helpfully summarises the distinction between 'falling in love' and 'being in love':

> The person in love sees his beloved's personality in all (her) acts and gestures, and is, as we might express it, spellbound by them. The person who *falls* in love . . . sees gestures and features which awaken his desire, and . . . he imagines a personality to fit what he sees.[12]

It is, of course, this 'imagining' of 'a personality to fit' what is seen that pinpoints the dangers of 'falling in love'. Although the pull of sexual attraction can be overpersuasive at almost any stage in life, it is in adolescence and early adulthood that body chemistry can be specially compelling. And it is here that Western, romantic notions of love can so easily overlay physical arousal and somehow justify all manner of folly – including sexual intercourse outside marriage or a dogged 'commitment' to someone who is quite unsuited as a close companion.

It is in early and mid-adolescence that romanticised ideas of 'falling in love' can pave the way for mistaken choices later in the teens. Further, European and North American idealisations of sexual desire have been exported world-wide, as well as being seen on our doorsteps among the younger generation of ethnic minorities. Roy Kerridge, writing in *The Independent*, comments on the 'Valentine Bhangra', a special edition of the blend of disco sound and traditional Punjabi music which he witnessed in central London, just before Valentine's Day, 1988.

Here there was a mixture of Eastern celebration (as one young Pakistani put it, '. . . it's all for joy. Not for serious courtship.') and Western physicality ('Behind me, in corners, young couples sat cuddling and holding hands in romantic bliss').[13] Even so, as we noted earlier, Asian young people in this country are still largely held within the more stabilising framework of longheld views on strong parental influence on the choice of life partners.

My main point here is for caution about 'falling in love' – whether at 15 or 50, and whatever one's cultural background. Within adolescence, it is not too difficult for emerging sexual awareness to be pushed, by the mass media, advertising and by peer pressures, to letting newly-awakened desires have the last word. It is only as young people let time pass that their opposite-sex friendships can find an appropriate level. The need to be able to do things together in mixed groups from mid-adolescence onwards is paramount, since in this way teenagers are freed to find out just *who* their friends are. Personal qualities, attitudes and understandings can be discovered and appreciated without allowing sexual urges to dominate and obscure the relationships. In the last chapter, we shall pick up once more with the distinctions between 'falling in love' and 'being in love' as we consider the question of life partnership.

Elizabeth, at 17, in answering the question, 'As far as

having a boyfriend is concerned, what do you think are the problems that people of your age have to face?' seemed to declare a healthy view which would not be too readily dislodged by premature, romantic notions:

> I think boyfriends are one big problem . . . I mean they can try and change your views in a very subtle way. 'Oh, if you liked me enough you'd do this.' It's really frustrating you know . . . and I don't see why my values and my views should be changed by someone else however much you like them. You know what I mean, and this can clash sometimes.[14]

Masturbation

Although Woody Allen once said of masturbation: 'Don't knock it, it's sex with someone you love!'[15] for many adolescents it is no laughing matter. A great many may find themselves trapped in a vicious circle of fantasising, masturbating and feeling guilty that leaves them anxious and unsettled. For this reason, let us immediately seek to dispel some of the myths attached to the practice.

First, masturbation (also called self-manipulation, auto-eroticism and solo-sex), in which a person achieves an orgasm by stimulating his or her own sex organs, is so common as to be regarded as a normal part of life. James McCary, in his *Human Sexuality*, declares that about 95 per cent of men and 50 to 90 per cent of women masturbate.[16] John Conger, the clinical psychologist, points out that in adolescence almost all boys masturbate and roughly half that percentage of girls admit to the activity.[17] It is worth saying that, in surveys on sexual behaviour, male prowess may sometimes be exaggerated to fit with a supposedly virile image.

Moreover, masturbation is not only widespread it is also physically harmless. In spite of traditional folklore that 'self-abuse' can lead to spinal weakness, insanity or blindness, there is no medical evidence to support any link between masturbation and bodily harm. By the same token, the Scriptures can be searched from cover to cover and no incident or statement can be found which forbids 'solo-sex'. The one event that used to be cited by finger-wagging clergy comes in Genesis 38:8–10 where Onan, Judah's second son, fails to fulfil his obligation as a brother-in-law by refusing to inseminate his brother's widow, Tamar. The term 'onanism', coined in the eighteenth century, should be used for the withdrawal method of contraception rather than masturbation!

From all this, we might be tempted to conclude that masturbation is 'a bit of a yawn' and about as worthy of comment as scratching one's head or sneezing. And yet, it is a practice that many, including a lot of young people, find problematic. This dilemma is not necessarily helped by the contemporary trend to see masturbation as not only common and harmless but positively health-giving. Thomas Szasz, the critic of traditional psychiatry, for example, has said:

Masturbation: the primary sexual activity of mankind. In the nineteenth century it was a disease; in the twentieth, it's a cure.[18]

For those who are in difficulty over masturbation, there will be a number who can be simply reassured about its normality. For others, though, their concern may relate to one or other of the ways in which the practice can become too central: where it is lustful, obsessive or self-centred.[19] We shall look at each of these in turn.

Although, for some, 'solo-sex' can give a quick release which is virtually imageless, for many masturbation is almost always accompanied by suggestive mind-pictures. In fact, erotic fantasies can be a wholly appropriate part of our sexual desire in the context of, say, the absence of one's marriage partner. None-the-less, for many the imagery entertained can be anything from frankly pornographic to an imaginative seduction of a friend, someone seen that day in the train or on the screen. It is here that masturbatory activity can be guilty before the words of Jesus:

> But I tell you that anyone who looks at a woman lustfully has already committed adultery with her in his heart (Matt. 5:28).

In this passage, the Lord then went on to challenge his hearers to remove and throw away the 'eye' or 'hand' that causes them to sin. In the context of masturbation, this is not a call to castration (!) but to genuine repentance and resolute change. The sinning is in the thought-life and so anything which feeds wrongful fantasy – certain books, photos, magazines, films, visiting places and people that overstimulate – needs to be 'out of bounds'.

Second, masturbation can become an ingrained habit that makes an imperious demand for frequent gratification. A repeated sequence of giving way, feeling bad about it, giving way again, and so on, can become profoundly undermining of self-esteem through a sense of continual defeat. Sometimes the impasse can be broken by sharing the dilemma with a wise counsellor or spiritual director, or by just realising that masturbation will not cause physical damage and is certainly *not* the sin against the Holy Spirit.[20]

Third, masturbation can become a highly self-centred activity. John White has called it 'sex on a desert island'[21] and Richard Foster has referred to it as 'sexual solitaire'.[22] Here we are back to Woody Allen's quip of 'it's sex with someone you love!' And herein lies the dilemma of masturbation. By definition, it seeks self-gratification. It is sex turned inward. And yet, for many lonely or isolated people, it provides a natural outlet for sexual energy. Where masturbation is becoming egocentric, the mould can be broken by a new openness to God and others. It is as the personality becomes more worshipful and caring that a great deal of inner passion can move upwards and outwards. Masturbation as a lustful, obsessive or selfish enterprise can give way to being the occasional release for pent-up sexual energy.

For the adolescent journeying towards adult sexuality, Richard Foster sums up the position well:

> . . . masturbation does help compensate for the un-even development that many adolescents experience in their physical, emotional and social maturation. Many teenagers are physically ready for sex far sooner than they are for social intimacy and the responsibilities of marriage. Masturbation provides a natural 'safety valve' while nature is synchronizing growth in the various aspects of life.[23]

Sexual Identity

In Chapter 2, we considered 'changing identities', and saw how essential coming to terms with sex and gender is for the adolescent as he or she heads towards maturity. For the vast majority of young people the sense of 'I am a man' or 'I am a woman' comes about with comparatively little difficulty. Further, for most, by the time the early twenties are reached, that sense of sexual identity includes an attraction towards the opposite sex. A primarily heterosexual orientation is the path for the many for their adult years, whether this leads to marriage or not. However, it is variously estimated that one in ten to one in twenty adults is essentially homosexual, with rather fewer women than men expressing gay preferences.[24] An indeterminate number of other people seem to be bisexual by inclination. Let us, then, examine the roots of homosexual leanings within the earlier years.

Homosexual Play

First, it is important for everyone to realise that, during the 'same-sex' period of late childhood and early adolescence, an element of homosexual play is normal. With the awakening of sexual feelings at puberty it is by no means unusual for young people to find their curiosity aroused about each other's sexual organs. Earnest comparisons may be made about the size of breasts or penises and competitions over the distance that seminal fluid can be ejaculated may be entered into. It is reckoned that about a third of 13-year-olds play with one another's genitals within same-sex groups. Such homosexual activity is commoner in boarding than in day schools, as well as in other situations where boys or girls sleep in close proximity – such as on camping and hostelling holidays.

I want to stress once more the normality of this period of experimentation in early adolescence. In fact, something like one in two adult people can look back to at least one experience, often in their teen years, of engaging in some sort of sex play with a member of the same sex. Such involvement, in itself, has nothing to do with being gay.

Homosexuality

Although many young people fear they may be developing lifelong homosexual or lesbian tendencies, it is crucial to see that very often such predispositions are simply part of the phase of development just described. However, among those who eventually conclude that they are gay a number begin to realise this during their late teens. One of the spin-offs of a wider acceptance in society for homosexuals to 'come out' and be open about their orientation, has been, I suspect, the premature conviction among the young that they are gay. Such mistaken bravura can of course lead to a living out of a half-formed inclination which soon becomes a wholesale commitment to being homosexual or lesbian.

Against this openness, the spectre of AIDS has brought in sinister social influences: paranoid, and even vicious, reactions from 'straight' people and a new fear of victimisation and exclusion among gays. It is here that the practical compassion of Christians – like Elisabeth Kübler-Ross in the United States, with her care for babies born with AIDS, and the staff of the Mildmay Mission Hospital in East London, offering medical and nursing help to sufferers – needs to be in the vanguard of concern. In this context, the story of the good Samaritan – breaking down barriers between people through a love that 'gets its hands dirty' – offers perhaps its greatest test in modern times.

The sense of ostracism in being gay, made a thousand times worse by the AIDS epidemic, can be crippling. For Neil, a young Christian student battling with homosexual leanings, the ground was cut from beneath the feet of his slender self-esteem by his parents' attitude. They had adopted him and, seeing how he was turning out, declared, 'Well, you're not ours – so we're not responsible for the way you are.' The feeling of isolation which being homosexual can bring is further seen in this letter by Jim, written in the 'Requests' Book' of a hospital chapel:

> Dear Jesus,
> I am a homosexual and I get very depressed as I have no one to love and care and respect . . . Please help me to find someone to love (a homosexual) and help me.
> Jim

How is it that people like Neil and Jim become homosexual? Before attempting to answer this question I should like to look at two common misunderstandings about being gay.

Kinsey in his reports on human sexual behaviour concluded that all men and women are somewhere within a spectrum of sexual propensity, ranging from a virtually complete heterosexuality at one end to a single-minded homosexuality at the other.[25] We can conclude from his findings that the majority lie somewhere between the extremes, though inclining more to an attraction towards the opposite sex. Putting this another way, most of us, adolescent and adult, are drawn towards members of both the same and the opposite sexes. Inevitably, because our sexuality is an integral part of who we are, these friendships include sexual attraction. It is helpful here to distinguish between relationships where there is a same-sex *responsiveness*, in terms of companionship and warmth of affection, and same-sex *preference*, the hallmark of an intrinsic homosexuality. As we have already stated, something like 5 to 10 per cent of the population have this constitutional inclination, in which there is an inner drive towards same-sex genital involvement. Such is the fear of being gay that many may not only exaggerate their desire for the other sex but may trap themselves into trying to disprove any vestige of homosexuality by seeking heterosexual conquests. Mike, though showing gay tendencies from his late adolescence, admitted to looking for 'Miss Perfect' among fellow college students; such potential heterosexual relationships made him feel tense, and he 'opted out' of them, one by one.

Second, another everyday myth is that effeminate men and mannish women must be homosexual or lesbian. Again, this is part of our stereotypical view of one another – fostered a great deal by music-hall clichés, depicting gays as heavily made-up men, who strut around with mincing steps and provocative side glances, or as 'butch' women, dressed in aggressive suits and barking out imperious orders.

Without denying that there are those who perversely *choose* homosexual activity as an extension of their promiscuous course through life, let us consider some of the factors which may contribute to inherent homosexual leanings. Traditionally, the powerful mother and the overwhelming father have been blamed for producing homosexual sons and daughters respectively. Among recent theorists, the writings of the Christian psychologist, Elizabeth Moberly, have been particularly persuasive. Her own research has led her to conclude that the gay person has often had difficulty from an early age in relating to the parent of the *same* sex.

To take the example of the male homosexual, there is

frequently a history where the father is seen as a remote figure – due to a break-up of the parents' marriage or the father's occupational absence, emotional coolness or early death. Thus the growing boy and adolescent experiences a detachment from the father in which his psychological needs, for an older man on whom to model his development, are not met. Moberly concedes that, as a result, the son is often very dependent on his mother, for where else can he go to find solace and personal warmth? Consequently, such a young man may grow up into an adult who is basically ambivalent towards his own sex. On the one hand, there is an aloofness in relation to other men, which may include an unease with male authority figures – like the headmaster, a games coach, a local Christian leader, an unemployment officer or the boss at work. On the other hand, there is a deep longing for physical and emotional closeness to men to make up for what was lacking during childhood and early teen years. Such a young man may thus be nervous with strong and successful older men and yet search out a homosexual companion, and perhaps lover.

What is the solution for the late adolescent or young adult who finds himself or herself drawn inexorably towards the same sex for love and comfort?

Before discussing this question in practical terms it is worth underscoring briefly what the Bible does and does not teach in this area. This is not the place for a detailed exposition but rather simply to point out first that the Scriptures clearly condemn genital sex between homosexuals. Along with adultery, fornication, incest and bestiality, homosexual *practice* is seen as contravening God's ordination that the norm for sexual intercourse is within the bond of marriage.[26] Nowhere in the Bible, either by statement or inference, do we find the homosexual *condition* castigated. The Scriptures, on the one hand, rule out homosexual genital activity and, on the other, are quite straightforward about attraction and friendship between men or women. We, the onlookers, are often ignorant of the exact sexual orientation of those we read about. This orientation is not called into question unless the situation is one of lust or overt sexual sin. As a case in point, the close emotional attachment between David and Jonathan is legendary. At their first encounter, we read: 'Jonathan became one in spirit with David, and he loved him as himself' (1 Sam. 18:1) and, following the death of his friend, David cries:

> I grieve for you, Jonathan my brother;
> you were very dear to me.
> Your love for me was wonderful,
> more wonderful than that of women (2 Sam. 1:26).

The point to draw from this deep mutual affection is not that David and Jonathan were homosexual. David's exploits with women, including his eight marriages, are stamped indelibly into history. Less is known about Jonathan's sexual proclivities although, at his death, he left a 5-year-old crippled boy, Mephibosheth (2 Sam. 4:4). It is, rather, that a same-sex relationship, in its own right, can be profoundly enriching and satisfying *without any implications of genital involvement*.

Let us return, then, to the dilemmas facing the young man or woman with entrenched homosexual or lesbian leanings. Despite the understandable pleas of the gay lobby in the Church of England, for instance, there is no way that the rightness of sexual intercourse between consenting homosexuals can be unequivocably argued from the Bible. Having said that, it is tragic to find so many Christian people who are judgmental and even vindictive towards the plight of their homosexual brothers and sisters. As with Jesus' handling of the woman taken in adultery, here is a situation for compassion and sensitivity rather than stone-throwing.[27] And comparisons between straight and gay single people, though valid up to a point, are not always expressed with understanding. The reality is, though both are called to sexual continence, the homosexual who follows Scriptural teaching cannot anticipate even the possibility of genital satisfaction with the same sex.

Without disputing the social difficulties facing homosexuals, Elizabeth Moberly's thesis brings hope by redefining the issues. She argues that homosexual tendencies, because their roots lie in a childhood deprived of fatherly love, are not, in essence, sexual so much as relational. It is the legitimate and unfulfilled desire for 'same-sex' affirmation, rather than the quest for genital conquest, that is the heart of the gay condition. She puts it like this:

> The solution to the problem of the homosexual condition is not sexual activity. Unfortunately, mere abstinence from sexual activity has often been mistaken for the solution, without the realisation that there are certain legitimate psychological needs involved, which ought not to be left unmet. One should neither ignore unmet needs (the 'conservative' mistake), nor eroticise them (the 'liberal' mistake). It is the failure to understand this that has led to the polarisation of the debate on homosexuality.[28]

In other words, the homosexual has a need to relate to other men, and the lesbian to other women, not primarily because of overwhelming sexual desire, but because same-sex relating has been, in many cases, at fault since childhood. Dr Moberly argues that all is not lost, for the 'normal process of psychological growth' can be recovered. She goes on to state that this process has 'heterosexuality' as its 'end result', where heterosexuality is defined as 'the ability to relate to *both* sexes, not just to the opposite sex, as a psychologically complete member of one's own sex' (italics mine).[29] It may be hard for many homosexuals to accept that their state is one of arrested psychological development; however, this realisation confirms the Biblical emphasis on healthy, normative relationships between the same sexes *and* the opposite sexes.

Any substantial degree of change may involve a long

haul, because the emotional needs of the gay person should
be met first with people of the same sex. This may come
about through friendships which are rewarding and yet able
to stop short of genital expression. For others, long-term
counselling or psychotherapy with a member of the same
sex may bring progress through a measure of affirmation
within the therapeutic relationship. At times, spiritual
counsel may enable the homosexual to find reconciliation
with his father, or her mother, through forgiveness offered
and received. Where the relevant parent is dead, peace can
be found by declaring a forgiving spirit in the Lord's
presence. Ultimately, it is the restorative work of the Holy
Spirit which strengthens the homosexual, not only by healing the past, but in and through everyday friendships with
the same sex – and, in time, by helping towards a safer
relating to both sexes. Elizabeth Moberly sums up this
difficult but promising path with these words:

> Love, both in prayer and in relationships, is the basic
> therapy. A defensive detachment from the same-sex
> love-source, and consequent unmet needs for love,
> constitute the homosexual condition. Love is the basic
> problem, the great need, and the only true solution. If
> we are willing to seek and to mediate the healing and
> redeeming love of Christ, then healing for the
> homosexual will become a great and glorious reality.[30]

Sexual Activity

As we have seen throughout this book, one of the hallmarks of adolescence is change in coming to terms with sex
and sexuality. This is not to dispute the sexual awareness of
children, but to emphasise the uniqueness of the teen years
in adjusting to changing bodies and changing desires. And
this highly-charged consciousness, as we noted in chapter
1, seems to start earlier and earlier. One 13-year-old boy,
seeking to impress his biology teacher, answered, 'The soil
is fertile, sir, because it is full of micro-orgasms.'

Whether this pupil's reply was the most innocent of mistakes or a true Freudian slip of the tongue, the fact is that not only sexual awareness but sexual activity, of varying degrees of intensity, is integral to the lives of adolescents at some stage or other. In mid-adolescence, many young people move in and out of 'being in love' relationships, where holding hands, kissing and cuddling may be the faltering expressions of new and disturbing feelings. Commonly, it seems, within these friendships girls are especially moonstruck while boys adopt a cooler stance. One break-up between a 16-year-old boy and a 15-year-old girl led, it appears, to a greater heartbreak on her side. In fact, the former set of parents spent more time consoling the girl's mother and father than their own son.

The reality is, though, that as the mid-teen years give way to the later teens, many young people are more and more likely to engage in more intimate sexual contact: from protracted kissing and embracing, through the fondling of breasts, clitoris and penis, with or without mutual masturbation, to full sexual intercourse. One survey, on British young people in the middle 1970s, showed that, among the females, 39 per cent of the 17-year-olds and 67 per cent of the 19-year-olds had had sexual intercourse.[31] The comparable figures for males were 50 per cent at 17 and 74 per cent at 19. As a generalisation, studies suggest that American girls are less sexually experienced than British ones, while the opposite seems to hold true for boys.[32]

Mark Twain once said that there are three sorts of lies: 'Lies, damned lies and statistics' and the above figures need to be taken with caution – not least because enquiries into sexual activity are remarkably prone to exaggeration and bias. Even so, there is considerable evidence that the proportion of young people who experience genital sex outside marriage has increased markedly since the Second World War.[33] And this is hardly surprising when the range of social and psychological pressures are thought about: the fact that late adolescence and early adulthood are times of peak physical and sexual condition; the increasing earliness of puberty; the huge numbers of young people who, through further education and inadequate employment, may defer marriage; the widespread questioning of the validity of matrimony, along with many other traditional patterns of life; the commercialisation and exploitation of adolescent sexuality through the mass media; and, not least, the influence of contemporaries on the individual to conform to 'liberated' views on sex.

Martin Herbert, in *Living with Teenagers*, points to some of the realities behind the statistics. He notes, for instance, that first experiences of sexual intercourse are usually not enjoyed and often leave girls feeling guilty and boys disappointed.[34] This may be due to the sullied romanticism of female mid-adolescents and the sorry tendency for their boyfriends, who are often older, to treat sex as pleasure without responsibility. Herbert also comments on the 'intense anxiety' of teenage sex and the observation that 'harmonious sexual relationships are relatively infrequent' among adolescents.

Having said this, it is worth pointing out that if, for example, nearly 40 per cent of 17-year-old girls have experienced coitus, then 60 per cent have not – either through choice or circumstance. Further, during my work with students I met many young people in their late teens and early twenties who were committed to keeping the precious gift of love-making for the possibility, one day, of marriage. I remember one couple, for example, who, though not Christians, were determined to remain virgins until their wedding two years away.

These two were fortunate in that they were of a common mind. Others find that a friend of the opposite sex is less considerate or is, frankly, exploitative. Sumali, a beautiful young woman from South-East Asia came to see me for the Pill. It was my custom to probe gently, when a student sought contraceptive advice, to find out something about the person and attitudes behind the request. On this occasion, I sensed her uncertainty about the ways of British university life and said, 'You can say "no", if you want to.'

The sense of relief in her radiant smile spoke eloquently. She left without a prescription but with a rediscovered confidence.

Liz had also been pursued but, unlike Sumali, she became trapped by circumstances. She came to the health centre in a distressed state because, the previous day, she had had intercourse with a fellow student for whom she had no affection, and who had badgered her over the past eighteen months or so. She was aware that she had given way out of some sort of protest against her parents' traditional values. She said to me, 'It seemed right at the time, but now I very much regret it.' In contrast to Liz and Sumali, Jane, another student, had the simplest of philosophies on sexual morals: 'Surely it's always right to give. If he wants it, I give it!'

It would be wrong of me to give the impression that college life is entirely made up of lusty young men who chase the women until they meet someone like Jane! In fact, the surveys suggest that sexual activity among adolescents is tending to move away from the classic 'double standard' where male adventurism was condoned and female submission was frowned upon. Young men, as well as young women, battle with the permissiveness of their peers. Tim, for instance, came to see me full of concern that he was being left behind by the conquests of his male flatmates. They boasted readily of their sexual exploits, leaving Tim bewildered and anxious about his own potency. We were able to discuss not only his fears but some of the ethical issues involved. In time he went on his way, let off the hook, it seemed, of the terrible, but mistaken, need to prove his virility to himself and others.

The Bible and Premarital Sex

What do the Scriptures have to say to the likes of Sumali, Liz, Jane and Tim?

To put our discussion once more into context, it is good

to remind ourselves that the Bible celebrates human sex and sexuality. To be human is to be a man or a woman, to be a sexual being. And this sexuality is part and parcel of everyday life, and how we see ourselves and in our relating to one another. Indeed, sex and gender are integral to our image-bearing as God's representatives and representations here on earth:

> So God created man in his own image,
> in the image of God he created him,
> male and female he created them (Gen. 1:27).

It is important that we all see, whether we are adolescents or adults, that our sexuality is about *who we are*, rather than whether or not genital sex is part of God's pattern for us. Single people within the Biblical record, including Jeremiah, Jesus and, it seems, Paul, were in no sense lesser mortals because of their call to celibacy. In fact, of course, our Lord himself, fully God and fully human, lived out a perfect life of loving obedience which, though excluding sexual intercourse, nevertheless included a rich fabric of relating as a sexual being to many male and female friends.

Within the overall framework of sex and gender, sexual intercourse is seen as the most intimate form of communication between a man and woman and is placed squarely by the Scriptures into the context of lifelong married commitment. The genital expression of that troth (an Old English word signifying covenant faithfulness) is acclaimed unashamedly from both male and female perspectives:

> May your fountain be blessed,
> and may you rejoice in the wife of your youth.
> A loving doe, a graceful deer –
> may her breasts satisfy you always,
> may you ever be captivated by her love (Prov.
> 5:18–19).

My lover is radiant and ruddy,
outstanding among ten thousand . . .
His mouth is sweetness itself;
he is altogether lovely.
This is my lover, this my friend,
O daughters of Jerusalem (S. of S. 5:10,16).

But the question remains. How about Sumali, Liz, Jane, Tim and any other young person pressingly aware of their sexual urges? Marriage is not on their agenda – either immediately or, perhaps, ever. Is sexual intercourse outside of wedlock wrong for them?

First, the Old Testament says comparatively little in a direct way about this modern dilemma. As we saw in chapter 1, young women, in particular, married as soon as they were marriageable – in other words, as soon as they could conceive and bring forth children. If they did not marry then, generally, their destiny seems to have been that of a maid-servant or, at certain stages in Israel's history, a concubine (who was available sexually on a regular basis to her master) or a prostitute. This system was both patriarchal and sexist: for example, a man could divorce his wife, often on extremely slim grounds, but this freedom was unavailable to her. Within these societal inequalities, none-the-less, an Israelite bride was expected to be a virgin and, if accused otherwise by her husband, had to produce the blood-stained garment as evidence of a ruptured hymen.[35] The prohibition of premarital sex is further implied in that, if a man had sexual intercourse with a virgin who was not betrothed, his 'punishment' was to give her father 50 shekels of silver and marry her![36]

In the New Testament we find an equality which picks up, as it were, with the harmonious and symmetrical relationship between man and woman as typified in the story of Adam and Eve. The unequal yoke between the sexes which had burdened humankind since the Fall (though here and there we find glimpses of something better) could now be broken and reassembled in Christ. And part of the calling of this renewed humanity is a further underscoring of the sanctity of marriage and the sinfulness of extramarital sex.

The word *porneia* is a general one used in the Gospels and Epistles to cover a wide range of sexual immorality, including, at times, both fornication (sex between unmarrieds) and adultery, as well as incest and prostitution. When, for example, Jesus explained to the disciples that real defilement is not about neglecting religious ceremony, but concerns the corrupt nature of our inner life, he said: 'For out of the heart came evil thoughts, murder, *adultery*, *fornication*, theft, false witness, slander' (Matt 15:19/RSV; my italics). Here the inclusion of both fornication and adultery indicates God's condemnation of all extramarital sexual intercourse.

Many Christians today, when asked why premarital sex is wrong tend to give *secondary* pointers. They say, in effect, 'Well, it's wrong because young people might get pregnant, make one another unhappy, catch VD or, worst of all, AIDS.' All this is true, and we shall look at some of these grave issues in the next chapter, but the Bible gives more fundamental reasons than these. The above are outworkings of 'sex gone wrong' but the Scriptures put their finger on the intrinsic wrongness of premarital sex.[37]

This is, perhaps, at its clearest in 1 Corinthians 6:9–20. It is worth a word or two on the context of Paul's relentless logic in this passage. Christians in Corinth in the first century were particularly set about by a plethora of sexual temptations. Cultic prostitution was rife (it is said that 'over a thousand courtesans consecrated to Venus lived in Corinth alone')[38] and the port had a thriving 'red-light' district. Further, the Corinthian church was continually threatened by Greek Gnostic views, in which the human body was seen as already decayed and therefore of no consequence. Thus all physical appetites, including the sexual, could be satiated without a second thought.

With this permissive milieu in mind, we can see Paul's

argument, in 1 Corinthians 6, against premarital sex in four stages:

(i)   Men and women do not 'have' bodies, they *are* bodies. Each individual is an indivisible unity. When Paul uses the Greek word *soma* (body) here and elsewhere he handles it in the sense of the total person.

(ii)   Paul reasons that the Christian, in his or her entirety, is united in every aspect of life with our trinitarian God – indwelt by the Spirit, joined to the body of Christ, called to glorify God the Father. We see this rich experience of belonging in these verses:

> The body is not meant for sexual immorality [fornication], but for the Lord, and the Lord for the body (13).

> Do you not know that your bodies are members of Christ himself? (15).

> Do you not know that your body is a temple of the Holy Spirit, who is in you, whom you have received from God? (19).

(iii)   How, then, can the Christian live a lie by taking what is the Lord's and giving it to another in disobedience? How can a believer take himself or herself – sacred temples of the Holy Spirit – and commit fornication? Paul gives question and answer – and his answer is most emphatic:

> Shall I then take the members of Christ and unite them with a prostitute? Never! (15).

Paul cites a prostitute since that was the Corinthian context. In doing this, he takes what, to us, might be an extreme example but, in the light of the wider Biblical teaching we have examined, it is likely that Paul is condemning all extramarital activity rather than intercourse explicitly with a prostitute. Today, he might ask, 'Shall I then take what belongs to Christ and unite myself with this girl, or boy, outside of marriage? Never!'

(iv) We can generalise from this first-century situation because, in verse 18 and elsewhere in his letters, Paul writes, 'Flee from sexual immorality [including fornication].' Here is a plain command. But, second, Paul taps the mystery behind the straight words with his third 'Do you not know' question:

> Do you not know that he who unites himself with a prostitute is one with her in body? For it is said, 'The two will become one flesh' (16).

This is the strangest of statements. The 'one flesh' phrase, used originally in Genesis 2:24 for the deepest intimacy of married love, is here used of the most sordid of heterosexual liaisons!

The inference seems to be that sexual union is meant uniquely for the commitment of marriage, in which there is a 'marrying together' of two bodies, of two people. Even where coitus takes place outside wedlock there is, it seems, a 'one flesh' dimension to love-making. As someone put it, you cannot experience extramarital sex and leave your soul parked outside. You give *yourself* in sexual intercourse. Lewis Smedes, commenting on this passage, makes the point clearly: '. . . when two bodies are united in sex, two *persons* are united. The body is the person, the outside person that touches the world around him.'[39]

We can say then, from the Bible, that premarital sex is wrong for two basic reasons. It is wrong for *everyone* because it flouts God's plan for 'one fleshness', given for the bond of marriage at the beginning and for the whole of humanity. It is doubly wrong for the *Christian* because, in fornication, he or she gives away the very self that is united to Christ.

It would be neglectful to finish this chapter without emphasising that all wrongdoing, including premarital sex, is open to the Lord's forgiveness and renewal. There is something in human nature, often relating to people's hang-ups, fears and voyeurism, which revels in sexual misdemeanour. Many Christians are contaminated by these attitudes – either condemning sexual sin as the ultimate disgrace or condoning it as outside the reach of God's concern. Jesus kept his harshest words for the pride and hypocrisy of the religious and showed a blend of deep compassion and encouraging firmness towards those who sinned sexually. His words of reconciliation and hope to the woman taken in adultery can be seen as a blueprint for every young person caught up by illicit sex: '. . . neither do I condemn you . . . Go now and leave your life of sin' (John 8:11).

7

CHANGING MORALS

No sex without responsibility
Lord Longford

The rise of the permissive society of the 1960s has been well documented. My own work in student health began at the end of that decade and I vividly remember picking up with the world of student sit-ins, marches against the bomb, the recently passed Abortion Act, the Pill, the early bra-burning days of a new feminism, the mini- and midi-skirt, the commune movement, black power, flower power, loon-pants, the euphoria of Woodstock and the Isle of Wight Music Festival, the preoccupation with Tolkien, the idealisation of pot and LSD, and the whole gamut of the alternative society voiced in the 'underground' press of papers like *Oz*, *IT* and *Friend*. These were heady and exciting days to be among the young since, in spite of the utopian optimism, there was a new spirit abroad of compassion for the needy and oppressed and a crusading zeal against the hypocrisy, facelessness and materialism of our bureaucratic and technological society. And yet, of course, there was a seedier and darker side to this 'counterculture' where obsessions with Eastern fanaticism, the occult, psychedelic drugs and perverted sex ruled the day.

Twenty years on, the point I want to pick up from all this is that however we view the post-war years in general, and the swinging sixties in particular, today we inherit a legacy which can be described as a 'mixed blessing'. Certainly the decade in question saw the beginnings of much that we, as

Christians who are aware of God's concern for justice, righteousness and the right stewardship of his world, can be grateful for: assaults on racism, sexism, class division, deprivation in the Two-Thirds World and ecological spoliation, for example, all had their mainspring in the 1960s.

I want, though, in this chapter to concentrate on an aspect of the more negative side of the shifting attitudes of the second half of the twentieth century – namely on that of the outworkings of changing concepts of sexual morality. This is not to deny that the whole history of humanity has seen a sequence of periods of permissiveness followed by times of reaction and repression. With this in mind, it is important that in examining some of the outcomes of sexual laxity in the lives of young people today we seek the Biblical 'third way' – not one of either prudery or promiscuity, but, as we have tried to lay down already, one of responsibility and celebration for our God-given sexuality.

In previous chapters we have thought much about the physical, psychological and moral aspects of sex and sexuality. Now we need to examine some of the outcomes of premarital sexual activity. Given the degree of genital involvement between young people that we discussed in the last chapter, we must first look at the matter of *contraception* before considering *abortion* and the *sexually transmitted diseases*.

Contraception

There are, of course, Christians, especially from the Catholic tradition, who hold that all artificial methods of contraception are wrong in any and every context. Many others, though, state that family planning within marriage is a responsibility which fits well with Biblical principles of the stewardship of health and material resources. However, birth control for the unmarried is one of the classic 'grey areas' of practical morality. We have argued that extramarital sexual intercourse is always sinful (see pp. 124–127). Is it, therefore, automatically wrong to use contraceptives in such a context? In some ways, this is rather like asking, 'Is it wrong to wear a bullet-proof vest while burgling a house?' After all, the vest might protect against complications should the thief be spotted. Putting it differently, given the immoral activity (sex outside marriage or burglary), can we see any secondary decisions, which make the enterprise 'safer' (birth control or protective clothing) as anything more than common sense?

Perhaps a more pressing question is to ask whether the provision of contraception not only prevents unwanted pregnancies but actually encourages genital involvement. The answer to this has been hotly debated throughout the 1970s and 1980s. Broadly speaking, the Family Planning Association, youth advisory centres and many doctors have argued that there is no evidence that, for example, the prescribing of the Pill fosters promiscuity. Others, including Family and Youth Concern (formerly, the Responsible Society) and a number of Christians in the field, have declared the opposite.

Some of the confusion may have arisen because quite different points are being made. The first line of argument sees the issue as 'promiscuity' (casual, indiscriminate sex with a range of other people) and thus reasons that most young people using contraception are faithful to one partner over, say, at least six months. I saw a great deal of this viewpoint during my work with students and must say that the perspective often looked like a rationalisation. Young people, often backed by their advisers, would frequently argue that they were 'going steady' and that their relationship was a 'stable' one. I recall Tina, a postgraduate student, who had moved through three consecutive 'stable' sexual involvements and then found an insoluble dilemma when the third of her men proposed marriage. She was unable to disentangle the memories of three love-affairs and could not, it seemed, commit herself to the one person. The second, and essentially Christian, approach tends to regard the debate as about *all* premarital sex and, naturally enough, concludes that the provision of the wherewithal to make intercourse 'safe' does just that: gives the adolescent permission to go ahead because pregnancy is rendered unlikely.

However, in practical terms, the dilemma remains. Where teenagers are already sexually active, they have simple but difficult choices to make. As we have said, their best decision is to abstain and keep such intimacies for marriage, if that state is to be part of the future. Others, though, may either find such a course, even if desired, next to impossible within an established sexual relationship or may see the bid for continence as irrelevant or foolish. Either way, the last two groups will at least need to think about contraception, unless having a child out of wedlock is their intention. The alternative of seeing an abortion as a form of birth control, if the situation should arise, seems not only careless but plainly wrong in terms of needlessly sacrificing a future human life for today's pleasures. These are the dilemmas of disobeying God's mandate for human sexuality.

With respect to the practice of contraception among the young, there is strong evidence that only one person in two uses a method of birth control in the first sexual encounter.[1] With increasing age and experience there is a trend, not surprisingly, towards a wider use of safer contraception. Even so, the reality is that no method is completely reliable in preventing pregnancy and, furthermore, a number of the techniques are potential health hazards. Among these, the complications that can arise with the Pill – including weight increase, depression and high blood pressure – are well documented. Conversely, of course, the spread of the AIDS virus into the heterosexual community gives the sheath, or condom, the double function of preventing an unwanted pregnancy and an unwanted killer disease. All in all, the advice of Dr David J. Hill, a consultant anaesthetist, seems to set the right tone from the points of view of both health and morality:

It is still true that the best contraceptive advice is to take a glass of water, not before or after, but instead of.[2]

It is the ability to say 'no', despite all the pressures to conform to the sexual mores of society's more permissive lobby, that is a mark of true personal freedom.

Abortion

In spite of the ready availabilty of contraceptive advice the numbers of abortions and illegitimate births have risen steadily among young people over the last thirty years or so. In looking at the figures for the 1970s and 1980s we find, for example, a clear change in the outcomes of premarital conceptions. Among pregnant women under 20 in England and Wales, in 1975 more than half either conceived within marriage or married between conception and birth, whereas in 1985 there were about a quarter in these categories. In other words, by the mid-1980s many more women avoided the traditional remedy of the 'shotgun' wedding. They either opted for termination of pregnancy or an illegitimate birth. With respect to the latter, there has been a rise in joint registration of births over this period (37 per cent in 1975 and 59 per cent in 1985). As *Social Trends 1988* puts it, with respect to the total figures of illegitimate births:

> . . . at least half the children born outside marriage in 1986 had parents who were living together and were likely to be bringing up the child within a stable non-marital union.[3]

Before looking at the statistics for legal abortion among adolescents it is worth pointing out that the remaining route for the girl who is pregnant outside marriage, adoption, has been declining over a similar ten-year period. Whereas in 1976 there were nearly 20,000 registered adoptions in

Great Britain, the number in 1986 was just under 9,000. None-the-less, in spite of the potential trauma of handing one's baby over to others, the choice of adoption – along with keeping the baby – must be seen as a more humane venture than termination. Details of organisations such as the Society for the Protection of Unborn Children, LIFE – Save the Unborn Child and CARE trust, which are willing to advise on adoption, are given at the back of the book.

Since the introduction of the liberalising Abortion Act of 1967 there has been a steady rise in both the total number of legal abortions and the quantity carried out on teenagers. Among the latter the figures have doubled: for those under 16, 2,000 in 1971 and 4,000 in 1986; and for those aged 16 to 19, 19,000 and 36,000 respectively.[4] In 1971 teenage abortions comprised 21 per cent of the total, while in 1986 the figure was 25 per cent. The vast majority of legal abortions are arranged (87 per cent of the total in England and Wales for all ages during the first quarter of 1987) under a particular clause of the 1967 Act which gives the grounds for abortion as the risk of 'injury to the physical or mental health of the pregnant woman'.

On a Thursday evening in January 1988, the day before the first reading of David Alton's Bill (to bring down the legal age limit of an abortion from 28 to 18 weeks), the nation sat agog to watch *EastEnders*. Michelle, aged 18 and 'old before her time', already the single parent of 'Dirty' Den's daughter Vicky, is pregnant again. This time the father is her husband, Lofty, who eagerly awaits a son or a daughter. But Michelle is in a quandary: she has broken with Lofty, though he wants her back; and, behind the scenes, Den is willing to finance a bed for a private abortion. How will she decide? The nation sits forward in its armchairs.

Somehow it all seemed a foregone conclusion. The money and bed were there, Vicky was a big enough strain and Lofty was out of favour. Neither husband nor parents were consulted. Michelle, recuperating afterwards, meets a chatty 16-year-old – also 'post-abortion'. After a little weep, Michelle tells the schoolgirl, 'I feel fine now.' Lofty is less easily assured. Learning the truth, he accuses Michelle: 'Weren't the best for me, nor the best for the baby. You never even asked me!'

Therein the nation was given a powerful example of the dilemmas of teenage pregnancy. What guidelines, if any, are there in this area? Or, must each instance simply be decided on its own merits? If so, what are the parameters? Is it basically just a matter of the woman's right to choose? Or are the issues such that the decision, either way, is essentially a medical one? Whatever the pregnant woman or the doctor believes, does the fetus have any rights within the debate?

These are hard questions and, perhaps not surprisingly, Christians, among others, are divided in the conclusions they draw. The vast majority agree that when the mother's life or health is clearly endangered then a termination of pregnancy is the lesser of two evils. Another considerable section will allow abortion where there has been rape or the fetus is known to be seriously handicapped – although these views are seen to be controversial by some. But the divergence of opinion comes to a head over the preponderance of terminations which are carried out under the widest possible interpretation of the Abortion Act of 1967. Here the risk of 'injury to the physical or mental health of the pregnant woman' may be seen to include, for example, a student approaching important exams, a sixth-former who cannot bring herself to discuss matters with her parents, or an up-and-coming trainee destined for a career as a beautician.

Let us examine two main views held by Christians – both frequently defended on Biblical grounds: a *purist view* and a more *pragmatic view*. Both these terms can be used pejoratively but, as we shall see, that is not my intention. Each position can be held with logic, compassion and with reference to Scriptural perspectives. There is a tendency for the first view to be held by moral philosophers and theologians and for the second to be maintained by those in the front-line situations of general practice and gynaecology.

The purist view

Although this is the stance which is usually referred to as 'pro-life', I have tried to avoid that phrase as, in many ways, both the purist and pragmatic arguments among Christians are *for* the life of the fetus – the former always, the latter as often as seems right.

The linchpin of the purist case is in the nature of the life within the developing embryo from conception onwards. As E. L. Mascall has written of the fertilised ovum (or zygote):

> . . . in that minute speck there is coded all the in-
> herited physiological complexity of the adult human
> being.[5]

It is because the earliest stages of development are regarded as just as intrinsically human as, say, a 28-week-old fetus or, for that matter, a 6-month-old baby, that the purist view regards certain forms of birth control as causing very early abortion. Both the intra-uterine device (IUD) and the 'morning after' pill are seen this way, since they work by shedding the zygote before it can embed in the lining of the womb. Interestingly, there are others who point out that the zygote remains mobile within the Fallopian tube and womb for seven to twelve days before implantation. During this time it may divide into identical twins. Thus, some argue, the fertilised egg cannot be regarded as an individual in the first week or two of its life since it may be destined to become two!

Whether the particular person's beginnings are dated from conception or implantation, the nub of the argument is well expressed by L. W. Sumner:

> The central question in the abortion issue is not
> whether fetuses are human, but whether all human
> beings, including fetuses, have the same moral status.[6]

Many Christians, as we are seeing, not only say 'yes' to Sumner's query but seek to argue their case from the Bible. This is not as straightforward an enterprise as many declare. None-the-less, there are a number of Scriptures which demonstrate, often in poetic language, the Lord's tender moulding of fetal life within the womb: Job said to God, 'Your hands shaped me and made me' (Job 10:8); David praised his Maker with the words, 'you created my inmost being; you knit me together in my mother's womb' (Ps. 139:13); and the 'word of the Lord' came to the reluctant Jeremiah: 'Before I formed you in the womb, I knew you' (Jer. 1:5).

Another passage often quoted in the abortion debate is Exodus 21: 22–5, in which the Mosaic law has some strong things to say about the outcome of a brawl between men, in which a pregnant woman is hurt and thus miscarries. Unfortunately, it is not clear whether the resulting 'serious injury' refers to the aborted fetus or the mother. On the whole, the harsh judgment of a 'life for life' makes it more likely that the woman's accidental death is alluded to.

Perhaps the strongest anti-abortion argument from the Scriptures is that of God's far-reaching concern for the helpless. The theologian J. W. Rogerson makes the case well in pointing out that the Bible 'has much to say about minorities and the defenceless'.[7] Among other passages, he quotes Psalm 82:3–4. We read:

Defend the cause of the weak and fatherless; maintain the rights of the poor and oppressed. Rescue the weak and needy; deliver them from the hand of the wicked.

Rogerson draws this valuable conclusion for the purist's use of the Scriptures:

The Bible does not address itself directly to this latter problem [of abortion]. What it does is to challenge us to include unborn children along with the defenceless and minorities whose task it is for the strong to defend.

What it does is to ask us whether at one and the same time we can assert our faith in a God who seeks the unworthy and the unwanted, and be indifferent to the fact that thousands of unwanted unborn children have their individuality terminated.

The pragmatic view

Among those Christians who hold more pragmatic views there will be few who would basically disagree with Rogerson's summary. If every pregnancy was simply a matter of fetal rights then, on the whole, decisions about the outcome would be straightforward. However, there are instances, by no means rare, when the hazards of continuing to carry a fetus jeopardise the physical or mental health of the woman to a serious extent. Both those who hold 'purist' and 'pragmatic' views will agree that where a mother's life is in real danger, as when there is an ectopic pregnancy or a cancer of the womb, then her well-being must take precedence. Termination is the responsible and compassionate route.

There are other circumstances where many purists would argue consistently against abortion on 'pro-life' grounds while those with more pragmatic thinking would want to weigh up the pros and cons in the individual instance. Examples of such dilemmas include pregnancies in those under 16, in women who have been raped, in the mentally subnormal and where the fetus is known to be seriously handicapped. In these and other complex situations that many young women find themselves in it is argued that there can be no carte-blanche approach.

It may be helpful to mention two examples, given in Rex Gardner's *Abortion: the personal dilemma*, to indicate something of the uniqueness of each story. In one instance, a pregnant girl of fifteen years and eight months and her boy friend, about three years older, wished to keep their future child. They also wanted to marry, but the girl's mother insisted that her daughter was too young for either eventuality and must submit to a termination. Gardner writes that both the family's GP and the gynaecologist 'felt that it would be unforgivable to force a girl to have her womb emptied against her will, such a course being likely to lead to severe mental trauma both now and in the future.'[8] Quite a different example seems to indicate, many would reason, the need for a legal abortion:

> A single girl was referred for abortion with the story that her mother had recently died. The patient was the only child. Her father was suffering from a malignant condition (the general practitioner's letter added that the girl did not know this) and although at present apparently well, would be expected to become bed-ridden shortly. The patient would then have not only to run the house but cope with a good deal of nursing.[9]

More pragmatic views on abortion among Christians tend to hinge on whether the fetus can be truly considered to be a *person*, or not. Some regard quickening as pointing to a crucial stage of development within the womb, as exemplified by the movements Elizabeth experienced when, albeit at a later stage of her pregnancy, the fetal John the Baptist leapt at Mary's greeting (Luke 1:41). Others take the account of the Lord God forming 'the man from the dust of the ground' and breathing 'into his nostrils the breath of life' (Gen. 2:7) as indicating that it is the newborn baby's first gasp of air that clinches God's gift of personhood. With respect, for example, to Jeremiah's understanding of the Lord's knowledge of him, even before conception, it is argued that the idea of being a person in anticipation can only be concluded *in retrospect*. As Donald MacKay put it, referring to Psalm 139:

> Once you *have* a person, you must reckon with his whole life-history (and, indeed, the history of his ancestors before his conception) as a linked sequence of processes and events divinely guided and appointed.[10]

We do not have the space to develop either the 'purist' or 'pragmatic' argument fully.[11] However, in terms of the teenager who is pregnant outside wedlock there is a pressing need for compassionate and sensitive counselling. The feminist view of a 'woman's right to choose' can tend to regard the fetus as a mere extension of the mother's body, but, as we have seen, Christian opinion contrastingly argues fetal rights too. Nevertheless, it is important that the pregnant adolescent – and anyone else integral to the discussion, including the putative father – has the chance to weigh carefully the pros and cons of her choice.

In my own experience of advising students I have found it essential that the young woman involved (and her boyfriend where he is prepared to stand by her) is given the space to consider the possibilities of marriage, keeping the baby and adoption, as well as legal abortion. Sadly, though understandably, many parents, as well as the adolescents involved, opt reflexly for the 'easy way out': termination of pregnancy. In so doing, the uniqueness of the growing life in the womb and the possibility of anguish and remorse later are barely considered. In fact, all surgical procedures have an inbuilt risk and abortion is no exception. Physical complications include infection, prolonged bleeding and the possibility of long-term infertility. Further, something like one in five or six 'will have reproach or mental symptoms which in the majority will gradually fade, but in some be long-lasting.'[12] Without wishing to belittle the painful dilemma of teenage pregnancy, and without dismissing the possibility that at times abortion will be the lesser of two evils, the aim of wise counsel will be to help more 'unwanted' pregnancies become wanted children.

Sexually Transmitted Diseases

In recent years there have been both an increase in the range of diseases passed on sexually and in the numbers affected worldwide. For instance, in 1916 in the United

Kingdom the only recognised venereal diseases were syphilis, gonorrhoea and chancroid. This was still broadly true when I was a medical student in the 1950s. However, by the late 1960s there were thirteen conditions acknowledged by the Department of Health and Social Security as sexually transmitted. It is reckoned that in the late 1980s this figure has doubled.[13]

Although there was a steady rise in the number of men and women infected by gonorrhoea in the 1970s, the statistics for that condition had more or less levelled out by the mid-1980s. Syphilis is comparatively rare in Britain and its incidence is reasonably constant. However, in 1986 there were 700,000 *new* cases of sexually transmitted diseases seen in clinics under the National Health Service. This figure signifies a major increase in the number of so-called 'non-specific' venereal infections, including non-specific urethritis (NSU).

Among adolescents the most common diseases passed on by sexual intercourse are gonorrhoea ('dose', 'clap' or 'drip'), NSU, herpes simplex, genital warts, candidosis (thrush) and trichomonas. Other infections, such as scabies and pubic lice, can be passed on by simply sleeping together. This is not the place to give a detailed account of these disorders, but it is vital that young people who suspect they are infected see their doctor or attend one of the local clinics. Symptoms which should arouse suspicion include penile, vaginal or anal discharges, irritation, lumps, sores or rashes in the genital regions, and lumps in the groins. There are clear links between sexual activity and the incidence of such disease. The risks are greater where there is more than one sexual partner and greatest within the most promiscuous relationships.[14]

It is important to realise that all these conditions can be passed on through either heterosexual or homosexual liaisons. Many of the 'new' infections are found among the latter, particularly in men, and include the hepatitis B virus and, of course, AIDS (acquired immune deficiency syndrome). The Human Immunodeficiency Virus (HIV), which causes AIDS, can be transmitted from using contaminated syringes and needles or receiving an infected blood transfusion, as well as through sexual intercourse. Generally, its incidence has been commonest among male homosexuals, intravenous drug abusers and haemophiliacs – though the epidemic in Africa has been largely among heterosexuals and the passage of HIV between men and women is now becoming apparent in the West. Even though not all those with a positive blood test will necessarily develop the full-blown disease, AIDS itself is a condition in which the virus attacks and overcomes the body's natural defence system against other infections. Fatalities from AIDS can thus be due to a host of different afflictions, including pneumonia, meningitis and various forms of cancer.

The social and moral implications of AIDS are, of course, immense. Depressingly, in spite of advertising campaigns for 'safe sex', there is little evidence of any radical change in sexual behaviour among many in the West. Studies in the United States of homosexuals and bisexuals who know they have a positive blood test have revealed no change in the overall number of sexual partners.[15] A government survey in Britain, published in the autumn of 1987, though showing a wider use of condoms among homosexual men, also demonstrated that the rate of promiscuity in men and women more generally was unaltered. It was further shown that young people in the 18–21 age range have the most partners: one in five had more than one sexual partner over a one-year period. Among 16- and 17-year-olds the figure was one in eight.[16]

While God's clear mandates for human sex and sexuality go on being spurned, the figures for the spread of AIDS rise menacingly. Although not first suspected until the summer of 1981, in the United States, what came to be known as the AIDS virus has had a devastating impact throughout the world in the intervening years. In 1986, for example, the global figure for AIDS sufferers was estimated as 100,000, with a total of between 5 and 10 million people thought to be symptomless carriers of HIV.[17] The World Health Organisation predicts the latter figures could have multiplied tenfold by 1991. In the United Kingdom, the number of those reported to have AIDS more than doubled from mid-1986 to mid-1987 to a total of 870; it is estimated that the number of new cases identified in 1988 will be 1,500. It is thought that the complete number of people who were 'HIV positive' in Britain in the summer of 1987 could have been 30 to 40 thousand.[18]

We have already seen something of God's blueprint for our sexuality. Writing in the context of Christian attitudes to sexual activity, Dr Caroline Collier quotes Dr Malcolm Potts, who sees that young people in their late teens and early twenties are at greatest risk. He writes:

> [Young people] are both the most sexually active and often believe themselves immortal. Risk-taking and AIDS are not unlike risk-taking and pregnancy – neither AIDS infection nor fertilisation are certain, the gambler often survives, and the penalty is remote – at least nine months in the case of pregnancy and maybe years in the case of AIDS.[19]

8

CHANGING EMOTIONS

Youth would be an ideal state if it came a little later in life

Earl Asquith

Many of us who have left our teen years behind feel, from time to time, 'Yes, given a chance, I'd like a rerun of my adolescence. I'm sure I'd get it right second time round.' Such wishful thinking may be strongest in those who reckon they have missed out somehow on what being a teenager is all about. Judy, now in her late twenties and an experienced midwife, looks back at the repeated, unsettling moves her family had to make throughout her teens; she feels she has only recently emerged from the delayed experience of adolescent 'rebellion', and its stresses and strains.

Judy's retrospective view is typical of most of us. We believe that adolescence spells necessary turmoil – and if we do not go through the fire between the ages of 12 and 20 then we feel we are destined for trouble later. It was G. Stanley Hall who, at the beginning of the century, lifted the phrase *Sturm und Drang* ('storm and stress'), originally used to describe the writings of Goethe and Schiller, and applied it to the teen years. Anna Freud, in similar vein, wrote, 'Adolescence is by its nature an interruption of peaceful growth.'[1]

There is, of course, a great deal in this perspective. Many young people *do* go through times of considerable 'storm and stress' in which the comparative calm of late childhood is rudely disturbed. Although outwardly content at the time, I can vividly recall my own inner conflicts during my mid- and late teens: not so much a storm but, on occasions, a steady drizzle of greyness which seemed to sap energy and weaken resolve.

Even so, as I have argued throughout this book, adolescence is to be celebrated: it is a key transitional period which the vast majority pass through without too much disruption. None-the-less, there are hazards on the way and a minority of young people fall foul of them. Many of these pitfalls pockmark the road for the whole of life. And yet others present particular dangers for the susceptible adolescent. Although the proportion of youngsters significantly disturbed by these 'changing emotions' (10 to 15 per cent) is not greatly different from the figures for children and young adults, there is a tendency for teenagers to experience a certain range of relevant malfunctions. Of these, I propose to look especially at 'eating disorders' and a few other emotional conditions that disrupt the lives of young people.

Eating Disorders

The fact is that adolescence is normally a period of great fluctuations in body weight and I do not want to create anxiety by appearing to plead for some sort of average teenage figure of a particular volume and shape. Although Western society has tended to idealise slimness on aesthetic and nutritional grounds, some recently have begun to challenge such views, accusing them of undermining feelings of self-worth in those of plumper build. Susie Orbach's two books *Fat is a Feminist Issue* and *Fat is a Feminist Issue II* are a case in point.

Even so, within the teen years, both overeating and undereating can be expressions of inner turmoil. Let us look then, in turn, at *obesity* and *anorexia nervosa*.

Obesity

There are many theories as to why certain young people

overeat and thus put on an unhealthy degree of extra weight. John Coleman cites some of the research which puts forward four main ideas about obesity in teenagers.[2]

First, there is evidence that many adolescents have difficulty in recognising and interpreting normal hunger cues. Such young people may be relaxed, happy and confident but, unlike others around them who know when they have had enough, they are inclined to ignore or miss the body's signals. They seem to have established a different level of feeling full and may complain that they 'always feel hungry'. The remedy here lies in re-educating the appetite through more modest meals, avoiding 'in-between' snacks and taking regular exercise.

Second, some obese youngsters have problems about expressing their own desires and needs. In effect, it is only in overeating that they seem able to influence their destiny. Such adolescents are often especially eager to please, are passive in their response to situations and agree readily with the poor views that others appear to have of them. A third category is formed by those with a deep sense of loss – perhaps through the death of a parent or the moving away of a close friend. Sometimes such overeating is an attempt to stave off feeling depressed. And finally, there are teenagers who stuff themselves as a demonstration against other people's expectations. Subconsciously, there may be a wish to be less physically attractive and so ward off the opposite sex, or plumpness may be the passport to thwarting parental ambition for social or athletic success.

We can see from these last three causes of obesity that being overweight – whether at 15 or 50 – can be the expression of profound inner needs or conflicts. The very temporary nature of adolescence often means that the young person finds, in time, a degree of harmony and integration which leads to healthier eating habits. Others, of course, adjust psychologically and settle happily for the fuller figure. For a few, their compulsive eating is a continued expression of deep unhappiness. A way forward may be found through valued friendships or some wise counselling. Most profoundly, faith in Christ and the non-judgmental welcoming of his people may break the spell of low self-esteem and dietary overindulgence.

Anorexia nervosa

As with obesity, there are many theories about anorexia nervosa. Some of these see a continuity between the starvation impulse of this condition and the bingeing episodes of so-called 'bulimia', in which a huge intake of calories may be followed by self-induced vomiting or purging. Jill Welbourne and Joan Purgold, in their book, *The Eating Sickness*, argue that bulimia is simply a late stage in the development of anorexia, though 'the anorexic phase may have been slight enough to escape notice'.[3]

Classically, anorexia nervosa is diagnosed where there is a weight loss of 25 per cent or more and an all-absorbing preoccupation with keeping that weight down. Conversely, the sufferer believes she or he is obese even when to all others the appearance may be painfully thin. In young women the periods may have stopped for at least three months, though this feature is considered to be secondary to the obsession with not eating.

Anorexia is essentially a condition of adolescence. Although it may start at the age of 10 or 11, it most frequently emerges at or around puberty. Some experience its onset in their twenties or thirties. It is by far and away commoner in women, the sex ratio being put variously at ten to twenty women for every man with the disorder.

This disproportion between the sexes has led to many conjectures about the nature of 'the eating sickness'. Its frequency in women may relate to a number of factors which arise from society's expectations. On the one hand, women have often been regarded as the gatherers, preparers and providers of food. As Marilyn Lawrence puts it: 'What women are learning is that food is for everyone but us.'[4] On the other hand, there are enormous pressures, carried through the mass media, for beauty in women to be seen as centred on slimness. Images of men are allowed to be thickset, sturdy, chunky and even stout, but the male-dominated world of advertising requires women to be able to look good in size 12 dresses from the age of 16 to 60.

Arising from sociological notions like these, it is argued that anorexia nervosa is often about *control*. Whereas gross overeating may be a way of cocking a snook at others, a dangerous level of undereating may be an attempt to exercise power over oneself at the expense of those around. Either way there can be a perverse controlling of one's own body. Marilyn Lawrence, in her *The Anorexic Experience*, makes the point in relation to the adolescent need to begin to exert independence – an effort that, because of upbringing, usually comes easier to boys than girls. 'Therefore,' she writes, '[women] are more likely to be driven to producing symptoms such as anorexia'.[5]

Paradoxically, anorexia nervosa is not a disorder of the Third World: it is a condition that arises in a society where it is a virtue to be thin. By the same token, it is rare among the more deprived communities in the West. Typically, the anorexic adolescent comes from a middle- or upper-class family, is seen as a 'good' and acceptable daughter and has parents who expect 'great things' from her. She is often academically bright and a high achiever in exams and continuous assessment. This point is sharpened by the statistics: roughly one in a hundred girls at fee-paying schools and university are anorexic, while the figure for state schools is one in three hundred.[6]

Sheila MacLeod, in her *The Art of Starvation*, describes her own development of anorexia nervosa. The eldest of three sisters, she was regarded with special favour by her stern schoolmaster father and her much adored mother. She writes:

Achievement, especially academic achievement, was what being clever was all about. I was destined for great things – Oxford or Cambridge, a string of letters after my name, a successful academic career, and would no doubt end up being the first woman Prime Minister.[7]

Winning a scholarship to a girls' public school in the Home Counties, Sheila felt both 'pushed out of the nest' by her parents and, to some extent, accepted by the novelty of 'interesting' friends. Menstruation at nearly 15 took her by surprise and the ensuing physical changes filled her with disgust. Her newly-rounded figure and its sexual implications seemed to mean a loss of her true self. Pressures from her family to achieve, and the school's competitiveness and hierarchical disposition, aggravated her sense of lostness and she withdrew into herself. Coming up to O-levels, and following demotion at school and a dismissive letter from her father, she did the only thing she thought she could: become anorexic. She felt her parents would not understand if she complained, had no money for running away and lacked the recklessness to start smashing up the school – so she starved herself. She writes:

> There was nothing conscious or deliberate about my decision, if indeed it can be called a decision at all. Even my rejection of food was not embarked upon deliberately. All I knew was that my life was intolerable and that the only way not to be destroyed by it, or by 'them' as I called the adult, authoritative world, was to reject them and everything they stood for. I had to make some sort of last-ditch stand.[8]

Although the families of anorexic teenagers vary greatly, there is a tendency for certain features in the daughter's relationships with her parents. There may be a strong attachment to the father, but more often than not, as in Sheila MacLeod's case, he is a distant figure. The mother, according to Hilda Bruch, is frequently 'too good' and tends to have anticipated her offspring's every need.[9] The child thus grows up compliant and conforming until the unsettlements of adolescence threaten separation from the much loved mother. The anorexic teenager may consequently regard mother as the only one who understands and feels she cannot have enough of mother's company. I clearly recall Vivien, a student in my care, who originally started on the downward spiral of anorexia through a friendly competition with her glamorous, 'sisterly' mother for the ideal figure.

How can the anorexic adolescent and her family be helped through the agonising months and years of this pernicious condition? First and foremost, there is abundant evidence that the earlier the disorder is diagnosed and treated the better the outlook. When a daughter in her mid-teens not only misses breakfast each day but becomes intensely conscious of calories – both for herself in reducing weight and for others in encouraging them to overeat – then the early stages of anorexia should be suspected. Where she always leaves the table early to wash up, thus missing the sweet course, is increasingly active in routine jogging and taking the dog for longer and longer walks, and is seen to be losing weight alarmingly, then it is important for parents to challenge their daughter, caringly but firmly. The temptation is for the family to feel the problem can be contained, and for the sufferer to be terrified of any 'treatment' which will upset her continuing goal of weight reduction.

If the anorexic pattern is establishing, the general practitioner will probably refer the girl for counselling or psychotherapy. There is a range of different approaches, some offering physical treatment and others psychiatric help. Where the condition can be caught early, the best hope is offered through psychotherapy from a specialist with experience in the field. The haul may well be a long one since, as Jill Welbourne and Joan Purgold put it, changes for the better are slow 'because they cannot be imposed, but must start from inside the anorexic fortress.'[10]

There are great frustrations for friends and family during treatment – partly due to feelings of helplessness and partly because the specialists seem to be 'getting nowhere fast'. The outlook is always better where the family members can face their own responsibilities in the situation rather than scapegoating their emaciated daughter. Family therapy is sometimes offered and, again, can be rewarding where mother, father and siblings are all willing to share in the enterprise of the anorexic's recovery.

There are times of course when anorexia nervosa is life-threatening. In fact, fatality from the condition is fortunately rare, approximately one in a hundred literally starving to death. But this possibility is indeed a grim one where such young lives are at stake. There may come a point when the sufferer's wasting away and malnutrition are at such a pitch that the body's functioning is severely jeopardised. This is no time for the niceties of psychotherapy. There is a medical emergency at hand and hospital admission is essential. Friends and relatives may be filled with anguish but, once the anorexic's body chemistry is restored, then wise physicians will make sure that deeper needs and attitudes are explored and understood. Many hold somewhat bleak views about the incurability of anorexia nervosa. Let me close this section with the experienced words of Jill Welbourne and Joan Purgold:

> . . . the odds are about four to one in favour of recovery and . . . a well-motivated and optimistic anorexic will win the battle against the illness eventually. For some that eventuality may take longer to achieve than for others but, sooner or later, the majority should be able to claim a successful outcome.[11]

One young woman, Helena Wilkinson, describes in her book, *Puppet on a String*, something of her 'battle against the illness' of anorexia nervosa. Her story is, in many ways, a classic – one of fearful confusion and depression during her mid-teens, set within a girls' boarding-school as she tussles with low self-esteem and a desperate desire to love and be loved. Her personal account, culled from regular diary-keeping, charts the relationships which both supported and rejected her as she slides into bizarre eating patterns, the loss of her periods, steady decline in weight and increasing debility.

Following a mixed experience, as a patient, of understanding and ineptness at the hands of hospital staff and a series of personal crises, she is eventually linked with a counsellor who helps her explore more fully her attitudes and feelings towards herself and others. While on holiday in Bermuda and aided by Kathie, a much-loved cousin, she begins to see more clearly the relevance in her story of a loving but possessive mother and a father who had seemed too distant. Her book closes with a strong testimony to the way God's love, mediated through her mother's prayers, her cousin, various faithful friends and her new links with other Christians, has brought forgiveness and a measure of healing, while enabling her to resist anorexia nervosa and its baleful influence. She writes of this stage in her pilgrimage:

Although so much joy and hope was [sic] coming into my life I was well aware that we cannot for ever remain on the mountain top and that life has its difficulties. I see this as a spiritual battle of love and joy against despair and desperation; a realisation that we have to fight for true life, but that fight will not be beyond our strength.[12]

Other emotional disorders

Despite the normality of the ups and downs of adolescent life, there are occasions when young people can develop more serious forms of emotional and psychological disturbance. As we have indicated, the overall incidence of such states may be no different from childhood or the adult years. However, it has been observed that the sex ratio of mental disorders does vary with the broad age-groups:

before puberty, they are commoner in boys than girls; during early and mid-adolescence the proportions are equal; and in late adolescence and early adult life women begin to preponderate over men. Further, certain conditions and responses, like *anxiety*, *depression* and *suicide*, are more frequent in the teen years – and so I propose to look at each of these in turn. Other forms of psychological disturbance, including schizophrenia, obsessional-compulsive states and many of the phobias, though often appearing initially during adolescence, are just as likely to surface in the early adult years.

Before examining the three specific areas of anxiety, depression and suicide, it will be helpful to say a little about *stress*, since most, if not all, emotional disorders are related to it in one way or another.

Stress

Stress is one of those everyday words that has a range of meanings. We can see it, first, as a stimulus in our environment to which we have to respond. If a teenager experiences earache, failure at an exam, a family row, or the loss of a friend, then he or she is undergoing stressful situations. Second, depending on how the youngster handles these incidents, we might say that he or she is showing signs of stress, or distress. This might be demonstrated by complaints of pain and insomnia, acute disappointment and frustration, a response of angry shouting and door-slamming, or withdrawal and tearfulness, respectively in the examples just given. Third, stress can be understood as a misfit between a person and life's general conditions. Here there is a failure to adapt to, for instance, the biological, emotional and social changes of major transitional stages. As we have seen throughout this book, this is why the adjustments within adolescence can be so stressful. Broadly speaking, it is this third category of stress which is most likely to lead to an anxiety or phobic state, to depression, and even a suicide attempt, among young people.[13]

Anxiety

All of us experience feelings of anxiety at appropriate times: before a major filling at the dentist's, on the run-up to important exams, on the eve of a crucial interview, coming up to our first attempt at the driving test. This level of concern at life's uncertainties needs be neither crippling in its effect nor sinful in its content. It is where degrees of apprehension spill over into inaction, or into the 'anxious care' that will not trust or obey God, that we go wrong.

However, others of us can be trapped into a chronic tendency to worry unproductively that is called an 'anxiety state' or 'anxiety neurosis'. The word 'neurosis' needs some brief explanation. It has been said that a neurotic is some-one who adds two plus two and gets four – but is unhappy about it! It is this chronic uneasiness about everyday things which is the hallmark of many anxiety states. A grander definition is given by Andrew Sims, professor of psychiatry at the University of Leeds:

> [Neurosis is] a psychological reaction to acute or con-tinuous perceived stress, expressed in emotion or be-haviour ultimately inappropriate in dealing with that stress.[14]

In anxiety neurosis, the 'psychological reaction' is one of debilitating fearfulness at everyday events which are per-sistently seen as stressful. The young person may be tense, worried, nervous and fretful and tend to visit his or her doctor frequently with apprehension about this or that symptom. Any or every system in the body may contribute, as the frame is constantly being prepared for 'flight or fright' in response to anxiety: a dry mouth, constricting feelings in the throat, tight sensations in the chest, palpi-tations, interference with the depth and rhythm of breath-ing, headaches, pallor, cold sweats, loss of appetite, nausea, 'butterflies' in the stomach, bowel upsets, trem-bling, dizziness, weakness and, to cap it all, fears of fainting or panicking. Small wonder that the teenager can feel overwhelmed and exhausted by this condition.

For some, such manifestations of anxiety may be part and parcel of various phobic states, such as *school phobia*. This disorder needs to be distinguished from natural fears of, say, playground bullying or a general lack of enthusiasm for things educational. Although this phobia is commoner in 11- and 12-year-olds, who are at an early stage of adjusting to new schooling, some teenagers also go through difficult bouts of school refusal. Sometimes this state is triggered by a move and a change of school, at other times as a result of prolonged illness and getting badly behind with study and, most fundamentally, through a 'separation anxiety' in which a boy or girl finds it impossible to leave mother at home. Such a phobia, like anxiety states generally, may be expressed in loss of appetite, abdominal pains and fainting feelings.

Anxious and fearful teenagers, where schooling, college life, a job or everyday coping are disrupted, may well need more specialist help than teachers, tutors, employers, family or friends can provide. Attendance at the local GP's surgery or a student health centre may bring a great deal of relief to troublesome symptoms – by talking through the problems and, perhaps, receiving a prescription for a short course of tranquillisers to tide over a difficult stretch. The latter should be seen as temporary adjuncts to more fundamental help. That help may be found through counselling or psychotherapy over some weeks or months – perhaps from a school counsellor, a student counselling service, a youth advisory centre, a psychiatric department or a specialist seen privately. For those with phobic conditions, a clinical or educational psychologist may well bring a lot of improvement through relaxation exercises and other techniques which modify negative behaviour patterns.

Forms of emotional disturbance which can respond well to these general and more specific approaches include hysterical and hypochondriacal tendencies, disorders involving obsessive and compulsive behaviour, as well as a range of phobias such as the fear of school, spiders and insects, flying and heights, mixing with people, of thunderstorms, animals, illness and death, confined spaces (claustrophobia) and open areas (agoraphobia).[15]

Esther suffered from a recurring anxiety state in late adolescence which, during early adulthood, came to a head in a period of acute agoraphobia. In this latter condition, her 'fear of the market-place', to use the word's literal meaning, confined her to her top-floor flat in the northern university city where she studied. On the one hand, she was greatly helped by a clinical psychologist who re-educated her into a slower, deeper breathing when she felt panicky, and encouraged her, street-corner by street-corner, to extend gradually her range back into the big, wide world. On the other hand, and as her agoraphobic symptoms lessened, she received regular psychotherapy from a caring counsellor who helped her explore the conflicts within the ways she saw herself and related to others. Since those difficult months she has been able to return to her studies, hold down a part-time job and take a couple of train journeys from one end of the country to the other.

Depression

It is not surprising, considering all the changes of body chemistry, physical appearance, relating to parents and friends, all the while seeking to establish a clear sense of personal and social identity, that adolescents frequently feel depressed. Important work by M. Rutter and others has shown that almost 50 per cent of teenagers experience at least mild depression at some stage or other.[16] Amid breaking up with friends, feeling parents do not understand, and trying to adjust to exam failure or unemployment, such teenagers may well feel, with Woody Allen, that 'life is divided up into the horrible and the miserable.'

In *Coping with Illness*, I distinguish between depression

in terms of *mood*, *attitude*, *experience* and *illness* and it is worth briefly summarising these distinctions here.[17] Before doing so, there is the need to say that the boundaries between these conditions are often blurred in adolescence, due to the complexity of life's ups and downs in the teen years.

First, young people are notoriously susceptible to mood-swings related to hormonal changes and emotional adjustments. They commonly feel 'down in the dumps', 'fed up', 'gloomy', 'dreadful', 'bored' and 'crashed out'. Further, adolescents as well as adults can be afflicted by a cast of mind and general disposition which are melancholic. Sombre, pessimistic and negative personalities can run in the family, where inherited traits and a tendency to adopt a doom-laden view on life can reinforce each other. Members of such families may repeat to one another such maxims as, 'Nobody ever did *me* a good turn', 'Learn to expect the worst in life' and 'Didn't I say things wouldn't turn out well!' Third, a youngster may become depressed as a response to some experience or circumstance, such as following flu or glandular fever, after breaking up with a friend, failing to get into college or losing a job. It is the fourth category, though, that we are mainly concerned with in this section, where depression can be classed as an illness.

The classification of depression as illness has been a source of great controversy in psychiatry. Traditionally, the condition has been divided into: reactive or neurotic depression, where the state is triggered by outside circumstances or inner conflict; and endogenous depression (linked with manic-depressive psychosis), where the cause is thought to be at least partly due to genetic and biochemical factors. Nowadays, depressive illness tends to be seen as part of a continuum, within which a whole range of different causes might be relevant. The term 'clinical' depression is sometimes used as an umbrella-heading to describe a degree of depressive disturbance in which everyday functioning is disrupted.

Depression of this more serious variety in young people is often masked, partly because of adolescent mood-swings and reluctance to communicate feelings, and partly because the symptoms are carried over into unexpected behaviour patterns – like undue irritability, playing truant, persistent expressions of boredom, aggressiveness, petty theft, running away from home or withdrawal from friends and social events. Behind these sometimes misleading responses to life may lie a very unhappy teenager. Careful observation will usually reveal the hallmarks of true depression: difficulty in sleeping, loss of appetite, morbid thoughts, poor self-regard, unremitting feelings of guilt, inability to concentrate and a new tendency to take risks, including, for example, drinking heavily or reckless driving. It is the essential *change* from former ways of being and behaving to attitudes of helplessness and hopelessness that should alert friends, family, teachers and employers.

The same comprehensive range of help is available to the depressed adolescent as to the anxious or phobic one. When depression is triggered by a sense of loss – as with the death of a parent, sibling or friend, a move to an unfamiliar and unwelcoming locality, failing a crucial exam, getting dismissed from a job or encountering a period of prolonged illness – then the teenager needs to be able to work through an extended time of grieving. Sonia, one young woman I knew, had been discouraged from openly mourning the death of a childhood friend who had died of a form of cancer. Seven or eight years later, during her late adolescence, she came to see me for help, locked into a delayed grief reaction which had produced a chronic state of depression. It took many years to unthaw her frozen sense of loss and for her, once more, to find life worth living.

Where, like Sonia, the young person can weep and be angry and share his or her feelings with another, then a healing of the wounds can begin to take place. As Robert Burton wrote in the seventeenth century, in his *The Anatomie of Melancholie*:

. . . in melancholie . . . the best way for ease is to impart our misery to some friend, not to smother it up in our breast; for grief concealed strangles the soul; but when we shall but impart it to some discreet, trusting, loving friend, it is instantly removed for a friend's counsel is a charm, and it allays all our cares.[18]

Despite attempts 'to impart misery to some friend', sometimes adolescent depression is too deep-seated to lift through everyday relationships. Where there is any doubt about the youngster's state of mind, including the possibility of suicidal thoughts, it is essential to seek professional advice. The family doctor may offer counselling or psychotherapy, either directly or by referral to a more specialist service. Where depressive feelings are established, antidepressants may be given initially to alleviate symptoms in order, in time, to help the young person face up to inner conflicts, anger or the sense of loss which may lie behind the condition. Where the adolescent is in a crisis situation, hospital admission may be necessary to prevent suicide and, more positively, to help him or her function on a daily basis once more.

Stephen, aged 16, is pehaps typical of many teenagers who become depressed. He is one of the fortunate ones who is able to declare just how he feels to parents who seem to care and understand:

. . . there was a period when I felt empty in myself, and very depressed, and I didn't want to go out anywhere. One night I ended up going to bed really early, which is unusual for me, and my mother came in to see what was wrong and I almost ended up in tears. But you know I find I can talk to my parents, especially when I'm really down in the dumps, and that sort of makes all the difference.[19]

Suicide

Mary was a loner. She came to see me in her first year at university, at the age of 18. She was a shy, retiring girl who was clearly depressed. She said that her father had always exerted pressure on her to study, felt that neither of her parents really understood her and added that she could not discuss matters with either of them. In spite of initial treatment, she became more severely depressed, could not work and returned home to the care of the family doctor and local psychiatric team. Six weeks later, I heard that she had taken her life.

Mary's story is, in some ways, typical of the many suicides and suicide attempts (sometimes called 'para-suicides') which end or mar the lives of troubled young people. In fact, the suicide rate among adolescents has risen markedly since the 1960s throughout much of the more privileged parts of the world. Generally, it is established that boys, often using more violent and determined methods, are more successful at committing suicide than girls, though the latter make more attempts. Both suicides and parasuicides are commoner in mid to late adolescence and Gethin Morgan, for example, studying this age range in Bristol in 1972 to 1973, recorded 166 suicide attempts by boys and 660 by girls.[20]

John Wodarski and Pamela Harris, in a paper published in 1987, point out that adolescent suicide is often linked with a sense of alienation from others and a resulting form of 'tunnel vision', in which the young person fails to see life's options.[21] Certainly Mary's horizons were narrowed down by a feeling of isolation from family, friends and, presumably, from anyone else who might help lift her low self-esteem. It seems she came to a point in the tunnel where she felt the only way out was to make an end of herself.

Apart from its clear links with profound depression, suicide, according to Wodarski and Harris, is also connected with general stress. One survey showed that more than 50 per cent of teenagers who committed suicide had a history of moderate to heavy drinking and/or the abuse of illegal drugs. The strongly competitive ethos in schools in the United States and Japan, for instance, seems to foster the high suicide rates in these countries.

Studies in the early 1980s, which have looked at the family backgrounds of suicidal adolescents, reveal a number of key factors. Most prevalent are the ingredients of discord and frequent separations between parents. Unstable family units, particularly with mothers and fathers who seem to lack interest in their offspring, feature commonly in stories of young people with suicidal tendencies. One investigation showed 43 per cent of parasuicides had experienced a family argument preceding the suicide attempt and, further, there was a close correlation with parents who had a separation or divorce pending.

Besides stressful lifestyle and family disintegration, attempted suicide among the young is also associated with isolation from contemporaries. As we have seen, relating to other young people is essential in the growth of a sense of personal and social identity in the individual. The teenager will often gauge his or her own view of the self by watching other adolescents: where the youngster is already unhappy, the sight of peers enjoying themselves and being successful can be bad news. Young people who are suicidal will frequently try to select a friend for support rather than a parent, teacher, youth leader, brother or sister. If that friend is unavailable, unsympathetic or non-existent then the outlook may be very bleak.

John Conger has suggested pointers for recognising potential suicide in the young.[22] They are: the persistence of a depressed state, including, for example, a steady decline in school achievement; gradual withdrawal from social contact; disruption of relationships with parents and friends; and a history of earlier suicide attempts or accident proneness.

Having said this, it is sadly true that it is extremely difficult to anticipate and prevent a single-minded determination on the part of a depressed youngster to take his or her life. The tell-tale signs may be there but, ultimately, there is an unpredictability about many suicides. Nevertheless, any talk of 'ending it all' in an adolescent should be taken very seriously. The adage, 'People that say they'll take their lives, never do', cannot be trusted.

It is clear from what we have said that it is the depressed loner who is especially vulnerable. It is where a young person feels cut off from family and friends, and particularly when those support systems are themselves breaking up, that a suicide attempt becomes a possibility. Often the endeavour is on a mere whim: all else has failed so the teenager, on the spur of the moment, sees death as the only solution. Adult memories may be short for the kind of acutely painful feelings which might precipitate adolescent suicide: what may look trivial to the mature and unsympathetic can be profoundly disturbing to the young and inexperienced. The agony of heart in the 15-year-old boy who jumped off Clifton Suspension Bridge to his death, following his request for a psychiatric appointment to cure his blushing, can only be guessed at.

The paper by Wodarski and Harris on adolescent suicide is keen to point out the need for prevention programmes at the middle-school level. They argue that children of 12 and 13 are the best target for such enterprises by schools, churches and the wider community. Short courses could be launched to help not only the youngsters in their interrelating but to aid parents, teachers and other professionals in their listening, understanding and communication skills. Basic signs for spotting potentially suicidal teenagers need to be picked up – such as taking seriously 'stray' adolescent comments like, 'My life is empty' or 'I have these weird thoughts.'

Ultimately, as we are seeing throughout, it is where young and old listen not only to one another but to their Creator-Redeemer God that the distorted responses to life's stresses of anorexia nervosa, chronic anxiety, fear, depression and suicide can begin to melt away. There is much in the wisdom literature of the Bible (especially in the Psalms, Job, Ecclesiastes and Lamentations) about grappling with life's adversities and trying to cope with emotional conflict and spiritual darkness. Let us close this chapter with a few verses from Psalm 55 which remind us of the agonies of heart many young people go through during the 'storm and stress' of adolescence and, further, give us all the key to a message of hope as we turn to the Lord for light in the tunnel:

> My heart is in anguish within me;
> the terrors of death assail me.
> Fear and trembling have beset me;
> horror has overwhelmed me (4,5).

> But I call to God,
> and the Lord saves me (16).

> Cast your cares on the Lord
> and he will sustain you;
> he will never let the righteous fall (22).

> But as for me, I trust in you (23).

9

CHANGING BEHAVIOUR

In a society where you don't seem to matter it is easy to think that other people and other things don't matter

Faith in the City (1985)

In Leonard Bernstein's *West Side Story* there is a marvellous 'tongue-in-cheek' chorus sung by Baby John, Snowboy and other gang members to Police Officer Krupke. The gist of their song is to explain that the reason they are thought to be 'punks' and 'delinquents' is not because they are basically bad so much as 'misunderstood', 'psychologically disturbed' and 'sociologic'ly sick'. By imitating, in turn, a judge, psychiatrist and social worker the young toughs parade the whole gamut of 'reasons' for their law-breaking behaviour, including drinking too much, laziness, craziness and, perhaps most telling of all, the mere fact that they are 'growing'. And it is the last of these perspectives, the simple reality of adolescent development from puberty to adulthood, which is often blamed by the public for all manner of disruptive activity by teenagers.

As Christians who believe in fallen human nature, are we to conclude that, along with Officer Krupke, young people who get on the wrong side of the law are simply a bad lot? Without denying elements of foolish choice and irresponsibility, let us examine something of the background and circumstances of many of the adolescents who cause so much social concern. I propose to concentrate on two main areas of misguided conduct: *delinquency* and *problem drug use*.

Delinquency

Delinquency, a term once used of those who levied war for Charles the First, is now technically reserved to describe that behaviour of juveniles (youngsters aged 10 to 16) which is punishable by law. However, the word 'delinquent', along with 'hooligan', 'promiscuous' and 'addict', tends to be bandied about more widely by straight society as a dismissive 'buzz-word'. None-the-less, the fact is that there has been a huge increase in the crime rate among young people in recent years. In the United Kingdom, one third of all recorded offences is committed by those aged 16 and under; in 1988 there are more crimes perpetrated by 15-year-olds than any other age group. Put differently, the peak age for male offences is 15 and for female 14. Among older adolescents, one quarter of those in British gaols in the late 1980s are aged between 17 and 20. High crime rates, it is said, among the young in Britain and the United States are being exported eastwards: for instance, Moscow now declares that 10 per cent of its criminal offences are carried out by teenagers.

The most common reasons for conviction or cautioning among those under 17 in the United Kingdom are theft and the handling of stolen goods. There is also a marked increase in crimes of violence recorded throughout the teen years. Even so, among juveniles, the graver offences of burglary, robbery and violence against the person do not appear to have become more frequent over the last ten years or so.[1]

In recent years there has also been a clear increase in the numbers of adolescent girls cautioned or convicted of crime. In fact, according to a recent publication by the Prison Reform Trust, 'self-report studies have found that girls are involved in far more delinquency, across a wider range of offences, than would appear to be the case from official statistics.'[2] Generally though, it is important to remember that the vast majority of juvenile crime is at the level of petty theft and minor vandalism and that almost all former offenders gradually become law-abiding by their early twenties.

So what is it that will turn one 15-year-old to an almost routine breaking of the law while his or her classmates keep, generally, to the rules? Broadly, and not surprisingly, research has established that the main causes of delinquency relate to family, peers and social conditions. One important survey, carried out by Sheldon and Eleanor Glueck in poor areas of Boston, Massachusetts, showed that in the families of delinquent young people there were higher rates of separation, divorce, alcoholism, criminality and lack of supervision.[3] Other recent investigations bear out these general conclusions, but also highlight that it is *emotional conflict* within the home which is the crucial factor.[4] Teenagers seem to cope better with absent parents than rowing ones.

There are many aspects to this clear linkage between domestic instability and adolescent crime. These include the overall family contexts of unemployment and material deprivation with their tendency to increase disharmony and bickering among relatives. Resultant drink problems and law-breaking by older members of families aggravate further the road to delinquency. In effect, where young lives are subject to weak or antisocial parental models their own behaviour tends to follow suit – both by imitation and through the unleashing of pent-up frustration and irritation. To modify the quotation at the head of this chapter: 'In a family where *you* don't seem to matter it is easy to think that other people and other things don't matter.'

Furthermore, there is a close correlation between delinquent youngsters and their contemporaries. The Gluecks, for example, found that 98 per cent of the criminally active group had close friends who were official delinquents, compared with only 7 per cent among the non-delinquent group. It may be this cohesiveness between sets of antisocial teenagers which accounts for the fact that some schools seem to foster higher rates of delinquency than others. More generally, poor school attendance, low academic performance and high delinquency rates go hand in hand.

Although the everyday contacts of those who are criminally active tend to be young people who are similarly disposed, antisocial teenagers are usually disliked or rejected by most of their peers. Aggressiveness, rudeness and general social ineptness all seem to contribute. A vicious circle is readily set up in which delinquent adolescents, unpopular among their contemporaries and singled out for negative comment by their teachers, feel more and more hopeless and thus turn their resentment into increasingly disruptive behaviour.

Although family background and peer pressures can play their part in nurturing delinquency, there are also strong environmental factors which can act as a seedbed of trouble. Among these, as we have indicated, high unemployment, poverty, poor housing, a declining population and inadequate recreational facilities, all contribute to the delinquency rates of many inner-city areas. John, for example, when asked if he would ever commit crime, replied:

> Why not? Really, you've got nothing to lose. You might as well try a job and get some money. And why not? If you get caught and you get locked up, so what? It's like being in a prison being trapped in the house with nothing to do all day in any case.[5]

It is thought that similar social pressures have led to the increased crime rate among teenage girls. A number of recent writers point out that young women are particularly susceptible to the forces of consumerism and, in the face of economic difficulty, may turn more readily to petty theft (or 'tea-leaving'). Roz, at 19 and never having had a full-time job, declared, 'Quite honestly, if I didn't do a bit of tea-leaving now and again, I'd never have clothes or make-up or anything – I'd be a wreck.'[6]

In many parts of the world there are, of course, even more vicious factors at work in the lives of the young. The brutalisation of children and teenagers in the face of terrorism, rioting, military suppression and war is one of the obscenities of our times. In Northern Ireland, for example, the adverse effects of the Troubles on the young are well documented by Morris Fraser, in his *Children in Conflict*. He shows that anxiety and fear, often accompanied by sleep disturbance and bed-wetting, are common. Janet, a 12-year-old, said:

> I can't sleep at night for thinking about fires and burning. There are five of us in the bed, and I sleep nearest the window so as my small brother won't get hit with a bullet. Every time I hear a loud noise I shake all over.[7]

Depressingly, this apprehension can give way to a dangerous bravado which, nurtured by bigotry and encouraged by adult example, can lead to the child or teenager guerrilla. David, on the threshold of puberty, declared:

> The favourite game in our street is 'riots'. We use tomato sauce for blood. My friend went in to his mum with his face covered with tomato sauce and said he had been hit by a bullet. When she found out it was just sauce she was furious and kept him in.[8]

We can see from our examination of the causes of delinquency that the repercussions for family, school and community are enormous. Much of what we said in chapter 5 about types of parenting is relevant here, for it is the authoritarian or lax patterns that seem to encourage delinquency – especially where parents are harsh, unloving, aggressive and inclined to punish adolescents physically. So much antisocial behaviour is the result of unresolved family conflict and so parents need to foster a greater openness and willingness to discuss issues with their offspring. Where genuine affection, coupled with firm guidelines and the giving of responsibility, is the hallmark of a family then the path of crime is unlikely to be chosen.

Where teachers can avoid victimising the 'misfits' in the class and encourage other children to do the same, then juvenile delinquents might become better school-attenders and achievers. Affirmation and the chance to prove oneself responsible can do a lot for the self-image of the antisocial youngster who is already in trouble with family, friends and the police.

We shall look more fully at some of the environmental elements that fuel delinquency in the next chapter.

Problem Drug Use

Addiction, the habitual and excessive use of something or someone, can affect just about any sphere of life – from watching television to global travel, from collecting stamps to ski-jumping. Although, on the subject of adolescence, most people think in terms of 'problem drug use' there are other forms of addiction which can bedevil the lives of the young. Among these, gambling on fruit machines can be one of the hardest habits to break. Julian, for example, had gradually become hooked since his first visit to an amusement arcade with a friend at the age of 12.[9] At 17, earning good money with a finance broker in London and borrowing heavily from the bank, he would spend up to £250 a week on his addiction. The ephemerel solace of many habituations comes through in the words of this lonely young man: 'The machine's somebody who isn't laughing at me. It accepts me as I am. It's like a person I can relate to.'

Before looking in some detail at the taking of particular drugs by young people, it is worth making several more general points. First, it is helpful to understand that drug dependence may be either physical or psychological – though many addictions can be a combination of the two. In *physical dependence*, as with heroin, the body comes to rely on the substance for its functioning and reacts strongly to produce 'withdrawal symptoms' when the drug is stopped. In *psychological dependence*, as with cannabis, there is a more subtle reliance on the drug so that there is an emotional sense of loss when it is unavailable or cannot be taken.

Second, we should remember that, though we are now concentrating on the teen years, vast numbers of the older generations are dependent on a range of substances, including the ubiquitous cups of tea and coffee, as well as tobacco, alcohol, tranquillisers and sleeping tablets.

Third, throughout our consideration of adolescent drug-taking, we need to understand that many young people experiment with a number of different materials, depending on availability, inclination and peer-group pressure, rather than being tied to any one substance.

And fourth, though talk of drug dependence makes most of us think of the illegal drugs, it is the more accessible legal items that lead to the greatest and most widespread health risks. By way of illustration, in the mid-1980s the number of drug-related deaths in Britain were: 235 from illegal drugs (1984); 40,000 through alcohol (1985); and 95,000 as a result of cigarette smoking (1984).[10] I propose to look at these last two, widely used, 'social' drugs first, before examining the teenage drug scene.

Smoking

It is, perhaps, because the fatal results of smoking – including coronary heart disease, emphysema, bronchitis and cancers of the lung and cervix – are reserved for adulthood that many teenagers smoke as avidly as if they had found the elixir of life. In fact, in the early years of the introduction of tobacco to Europe it was sometimes seen as having health-giving properties. One writer in 1614 stated:

In tobacco there is nothing which is not medicine. It cures asthma. It heals an old cough. It stops migraine. It is a help against arthritis, gout and the stone in the bladder.[11]

The heyday of smoking in the United Kingdom was the mid-1950s when 80 per cent of all adult men indulged. The habit in women continued to grow in the following years so that by the mid-1970s 40 per cent of them smoked. With the clear public recognition of its serious health hazards, the adult population has gradually cut down on smoking so that, in 1986, 35 per cent of men and 31 per cent of women were reckoned to be smokers.[12]

These statistics are important for it is estimated that children with parents who smoke are twice as likely to start themselves. Up to the age of 10 or so, most children are strongly against the habit. However, over the next few years huge numbers of teenagers begin a lifetime of addiction to cigarettes. There is a lot of evidence that, in the late 1980s, more 14- and 15-year-old girls are smoking than boys of the same ages. One recent survey by Pam Gillies in Nottingham showed that, among 500 14-year-olds, one in three girls and one in five boys smoked.[13] A nationwide sample in 1986 of 18,000 teenagers revealed that, among the 15- and 16-year-olds, 66 per cent of girls and 62 per cent of boys had tried smoking at some stage or other.[14]

The reasons why so many young people are smoking are various. Parental example, as already mentioned, is important; in fact, where parents actually approve of their offspring smoking the likelihood of their doing so is seven times greater. The behaviour of close friends is also highly influential: it can feel antisocial not to light up when everyone else is doing so. It is found, too, that teenagers with generous amounts of pocket money are more inclined to smoke and there are clear associations between drinking alcohol and smoking. At a more psychological level, recent research has shown that, whereas boys are more inclined to smoke because their peers do, girls seem more susceptible to advertising, believing that smoking calms their nerves, gives confidence and controls weight. The Nottingham survey discovered that three out of four girl smokers said they did so to ease worries about the future. Their greatest concerns were about whether they would get a job on leaving school, finding someone to marry and whether their future husbands would be sexually faithful. One in four of them expressed fears of catching AIDS.

Behind such reasons for starting smoking is the hoary problem of addiction to nicotine. It seems that a teenager's intake of the drug per cigarette is similar to an adult's. The calming effect experienced through smoking, and the withdrawal symptoms of irritability, hunger and craving for a cigarette, are typical of a drug dependency. Rachel, aged 16 and from a comprehensive school in North London, started smoking at the age of 13. The addictive qualities of nicotine are indicated in her answer to the question of whether she considers herself a nervous person: 'No, not really. It [a cigarette] just makes me feel peaceful, especially when I haven't had one for a few hours.'[15]

The 1986 survey referred to earlier showed that two out of three smoking mid-adolescents would like to stop. However, giving up smoking is never easy. Typically, the most intense withdrawal symptoms come within the first twenty-four hours following the last cigarette and then diminish gradually over the next three weeks or so. It can help to decide in advance on a particular date for giving up, to make sure there are no surplus cigarettes available. It is wise to tell family and friends of the resolve and avoid situations where smoking is the norm. This might mean taking up jogging or other activities to avoid idle stretches of time and, further, keeping away from the pubs and wine bars. Where addiction is especially hard to beat, the local GP or a clinic that specialises in smoking problems may be able to help.

Alcohol

Alcohol has been described as 'Britain's favourite drug' and, in terms of the misery it brings through physical and mental deterioration, crimes of violence and accidental death, it can be seen as the most dangerous of addictive substances in relation to its popularity and availability.

Among juveniles in the United Kingdom alcohol dependence is a far greater social problem than the abuse of illegal drugs. The 'Adolescent Drinking Survey', carried out by the Office of Population Censuses and Surveys in 1984 for England and Wales, showed that the majority of children have had their first 'proper drink' by the age of 13.[16] Although the figures are thought to be an underestimate, it was reckoned that one in three 13-year-old boys and one in nine girls of the same age drank at least weekly; the ratios for 15-year-olds were one in two boys and roughly one in three girls. The youngest adolescents drank mostly in the homes of their parents or their friends' families; those in their mid-teens also drank in clubs and at discos; while the majority of 17-year-olds said they usually drank in pubs. Another sobering statistic, if you will forgive the pun, is that one in four of those arrested for drink-related offences is under 21.

Excessive drinking in adolescence tends to be among young people who have problems coping with aggression and who seem to feel the need for power over situations and others. Male teenagers who drink heavily often appear to want to demonstrate their virility and are loth to admit anxiety or the need for other people. A great deal of soccer violence seems linked with this mentality and its boosting by alcohol. There is, of course, always the danger of more secure youngsters slipping into addiction through experimentation. Yet again, families are enormously influential for better or worse: alcohol abuse is most common in teenagers where one or both parents have a drink problem.

For those young people who are trying to control their drinking habits, the psychologist John Travers, in his 1977 study, offered some useful advice.[17] The youngster needs to know the positive reason for any decision made about alcohol; he or she should not feel it necessary, for example, to apologise for abstaining; the convictions of others about drinking should be respected; sensible, social drinking habits should be acquired – for instance, learning to sip slowly and space, say, one or two drinks over an evening in order to relax in the company of others. Adolescents with a strong dependence on alcohol can find help through their GP, special psychiatric units and a wide range of centres for detoxication and rehabilitation; addresses are given at the back of this book.

Illegal Drugs

Perhaps alongside sexual promiscuity, pregnancy outside wedlock and delinquency, drug addiction is one of the aspects of the teen years most feared by the adult world. Sometimes this fear surfaces in most unlikely corners. At the age of 6 our son, Simon, was accused of peddling drugs. Auburn-haired, plumpish and almost cherubic, he did not look like the stereotypical junkie. One day in term-time we were phoned by a conscientious headmistress. An anxious mother had contacted the head urgently because one of the pupils at the local primary school had offered her son a mysterious pill during break. The culprit, Simon Hurding, worryingly the son of a local doctor, had been seen by the same boy to give similar tablets to several other children. Clearly a potential drug-ring of addicts was in the making at Highdown Infants'! Following this incident, we urged Simon to be less generous with the 'Setlers' he was taking for stomach-ache.

As we have already indicated, the more serious features of the abuse of illegal drugs are infrequent compared with health risks associated with alcohol and smoking. None-the-less, as we shall see, the hazards of 'problem drug use' are considerable and widespread. For instance, from 1981 to 1985 in the United Kingdom, the number of admissions of people with drug dependence nearly doubled.[18] As we have noted with delinquency and smoking, there is also a trend for more girls to become involved in illicit drugs: in the mid-1970s there were three male drug-takers to one female user; in the late-1980s the ratio is two to one.[19]

Such trends may, among other things, be one of the outcomes of the greater freedom which young women have in contrast to earlier generations. It is likely, too, that the rise in female drug abuse is linked with the range of personal and sociological factors that seem to foster drug dependence in adolescents generally. The teen years are years of experimentation, and the reasons for trying out illegal drugs are many and varied. Probably the most basic drive is that of curiosity – particularly among those who already smoke and drink regularly. The idea of extending the scope of pleasurable experience, especially when your friends urge you to join them, can prove irresistible. Other influences on starting the habit include the availability of the drugs, fads and fashions of drug misuse among contemporaries and the posturing of 'rebellion' against the Establishment.

It is one thing to give cannabis, cocaine or heroin a try, it is another to continue into a subculture of drug dependence. Clear links are established between addiction and social conditions. Young people from deprived areas are more readily drawn into drug abuse, crime and delinquent behaviour. Consequent 'labelling' as 'addicts' or 'junkies' by the authorities can lead to further deviance – fulfilling the expectations of 'straight' society. One survey in the Lothian region of Scotland, for example, followed up a thousand or so 15- and 16-year-olds through the early 1980s and has exposed a clear connection between unemployment and the use of illicit drugs.[20] Interestingly, extra involvement with the latter, rather than tobacco and alcohol, may be explained, at least partly, by their lower cost.

Once more, we also find a linkage between drug dependence in the young and strained parental relationships. One review, published in 1977, noted that the families of heroin addicts often demonstrate a father who is a shadowy and detached figure and a mother who is dominant and possessive.[21] However, the more widespread drug-taking is the more the offspring of well-adjusted and caring families can be affected, too. Impeccable child-rearing and marital bliss are no automatic guarantees that a son or daughter may not one day smoke pot or sniff coke. Conversely, of course, family strife does not inevitably lead to addicted teenagers. As we have shown, the reasons a particular adolescent becomes drug-dependent are many and various and concerned parents should not reflexly blame themselves for their offspring's irresponsibilities.

Space forbids too detailed an account of the various substances abused by adolescents, but I should like, nevertheless, to outline some of the salient aspects of illegal drug use among the young. It is worth saying, too, that the well-defined subcultures of the 1960s – pot-smoking hippies, 'pep pill' swallowing mods and alcohol-drinking rockers – have gradually lost their distinctiveness and blurred into the general morass of multi-drug use in the 1980s. Even so, for the sake of simplicity, let us briefly look at each of the main ingredients which make up the composite picture of teenage drug dependence today. Broadly, we can divide the items of problem drug use into three categories: the *hallucinogens*, the *depressants* (or 'downers') and the *stimulants* (or 'uppers').

Hallucinogens

The hallucinogenic, or 'psychedelic', drugs are substances which can alter perception, sensation, states of consciousness and mood. This distortion of how phenomena are experienced may include seeing, hearing, feeling, smelling or tasting things that have no objective reality. Although cannabis is mildly intoxicant, like alcohol, in high doses it can produce these hallucinogenic effects in susceptible individuals.

Cannabis Cannabis, usually in the form of 'hash' – the resin obtained from the tops and leaves of the female form of *Cannabis sativa* – is the most widely used illegal drug in Britain. Its use has spread from the 1960s onwards to pervade all sections of society, mostly among people in their late teens to early forties. In the early 1970s it was often said, 'Now the law students smoke pot it will soon be legalised.' Although the drug is still illicit, it has been estimated that there are at least one million regular users of cannabis in Britain. As well as hash, cannabis is also used in a dried, less potent form known as marijuana (pot, grass, weed, smoke) and as a powerful oil, obtained from the resin. It may be smoked, ingested in food or brewed as a drink. Basically depressing the nervous system, the drug can initially stimulate – though it does not readily give the user the desired effects of high spirits, talkativeness and heightened sensations of sight and sound. Regular use can lead to psychological dependence and lung disease.

LSD LSD, a man-made white powder derived from a fungus that grows wild on rye grass, is one of the so-called 'mind-expanding' drugs that were especially popular in the late 1960s and early 1970s. Recently there has been a new surge in its use – though mostly in weaker doses as a 'fun' drug. Taken as a tablet or capsule, or absorbed on paper, a sheet of gelatin or a sugar cube, LSD produces its so-called 'trip' after half an hour or so, the experience peaking in two to six hours. Distortions of a sense of space and time, together with visual and auditory hallucinations, are unpredictable in quality and apparent significance. A bad trip may take on the colour of a waking nightmare. One young woman saw spiders everywhere and could feel them crawling over her body. A student I once knew, under the influence of LSD, believed he was a motor-car and wandered the streets of Bristol in the small hours of the morning, parking himself in strategic corners. Another student, who fell to his death, was reckoned to be on a trip and may have believed he could fly. Others I have seen have reported the recurrence of unsettling fears and odd sensations weeks or months after the original bad trip.

Laughing mushrooms Certain fungi, like the 'Liberty Cap', contain the hallucinogenic drug, psilocybin. These 'laughing' or 'magic' mushrooms, eaten raw, cooked or brewed as a tea, can produce a mild form of LSD trip. There can be minor epidemics of getting high on these mushrooms among teenagers in rural communities during the autumn term, when the fungi are fruiting. The greatest danger of this habit is the accidental ingestion of one of the poisonous, potentially fatal, *Amanita* species of fungus.

Ecstasy   Ecstasy ('E', 'Adam', 'XTC') is a mildly hallucinogenic drug that can be either obtained from the natural oils of various plants or made synthetically. Its effects are a blend of those produced by LSD and the amphetamines. After 20 to 60 minutes this drug, taken in tablet or capsule form, produces a short-lived euphoria which merges into a state of calmness and the loss of hostility. As its name implies, Ecstasy tends to enhance sensual experience, although it does not in fact lead to any increase of sexual activity. This so-called 'love drug' first emerged on the American West Coast in 1968 and has in turn appeared in Britain during the late 1980s. Its use is associated with certain night clubs, especially in conjunction with 'Acid House' and 'Balearic' style music. Besides nausea, sweating and a dry mouth, Ecstasy can raise blood pressure and quicken the heart rate. Other serious side-effects include panic feelings, confusion and insomnia. More powerful, related 'hallucinogenic amphetamines' include DOB, which can cause fits, prolonged coma and even death.

Depressants

The depressants, or 'downers', produce their desired effect by slowing down the nervous system. They include alcohol and widely prescribed drugs like sedatives and tranquillisers, as well as solvents and the opiates.

Solvents   In the 1970s there was an explosion of solvent abuse, particularly among boys of 13 to 16 or so. Although glue-sniffing seems less newsworthy in the late 1980s, it is still a serious form of drug dependence. Inhaling a range of products, from adhesives and nail-varnish remover to butane gas and petrol, the youngster seeks to get 'high' and 'drunk' relatively cheaply. Again, the hallucinations that can be induced, variously described as 'dreams' or 'images', can be either pleasurable or frightening. In the early days of solvent abuse, glue-sniffing was something of a symbol among disaffected punks. Indeed, this particular form of drug dependence is often linked with long-standing social and emotional problems. Inhaling often gives young teenagers a sense of fleeting, but illusory, power and excitement in the face of the drabness and apparent hopelessness of their surroundings. Joe, a boy who was sent to a community home, used to see soldiers rising from the ground in front of him when he sniffed solvents.[22] He experienced some exhilaration, it seems, when he found he could push these figures back below the surface by placing his hand on their heads.

The dangers of both short- and long-term abuse of solvents are considerable. Acute effects include anything from headaches, nausea, vomiting, bloodshot eyes and bad breath through loss of memory, facial rashes and sleep disturbance to the grim possibilities of fits, heart failure and death through suffocation or swallowing vomit. With prolonged periods of regular sniffing the user may lose weight, become depressed and find daily functioning virtually impossible, besides running the risk of unco-ordinated limb movements and lasting kidney and liver damage.

Sedatives and tranquillisers   Apart from the huge numbers of adults reckoned to be dependent on sedatives and tranquillisers, as a result of legal prescribing, there are lesser but significant numbers of young people who take these drugs illicitly – obtaining them by breaking into pharmacies, stealing them from parental medicine cupboards or buying them on the black market. There is a wide range of preparations used, depending on fad, fashion and availability. Traditionally, it is the barbiturates ('goofballs' or 'sleepers') which have been most extensively used as 'downers'.

Up to and including the 1960s, vast quantities of these drugs were prescribed for anxiety states and insomnia. In the mid-1970s there was a great deal of publicity over the prevailing misuse of barbiturates, particularly among homeless young people in London. The death rate at that time from the intravenous use of these drugs was higher than that from heroin and other opiates. Since then, despite stricter controls on prescribing, committed drug users still acquire these dangerously addictive substances by break-ins and theft.

The drowsiness, unsteadiness and aggressiveness from taking barbiturates are similar to the effects of a heavy consumption of alcohol. Large doses cause unconsciousness and the possibility of death through respiratory and circulatory failure. Over the past twenty-five years, tranquillisers like Valium, Mogadon (Moggies) and Mandrax (Mandies) have become a somewhat safer source of drug dependence among the young. Even so, the hazards of accidental overdose, and mixing these drugs with other depressants like alcohol, are considerable.

Heroin Heroin (smack, junk, H, horse, jack, boy) is the most notorious of the highly addictive opiates. Other drugs in this broad category include opium, morphine, pethidine, methadone, codeine and dihydrocodeine (DF118). Heroin, though producing nausea and vomiting with its first use, can bring an immediate surge of pleasurable warmth (known as a 'rush') and strong feelings of relaxation and well-being. The need to increase the dose for the desired effect is marked and both physical and psychological dependence can be rapid. By the beginning of the 1980s, partly due to legislation against the widespread prescribing of barbiturates and partly due to the increasing availability of heroin from the Middle East, the current epidemic in the illicit use of opiates was under way.

The powerfully addictive qualities of heroin are made more accessible to young people by the comparatively new trends of smoking ('chasing the dragon') and sniffing ('snorting') the powder. It is, of course, the intravenous use of heroin, and other drugs, which can spread the AIDS virus through contaminated syringes and needles. By 1985 it was estimated that there were 60–80,000 using opiates regularly in the United Kingdom.[23] The numbers seem to be rising still and it is reckoned, for example, that Merseyside alone now has 15,000 heroin users. The life-style behind this addiction is seen in the words of Bob, aged 20 and unemployed, who first 'chased the dragon' at 16:

> I had to move out of home because I stole from my dad. I live in a flat with nothing in it now . . . I haven't seen my parents since.
>
> You can't buy smack on your Giro. We go out stealing every day, burgling houses or shop-lifting – it's dead easy.[24]

Stimulants

Caffeine, in the cups of tea and coffee and cans of Coca Cola of countless millions, and nicotine in tobacco are the most ubiquitous of the addictive stimulants. Let us look briefly, though, at the illegal use of two other 'uppers': cocaine and the amphetamines.

Cocaine Among stimulants, cocaine (coke, snow, C, charlie, girl, gold dust) is not used widely among adolescents in the UK. From the mid-1970s onwards the popularity of coke has risen, especially where there has been 'style, champagne and money'.[25] More recently its use has become more pervasive, particularly for occasional and recreational use. Although cocaine is usually sniffed, there is current concern that the especially addictive form of 'crack', which is smoked, is spreading from North American cities to Britain. Users of cocaine may experience feelings of great exhilaration and deceptively strong sensations of great physical strength and mental ability. Sometimes these desired effects give way to acute anxiety, panic and ideas of being victimised. Sleeplessness, fatigue and depression are not unusual after using coke. The risks of long-term exposure to the drug include chronic insomnia, loss of weight, hallucinations and profound psychological disturbance.

Amphetamines After cannabis, the amphetamines are the most widely used illegal drugs among teenagers. These were popular as 'pep pills' in the 1960s and early 1970s, went out of favour with prescribing restrictions in the mid-1970s, but are now seen in large numbers in the illicit market. Producing feelings of alertness and boundless energy, these drugs are nowadays mainly sniffed in powder form or injected as 'speed'. In contrast to cocaine, the amphetamines are said to be commoner among the 'working classes', as well as in certain colleges and other situations where young people might try to 'burn the candle at both ends'. There is a high level of physical addiction and the real danger of developing serious psychiatric illness, in which the victim has delusions of persecution, may hear threatening voices and may respond with violence. The profundity of such a psychosis led to the adage, 'Speed kills' among the laid-back, pot-smoking hippies of the late 1960s.

Drug Dependence in the Family

We have already indicated that the problems of drug dependence are much wider than the illegal drugs. As we have seen, many more families are troubled by the repercussions of drinking and smoking, as well as the effects of chronic addiction to legally prescribed tranquillisers and sleeping tablets. Nevertheless, how are families to respond when a son or daughter, brother or sister is trapped by problem drug use?

First, it is important to realise that there are different patterns in using drugs, ranging from 'experimental' and 'casual' through to 'regular'. Contrary to common belief, there is no inevitable development from taking drugs occasionally to using them frequently – or, for that matter, from smoking pot to a dependence on 'hard' drugs like cocaine or heroin. The adolescent who comes from a stable, caring family, whose friends are not involved with the drug scene, who has a range of interests and who is well-motivated at school or in a job, is unlikely to get 'hooked'. As Dr Annas Dixon puts it: '. . . for the majority of youngsters drug use is a passing phase, usually of a recreational nature.'[26] It is in this context that parents need to avoid overreaction – not least, because it is easy to push a sensitive teenager towards heavier usage by knee-jerk condemnation.

Where an adolescent is becoming a regular user there are a number of tell-tale signs which might be observed by parents, siblings, friends or teachers. Overall, it is a marked *change* in behaviour, in a certain direction, that may be the main clue. Relationships generally may become more strained as the young person becomes increasingly withdrawn and edgy. Former responsibilities and time-keeping may begin to slip, while continuance in education or employment may become seriously threatened. There may also be physical changes, such as a dip in appetite, weight loss, nausea, vomiting, drowsiness, excessive yawning, sneezing or coughing, and a general neglect of appearance. Further, a new tendency to borrow money and get into debt may indicate the flow of cash into drug-taking. This need for finance may lead to theft, fraud and the forging of doctors' prescriptions. The more desperate, intravenous addictions for opiates, speed or barbiturates may lead to more desperate attempts to make money. For example, the Scottish Communicable Diseases Unit published figures for Glasgow recently in which 75 per cent of the city's female, AIDS-infected, intravenous drug abusers admitted to funding their habit by prostitution.[27]

Where parents observe some of these changes in a son or

daughter, they will need to challenge him or her with their suspicion. The physical signs mentioned may, of course, have already taken some members of the family to the doctor for advice. It is important that any attempt to discuss the matter is open to the teenager's side of the story. There may be difficulties in relationships or other worries, as well as a clear medical condition, behind the deterioration of behaviour and general health. However, young people hooked on drugs will not be averse to lying in order to continue their habit. Where, for instance, household money is vanishing or there are direct evidences of drug-taking in, say, a teenager's bedroom, then there must be firm confrontation.

Many parents are uncertain as to where they stand with the law if one of their offspring is taking drugs. They can, in fact, be prosecuted if they knowingly allow the family home to be used in that way. However, if they find illegal substances on the premises they are not obliged to report the matter to the police. Failing that response, they must destroy the drugs. None-the-less, where parents know that a son or daughter is hooked on illicit drugs they obviously must, on grounds of compassion and morality, do all they can to help.

One avenue that could relieve the situation greatly is that of the statutory agencies. The general practitioner may be able to help directly or refer the young person to a social worker, clinical psychologist or psychiatrist for more specialist advice. As we saw with anorexia nervosa, such professionals may seek to involve the whole family in finding a way forward. Where the teenager is addicted to heroin he or she may be prescribed methadone tablets to help alleviate the 'cold turkey' symptoms of withdrawal. Supervision, counselling and support may be offered. Whether the drug-dependent youngster is at home or away, the wider family will have their needs, too. They can find a great deal of encouragement and understanding through a local self-help group for parents or through contacting an organisation like Families Anonymous.

Further, the local church, particularly where there is a ministry to needy young people out in the community, and Christian bodies and rehabilitation centres, like Life for the World in Bristol and the Coke Hole in Andover, may be instrumental in bringing the power of the risen Christ to change lives damaged by habitual drug use. Street-wise people like David Wilkerson, Floyd McClung and Jackie Pullinger have pioneered a work of God's love among countless young people held in bondage by a range of addictions.[28] Often, traditional church structures seem unhelpfully strait-jacketing for those adolescents who long to break their drug habits and find a deep sense of belonging. Kenneth Leech, in his *Pastoral Care and the Drug Scene*, challenges us all with these words:

> The Church must see its ministry to the drug scene as being a purging and a learning process. Perhaps the respectable, conventional Church must die before the living Body of Christ can arise. It must certainly cease to be the community of the 'good' and the 'respectable' and those who conform to the dubious standards of middle-class materialism, and become, as at the beginning, the brotherhood of those who are led by the spirit [sic] and are free.[29]

CHANGING SITUATIONS

The poor need justice, and the rich need restored sight

Jim Wallis

One of the titles I originally suggested for this book was *It Makes A Change*. We have seen just that throughout – how adolescence makes the change from childhood to adulthood in the areas of the physical, psychological, relational, sexual, emotional and behavioural. It remains, finally, to consider the situational and attitudinal and, in so doing, see the way the teen years anticipate and prepare for maturity. The future beckons and the young person, influenced by past and present, faces it with fear or confidence, reluctance or eagerness, despair or hope. While the days ahead are envisaged, the adolescent, for better or worse, has to make choices – choices about where to live, what to do, who to be with and what to believe. Let us therefore, in the last two chapters, think about these four crucial aspects of decision-making under the headings of *home*, *work*, *love* and *God*. As we do this we cannot avoid looking at the flip side of the coin to include homelessness, unemployment and isolation.

Home and Homelessness

We saw in chapter 5 how home needs to be a 'launching centre' for teenagers. Our youngest, Rache, had her twentieth birthday yesterday and so I have not quite succeeded in finishing this book while at least our youngest was still in her teen years. How well have Rache, Simon and Sarah been 'launched'? How effective has the nurturing home been in preparing them for the responsibilities, rigours and rewards of adult life? Only to ask the questions reveals that they cannot be answered – for time will tell. Each of these young people is on an individual journey and God only knows of the storms and calms ahead, who will be their respective travelling-companions and how each will fare day by day. In the earlier years of maturity they may return to the home-port from time to time. They will always be welcome, for the launching is rarely a clear-cut event. But the cutting loose and the voyage is *their* adventure and it cannot be gainsaid.

As we have seen, it is democratic families, rather than authoritarian or permissive ones, which pave the way for this journeying. John Halliburton, in his delightful account of his 15-year-old daughter's preparation for the future, gives the flavour of a family life which is loving and wise enough to know how to let go. He writes this of Rachel and her friends:

> It is their self-determination that has to be respected; and if for what seems an unbelievably long time their choices remain immature, apparently wasteful and (in our opinion) wide of the mark, then we simply have to bear with this. They will choose anyhow; and we shall do far better to remain friends with them and listen to their extraordinary expositions of life's purposes and ideals than to push them into an outward conformity which will either crush their spirit or induce the wrong kind of rebellion. Our moral life is of our own making and the good is only that which is freely chosen.[1]

This element of choice is, of course, always tempered by circumstance. For some, the environment is highly favourable: the family is democratic and supportive, parents love without being clinging, education has been stimulating and forward-looking, friends are a pleasure to be with, just the right qualifications have been achieved and the future seems to open its arms in welcome. For many, though, the passage is not so smooth: family life is riven by conflict and violence, parents are harsh and rejecting, friends are notable for their absence and schooling has been woefully inadequate. Veronica is a case in point. Her father left her mother and four children in order to go and live with another woman. Veronica, a problem drug-user, has drifted from one sexual relationship to another – in search, it seems, for a sense of belonging, of being 'at home'.[2]

The stress on the importance of family life has, as in the example of Veronica, been profoundly weakened in white, Western culture. Even so, there are many sections of society where traditional values and customs still greatly influence the young – not least within the Asian and Afro-Caribbean communities in Britain. Although here, too, European secularism and materialism threaten established ways of living, it is worth outlining something of the ethos of 'home' among the ethnic minorities.

Asian youngsters in this country from the Indian subcontinent, be they Sikh, Hindu or Muslim, Punjabi, Indian, Pakistani or Bangladeshi, come from close-knit communities where the extended family forms a nurturing and disciplining network which gives a great deal of security.[3] Home is a place of intense loyalty, where both a sense of duty and a respect for authority are strongly developed. Any stepping out of line is not to be tolerated and deviance is swiftly and summarily dealt with. One young Asian put it this way:

> My brothers, they can come in the house, say something – I've got to do it, whether I like it or not. Say, for example, I refused him once, which I did. This was when I was working at the market, and he just turned round and slapped me in the face. I was 19 then. See, if I'd been an English lad myself, I know this, I would have turned round and hit him one. But not me . . . I just turned, started working.[4]

This solidarity, though often punitive, is ultimately concerned with family honour – in contrast to white, Western competitiveness which stresses individual ambition and achievement. As a result, Asian adolescents, despite the challenge of needing to master two languages, frequently do well academically as they seek to do their best for the sake of those at home. The goal is to find steady employment – at the level of skilled manual work at least, if not in 'white collar' occupations or the learned professions. Aims like these are supported by kith and kin, whereby the young are more readily able to receive help in buying a house, attending college or starting a business.

There are, of course, many social pressures which undermine this process. Different aspects of white society, ranging from the exuberance and sexual freedom of many in the youth culture to the élitism and secularism of the middle class, can look alien and threatening. Further, what is valuable in Asian family life can prove irksome and repressive to the youngster who is beginning to taste Western liberalism. Although adolescent boys, for example, may have to give their wages to their fathers, it is the girls who experience the greatest restrictions. Basically, there is considerable curtailment of their comings and goings, and arranged marriages, though often continuing a welcome sense of security, may be seen as the death knell for any future freedom. Where Asian young people try to break away from family strictures they may, in effect, end up as moral outcasts.

Home for the West Indian, whether originally from Jamaica, Trinidad, St Kitts or Guyana, is a very different place from that of the Asian. In contrast to those from the Indian subcontinent, from a complex empire recently freed from colonial rule, people from the Caribbean inherit a history of slavery, within which they have been subject to the culture and language of their masters. Furthermore, the influx of Afro-Caribbeans into Britain in the post-war years was of a body of skilled, semi-skilled and unskilled workers who became part of the mainstream working class in this

country. Unlike their Asian counterparts, with strong traditions of mutual support and achievement, many West
Indians in Britain have inherited a demeaning legacy of
subjugation, coupled with modest educational attainment.

The basically poor sense of collective self-esteem, which
seems to have been the birthright of an enslaved people, is
exacerbated both at home and at school for the adolescent
West Indian. Although Caribbean families traditionally
rate British cultural values highly, there is little security in
home life for many teenagers. Generally, the relationships
between male adolescents and their parents are poor and,
as soon as secondary education is over, most young men
move out. Indifference at home is mirrored by indifference
at school and, though some West Indians do well against
the odds, the system seems to worsen the already
precarious sense of worth held by black pupils.

Selective testing, which a lot of white, working-class
children find hard enough, appears to underscore a downward trend and many Afro-Caribbeans find themselves in
remedial and disciplinary classes. It is small wonder that
feelings of personal value are sought elsewhere – particularly in vibrant and ecstatic black music, like reggae and
hip-hop, and, for some, in the world of Rastafarianism.
This latter movement, growing up in Jamaica in the 1830s
and stressing a longing to return to black roots in Africa,
sees the West as an avaricious and ungodly 'Babylon'. The
sense of belonging that Rastafarianism gives to many young
West Indians is brought out powerfully by the words of one
Rasta to a white researcher: 'Me no want you to understand
Rasta; it is I's faith, it is my life.'[5]

Whereas Asian girls are closely controlled by their
fathers and husbands, Afro-Caribbean young women have
much greater freedom. They are even, at times, able to
taunt and intimidate the men – and get away with it! At
school, adolescent black girls, though fun-loving and un-
conforming, often apply themselves diligently to study,
even though ridiculed by the boys. Marcia described these
pressures as follows:

I've always got my head in a book, I don't think they [boys in school] like it because they always commenting on it and they say, 'You won't get anywhere', and sometimes I think they don't want me to learn or something like that, you know, but I spoke to my mum about it, and she said I shouldn't listen and I should keep working hard.[6]

Whether the late adolescent is an Indian boy going away to college, a West Indian girl tied by maternity and planning to live with her man, or a white youth looking for casual work, the desire to set up home is written deeply into our human nature. The need to belong somewhere, to have a place where we can put up a favourite picture, hang up familiar curtains and listen to our choicest music, is an instinct that is often modelled on childhood experience. Where earlier family life has been disrupted and memories soured, a feeling of being 'at home' may still be rescuable where others are warm and accepting. Kate, a second-year student at university, had lived through the break-up of her parents' marriage and was invited to the family home of Nicky, a fellow student. Following her stay, she wrote to Nicky's mother and father:

You made me feel extremely welcome and I can't begin to express how good it was to be within a 'family' atmosphere. Even in your absence the house seems to exude a sense of security.

Homelessness

Tragically, unlike Kate and Nicky, there are many young people who are not only homeless but seem fated to stay that way. The overall figure for homeless families in Great Britain in 1986 was 120,000, though a further 56,000 enquirers were deemed 'non-priority'.[7] These are the statistics of officialdom and do not include the 'concealed households', where displaced people are not literally on the streets, but bed down in the established homes of friends or relatives. Further, these numbers do not reveal the rising proportion of youngsters who are homeless. Hackney's housing advisory centre in London's East End, for example, saw as many as 2,000 single homeless a year in the mid-1980s and four out of five of these were under 25. As Paul Harrison, the author of *Inside the Inner City*, puts it: 'Most single homeless . . . are getting younger and younger as the nuclear family shatters into its constituent particles.'[8]

Adolescents leave home prematurely and run the risk of homelessness for a variety of reasons. A number move out to escape the endless rows of so-called 'home', some to avoid violence or sexual interference, others because they have been kicked out by parents and yet others to replace boredom with excitement, or restriction with freedom. Life on the streets, unless help can be found promptly, is likely to prove rough and tough. Some may find meagre and, at times, insanitary accommodation in bed-sits or short-life tenancies, or track down a bed in a hostel among older vagrants. Others have to fend for themselves and may be drawn into prostitution, the drug subculture or petty crime in order to make ends meet. A residue become dossers and join the huddled figures of urban 'cardboard cities'. Brian, a 20-year-old, looked back over the long months of homelessness:

It's terrible! I've had twenty-three different addresses the last two years; bed-and-breakfast places; grotty 'hotels'; boarding-houses; and bed-sits. Being homeless is awful. Most people, when they're kicked out, don't know what to do – how to find a place not nothin'. It's bad. It's really hard.[9]

Fortunately, there are many agencies, both statutory and voluntary, which are highly committed to helping homeless adolescents – and a number of their addresses are given at the back of this book. Among these, certain Christian organisations are in the vanguard of care. Peter Stow, in his *Youth in the City*, writes out of his own earlier experiences on the streets of East London and outlines his work as a youth and community officer linked with the Hackney Marsh churches.[10] Next door to the club he runs, an old vicarage has been converted by a group of local Christians into a hostel to sleep seven young people in single rooms. This facility operates under the name of the Homerton Space Project and aims to give homeless youngsters a fresh chance to learn how to live. As part of this overall goal, every effort is made to encourage reconciliation with the parents involved, before a young person is admitted.

Peter Stow also offers some helpful, more general, guidelines to teenagers on the verge of leaving home prematurely. First, he urges them, if they *have* to go, to do so without saying or doing anything they might regret later. Although most youngsters facing homelessness prefer to stay locally, where there might be friends and landmarks are familiar, they still need adequate money: Stow, writing in the late 1980s, recommends a realistic figure of well over £100. Young people in this situation, under present government legislation, and depending on the designation of the area, can only spend up to two, four or eight weeks in 'bed and breakfasts' in any one town and so they are pushed towards the greater expense, and continual uprooting, of travel. If possible, a trusted companion will lighten the burden of the search for accommodation and work. Qualified youth workers can refer adolescents who are homeless to reception centres, night shelters, halfway-houses or hostels like that run by the Homerton Space Project.

It is the Christian ethos of the latter which gives it its distinctiveness. Unlike many secular hostels, the project is committed to giving the young people a measure of privacy, thus respecting their human dignity. The facilities of single rooms which can be locked and times for individual cooking must mean a great deal to teenagers who are longing for a sense of being at home. In such an environment, the homelessness experienced by Joseph and Mary in their early years together,[11] and by their eldest son, Jesus, during his itinerant ministry, can be brought to bear on the dislocated lives of the young.

In contrast even to the animal kingdom, where nesting birds and breeding foxes at least have a regular base, Christ declared to his would-be followers, '. . . the Son of Man has nowhere to lay his head' (Matt. 8:20). And yet, though he and his disciples were mostly 'on the road', there were places where he could relax and feel loved, like the house in Bethany run by Mary, Martha and Lazarus. Our prayer and concern for the footloose young of our inner cities is that they, too, will find friends who will welcome and care for them, so that they might, in time, find life worth living once more. Thus, at least some might discover, in a friendship with Jesus himself, that they have come home at last. As he says to those who turn to him: 'My Father will love him, and we will come to him and make our home with him' (John 14:23).

Henri Nouwen describes this new homemaking as a movement from the house of fear to the house of love. He writes:

> To those who are tortured by inner or outer fear, and who desperately look for the house of love where they can find the intimacy their hearts desire, Jesus says: 'You have a home . . . I am your home . . . claim me as your home . . . you will find it to be the intimate place where I have found my home . . . it is right where you are . . . in your innermost being . . . in your heart.[12]

Work and Unemployment

One of the unexpected spin-offs of the high levels of unemployment within modern society is the need to revise our views on 'work'. In my own adolescence and early adult years, notions of work centred almost entirely on jobs that earned money. Even today similar perspectives are widely held, especially among those who are employed. The question, 'What sort of work do you do?' frequently posed when meeting someone for the first time, does not generally anticipate such replies as, 'Housework', 'Cultivate our garden', 'Write short stories for fun', 'Sing in an amateur choir', or, even, 'Study for exams'. The answer usually expected will be one of regular, paid employment.

Our idea of work has strayed a long way from the Bible. In Genesis 1:28 we see that God has ordained that men and women are to rule over and subdue the created order. Response to this edict requires planning, reflection and imagination as well as endeavour and productivity. In Genesis 2:15 we find that the Lord 'took the man and put him in the Garden of Eden to work it and take care of it.' Further, in the following verses, the creation of woman as a counterpart to Adam indicates their combined and equal responsibility as co-workers for God. Thus we discover that 'work' is an intrinsic part of our humanity before the Fall. Just as the Lord God had worked with infinite care and boundless fruitfulness in the unfolding of the creation, so Adam and Eve are called to till, mulch, prune, train, raise seedlings, plant, graft and generally nurture within the garden. After the Fall, joyful work became a backbreaking and wearisome toil.

None-the-less, the point remains that God's call for us to work is a call to be good stewards of his world in any and every aspect of its complex life – even though we often battle with adverse conditions. Martin Luther held this panoramic view of what we do and challenged our tendency to narrow down the vision of work to a checklist of 'higher' and 'lower' callings. He argued that work 'is a part of the order [God] established for man' and declared that 'in making shoes, the cobbler serves God, obeys his calling from God, quite as much as the preacher of the Word.'[13]

This is not to deny that a crucial aspect of our working day is to 'earn a living' and 'make ends meet'. Jesus himself, as a carpenter, seems to have been the provider for his mother, brothers and sisters through much of his adult life, and Paul was not averse to picking up his craft of tent-making in order to pay his way: 'labouring and toiling so that we would not be a burden to any of you' (2 Thess. 3:8).

From these Scriptural principles we can see that who we are as people does not depend on whether we have a waged or salaried job, or not. Although there can be a measure of fulfilment in earning money as a plumber, car mechanic, secretary, hairdresser, shop assistant, teacher or solicitor, we are *all* called – employed, unemployed and retired alike – to see life as a rich pattern of work and rest under the lordship of Christ. Michael Moynagh, in his *Making Unemployment Work*, in citing the examples of Terry and Gill, points to this broad perspective on work as obedient stewardship of the created order:

> So when Terry was encouraged on his youth training programme to improve his skills in writing and maths, he was trying to master the laws (or rules) of these subjects. Likewise, Gill's use of the word-processor involved her in mastering the laws of that machine. Both, as far as the Bible is concerned, were engaged in work. According to the Bible, though, Gill is also at work when she is strumming the guitar in her bedroom because this involves mastering the laws of music. Equally, when Terry used to play football, he was at work since he was 'subduing' the laws of physical movement.[14]

Many young – and not so young – people reading this book may feel that it is all very well to hold a lofty concept of work which covers all sorts of creative activity, but holding down your own job is still very desirable – not only to help pay the rent and buy food and clothing but to give identity and a sense of purpose in life. Let us, then, look at the situation for the young who face unemployment.

Unemployment

The high statistics for unemployment in Britain during the late 1970s and 1980s are well known. The figures doubled to nearly 2 million between 1979 and 1981 and reached their peak in the summer of 1986 with virtually 4 million out of work. Since then the numbers have slowly declined so that in May 1988 the level, for the first time in seven years, was less than 2½ million. The distribution of this huge number of unemployed people is very uneven. Broadly speaking, the percentage of those out of work is higher among blacks than whites and in the North rather than the South. Regional variations in June 1987, for instance, gave the unemployment figures of 8.3 per cent in the South-East, 16 per cent in the North and 21.6 per cent in Northern Ireland. Within each overall area there is a further range, depending on degrees of affluence or deprivation: for example, in Scotland in the summer of 1986, the statistics for Galashiels were just over 7 per cent while in Cumnock and Sanquhar not far off 30 per cent were without work.[15]

Young people have been hit particularly hard by these high levels of unemployment – partly because the most junior are often the most readily laid off and partly because of the difficulty of climbing on to the job ladder in the first place. Michael Moynagh points out that, in 1984, if the government's Youth Training Scheme is left out of the equation, over 50 per cent of the 16- to 18-year-olds who were not still in education were on the dole.[16]

We have already indicated that the desire to get and keep a reliable and worth-while job is an integral part of wanting to develop into a competent and responsible adult – and so it is not surprising that many adolescents are affected badly by unemployment. As Erik Erikson has put it: 'In most instances . . . it is the inability to settle on an occupational identity which disturbs young people.'[17] Research has established clear links between unemployment and homelessness, crime, suicide and problem drug use.

Behind the statistics and generalities lie legions of individual youngsters who grapple with the everyday realities of unemployment. Dave, at the age of 18, had left school at the earliest opportunity, and had spent over a year looking for work in London. Originally from Manchester, he felt the prospects of employment might be higher in the capital. Disillusioned with the very limited possibilities, he eventually found a 'backroom job' in a casino, where he works long, antisocial hours for a low wage. Leslie Francis, the social psychologist, writes of him:

> The long period of unemployment and the unsatisfactory nature of his present job are both casting a long shadow over Dave's attitude to life. He says that, as things are, he completely lacks a sense of purpose and direction in his life. He lacks a sense of identity and self-worth. In short, life is not worth living.[18]

There are several Government schemes which attempt to bridge the gap between the high level of unemployment for the school-leaver and future work. These include the Youth Opportunities Programme, the Youth Training Scheme (YTS), the Restart Programme and the Job Training Scheme. There are plans to simplify the many existing projects under the umbrella body of the Employment Training Scheme. Such enterprises have come under a great deal of criticism – both in terms of 'milking' the unemployment figures and with respect to the quality of training provided. There seems to be no doubt, though, that the prospects of work following these programmes are raised to some extent. One study in the mid-1980s of 16- and 17-year-olds showed that about 20 per cent were still unemployed after being on the YTS, whereas roughly 50 per cent were without work among those who did not join the scheme.[19] Michael Moynagh lays down the following criteria for more successful training programmes:

> Training should be divided into modules of recognised skills. To give trainees an incentive to progress

through the modules, their cash allowance should be raised as they complete each one successfully. Qualifications should be standardised across the country, and where possible be matched with school and college qualifications. A comprehensive information system should record each person's progress so that if he or she drops out, training can be resumed later at the appropriate level. Meeting these tough criteria will ensure the best results.[20]

For those young people who face life on the dole there is an urgent need for discovering right attitudes and positive strategies. First, it is essential that those around the unemployed youngster exercise understanding and sensitivity. Each job an adolescent might apply for could have a hundred or more applicants and it is crucial that friends and family see that failure to be taken on is not failure as a person. Further, one of the greatest dangers of long-term unemployment is that of withdrawal and isolation. The teenager who is on the dole from leaving school into his or her twenties desperately needs companionship and, from time to time, someone who will listen and try to understand the pain of feeling discarded.

Besides care and support, those out of work should also have an agenda for making the most of their potential and of the time on their hands. In fact, it can be a helpful exercise, perhaps with a friend, to think hard about four or five jobs that one would really like to do if one had the skills and wherewithal. One book, *How to Survive Unemployment*, suggests the listing of different aspects of the job under consideration.[21] These include: the *social* (how important is the company of others to you?); *concern* (do you enjoy helping others?); *money* (how essential is being free of financial worry to you?); *success* (how strong is your need for responsibility and achievement?); *power* (how much of a leader are you?); *learning* (how keen are you to acquire new skills and knowledge?); *variety* (do you need frequent change in your work situation?); *independence* (are you committed to your own way of doing things or do you prefer being directed?); *creativity* (how readily do you generate new ideas?); and *lifestyle* (what sort of life do you want to lead in terms of place, surroundings and levels of involvement?). In evaluating what one would like to do it can be useful to arrange these ten features in order of priority. Such self-assessments can increase a young person's confidence – not only in job interviews but in the wider issues of making the most of life day by day.

And yet the challenge of unemployment is more far-reaching than just to the jobless. Nick, a young man from Sheffield, spoke of his life on the dole in these terms:

> It's just that I've been conned . . . by everybody really. You spend your life at school and they all say, 'work hard and you'll get a job, get all your results and you'll get a job.' And it's a lie . . . nobody's personally to blame, it's everybody . . . it's a community thing isn't it? Builds you up and lets you down.[22]

It is this 'community thing' that we all need to face up to: teenagers, parents, teachers, youth workers, Christian leaders, those in local and central government – indeed all who can have any influence on policy and action. Let me close this section with some hard-hitting words from Michael Moynagh's book:

> For those of us in work, the unemployed are not our problem. We are their problem. Too often we are ignorant, indifferent or unimaginative in the solutions we seek. If we want to stop being the problem, we need to get ourselves informed, commit ourselves to the jobless and be ready for some creative thinking.[23]

This challenge is for all who follow Jesus Christ, whose own experience of homelessness and life 'on the road' should spur us to compassionate prayer and creative action on behalf of those young people who face dislocation and disillusionment in their changing situations.

11

CHANGING LOYALTIES

Remember your Creator
in the days of your youth,
before the days of trouble come
and the years approach when you will say,
'I find no pleasure in them'
(Eccles. 12:1)

Perhaps the most far-reaching characteristic of adolescence is that, within the 'in-between' years, decisions and commitments are commonly made which are momentous enough to colour a lifetime. Many young people in their mid- and late teens, amid the melting-pot of ideas, attitudes and beliefs discussed, begin to shape up political, philosophical and religious convictions that may be, for better or worse, virtually immovable in later years. Older heads may see the changing loyalties of youth as illogical and idealistic and may murmur knowingly to one another, 'These youngsters don't realise what's coming to them. They'll learn though . . . all in good time!' Nevertheless, adolescence, despite its heady enthusiasms, often shows the adult world the way forward. Let us then explore some of the more visionary aspects of the teen years in the desire of young people to receive and express *love* and in their quest for *God*.

Love and Marriage

As young people grow towards maturity they need love as well as home and work. As part of their developing sense of personal and social identity they should somehow find a way to love and be loved. The more fortunate ones will have already experienced a great deal of nurture and care from 'good-enough' parents and will have expressed their filial affection in return. Those who have been deprived of maternal and paternal love may have found a source of caring elsewhere – through grandparents, an aunt or uncle, or another 'significant' adult. Contemporaries, too, will have provided varying degrees of companionship through the years. Sometimes one or two will have stood out for the loyalty and trust they offered. In late adolescence and early adulthood the process of learning to love and be loved – with all its consequent pains and misunderstandings – needs to go on.

In chapters 5 and 6 we looked at the changing relationships with parents and peers. We saw how there should be little or no 'generation gap' where families are democratic and God-centred; we considered, too, the importance of adolescent friendships and the dilemmas that can arise from 'falling in love' and misplaced sexual activity. I do not want to repeat that material here but rather to build on what we have said as we anticipate the transition from late teenage into the adult years. In doing this I should like to examine the adolescent tendency of *idealism* and counterbalance this with the need for *realism*.

Idealism

During mid- to late adolescence many young people discover the desire to make their mark on the unfairnesses in society. This is the time when CND badges are prominent, T-shirts against apartheid or for Nicaragua are worn, collecting boxes for Greenpeace are shaken at passing crowds, vigils for Amnesty International are entered into and countless 'trainers' are worn out on marches against oppression and injustice. It is sad, though, that this teenage crusading spirit is often a high point in the life of the individual, for youthful zeal can easily give way to disillusionment, selfishness or cynicism. The 'up and coming' have 'upped and come': marches have given way to mortgages, street campaigns to traffic jams, and ideals to bigger and better insurance.

At times, both adolescent and adult concern are strong on enthusiasm, but weak on application. The warmth of feeling and campaigning vigour are there, but the recipients of caring somehow get in the way of the enterprise. They turn out to be awkward, stubborn, ungrateful and, frankly, unlovable. As one anonymous writer put it: 'I love humanity, it's just people I can't stand!' Dostoyevsky took the point further and showed that it is not others who are the problem, it is ourselves. In *The Idiot* he puts these words on to the pen of Nastasya, who writes of her love for another woman, Aglaya: 'In abstract love of humanity one almost always only loves oneself.'[1]

It is this love of self, and 'not standing other people', that Christ came to rescue us from. In fact, his call to love others is a call to love *everyone*, since that most difficult category – our enemies – is included:

> You have heard that it was said, 'Love your neighbour and hate your enemy.' But I tell you: Love your enemies and pray for those who persecute you, that you may be sons [and daughters] of your Father in heaven (Matt. 5:43–5).

If by idealism we mean the pursuit of ideals, here is one of the loftiest of callings – to love and pray for those who mistreat, misunderstand, victimise or reject us. Such an exalted vocation can only be responded to as 'sons and daughters of our Father in heaven', members of his new family through the dying and rising again of Jesus, our elder brother.

As we have seen, this loving of others must be practical and rooted in the everyday. As the Father calls us to love, he calls us to a love in action. Earlier in the Sermon on the Mount, Jesus urged his followers with these words:

. . . let your light shine before men, that they may see your good deeds and praise your Father in heaven' (Matt. 5:16).

In this context the idealism of youth often shows up the cynicism of age as it gets its hands dirty in the name of Christ: an elderly man's bungalow is painted, a widow's garden weeded, handicapped children are given holidays by the sea, down-and-outs are visited on a soup-run, unjust immigration laws are campaigned against. Gustavo Gutierrez, a theologian who works among the working class in the slums of Lima, Peru, showed the down-to-earthness of the sort of loving God requires, when he wrote:

> Authentic love tries to start with the concrete needs of the other and not with the 'duty' of practising love . . . Works in [sic] behalf of the neighbour are not done in order to channel idle energies or to give available personnel something to do; they are done because the other has needs and it is urgent that we attend to them.[2]

Realism

The opposite of idealism is realism. Whereas idealism can be starry-eyed and moonstruck, realism can be hard-nosed and go-getting. If idealism was one of the hallmarks of the 1960s, then an aggressive brand of realism seems to be the spirit of many in the 1980s. A study of 15- to 25-year-olds, carried out by the market research company Mintel, declares that 'ten years of Tory rule' has led to young people achieving a 'well balanced and mature attitude', which is a 'far cry from the confused, misunderstood, alienated rebels associated with previous generations.' One of the ways this 'Thatcher's generation' likes to see itself is as 'sensible and responsible' (50 per cent) rather than 'romantic and impulsive' (8 per cent). Sadly though, human nature often polarises personal characteristics and an acquisitive, success-oriented society does not readily follow the ideals of self-giving love that we have just outlined. For instance, the Mintel study, as reported in *The Independent*, reveals that between 'one-third and a half of those questioned said they might evade tax, stay away from work when they are not ill, and cheat on a partner.'[3]

Even so, it may be a healthy sign that the desire to be 'romantic and impulsive' has been demoted among today's young people. Perhaps one of the most pressing areas where romanticism and impulsiveness can so easily wreak havoc is that of teenage marriage. It has been long established that wedlock between adolescents is much more likely to founder than where partners are older. The whole tenor of this book has been a commentary on why this is. Although two young people may be at their peak physically and mentally in an early marriage, it is unlikely that they will bring to each other a great deal of maturity at the psychological and emotional levels.

Teenage is a time of profound change in every aspect of the personality and matrimony is made vulnerable if that state of flux continues into its early years. Many of the married couples I have counselled have been in trouble because the two partners entered into marriage too soon. The years have slipped by and both have continued to develop as people. In time, the anguished cry has gone up, 'But he's not the person I married. I've changed, he's changed – and there's now nothing for us in the marriage.'

In fact, the number of teenage marriages has fallen by 75 per cent over the last fifteen years.[4] Given the trend for later first marriages in the late 1980s, mistakes can still be made! It is essential that young people, following the broad guidelines we gave in chapter 6, avoid rushing into marriage. Of all life's events in the West, matrimony is most readily romanticised and idealised. In Christian circles, there is often a great deal of pressure on youngsters to hear wedding bells as soon as they gaze into each other's eyes or tentatively hold hands. Such is the fear of sexual intimacy outside wedlock that many older believers seem to be on the verge of apoplexy when late adolescents of opposite sexes demonstrate physical closeness. The validity of Paul's maxim, 'it is better to marry than to burn with passion' (1 Cor. 7:9), is not denied, but this apostolic advice is best applied where two people of maturer years are sure of God's calling to married commitment. A good corrective against seeking out marriage too early and too eagerly is the comment of an old man who, when asked the secret of his long, married life, said: 'Frequent separations and a growing loss of hearing!'[5]

It is not the remit of this book on understanding adolescence to move into early adulthood and a discussion on singleness and marriage. Even so I should like to say a few words to those teenagers who find themselves caught up in a relationship which may well, in time, lead to marriage. In doing so, I should also refer the reader back to chapter 6 and the sections on friendship, falling in love and sexual activity. Further reading is given at the back of this book.[6] On this matter, I want to make brief comments in four areas: the importance of a range of other friends; the dangers of the 'in love' state; the need to give the situation plenty of time; and the limits of intimacy outside marriage.

(i)   Keep as wide a network of relationships with *both* sexes as possible. A rich pattern of interrelating can but be good and will teach you much about different personalities, lifestyles, attitudes, beliefs and activities. Some of the least worth-while marriages come out of excluding other people and living with narrowed horizons, so beware!

(ii)   Try to avoid seeing the state of 'being in love' as the last word on God's potential plan for your life. 'Being in love', though pleasurable, says as much about hormones and body chemistry as about compatibility and qualities of friendship. See that there is choice in this area. Many deliberately allow themselves to 'fall head over heels'. It is much wiser to stand back and see how the friendship is shaping in terms of common interests, sensitivity towards each other, the degree to which ways of thinking and seeing the funny side of things are shared, and God's overall will for your lives. The feelings of mutual attraction may continue and grow, or they may decline. Either way, such emotions – or their lack – need to be seen as confirming God's direction rather than dictating the way forward.

(iii) If your love and caring for each other is growing mutually, allow plenty of time to test out the situation. It is much healthier to continue in your job or complete your training or studies, while God's further leading is sought. Many young people have found the blossoming of love and commitment as a welcome by-product of serving the Lord and others together.

(iv) In the context of your friendship, discuss and seek to keep to sensible limits of physical intimacy. Be grateful for your sexual desires, but, as we argued earlier, remember God's blueprint for genital sex is within marriage. Your body is his. Allow him to be Lord of your sexuality. If the love within your friendship is genuinely caring then you will come to know of and respect each other's strengths and weaknesses. Avoid exploiting each other sexually. It may well be right to keep your expressions of endearment to kissing and embracing that are not protracted. Further, you will be wise to avoid fondling breasts and other genital areas. This is not so much a question of passion controlled by the rule-book and stop-watch as by sensitivity and good sense. If it is right for you to marry eventually, there will be plenty of time to explore each other's body tenderly and unhurriedly when you are husband and wife. If that is not to be the outcome, then you will not regret that you loved each other enough to respect the distance between you in the earlier stages of the friendship.

Perhaps the most important perspective in this area of loving another is to warn us all – whether adolescent or adult – that we should never make the other person 'the be-all and end-all' of life. There are few worse tyrannies than the idolatry of a love match which expects complete fulfilment in the other person. Only God can provide that. As Jean Vanier puts it:

> . . . it is more difficult for a man to live a permanent and deep relationship with a woman, and for a woman with a man, if they have not discovered the relativity of their relationship. Neither will ever be able totally to fulfil the other; they are not God for one another.[7]

God and Young People

Adolescence, along with the years of the mid-life crisis, is one of the cardinal periods in life when far-reaching decisions are made – about friends, career, lifestyle and, above all, about God. As the future unfolds, young people find themselves asking, 'What do I *really* believe?' 'What is life all about?' 'Is there any point in it all?' 'What am I here for?' 'Is there a God? If so, what claim, if any, does he have on me?' 'If there's a God, how can I find him? Or should I say "her"?' Many can look back to late childhood or the teen years to a turning-point in their lives when – perhaps hesitantly, perhaps resolutely – commitment was made to some ideal or belief. Youngsters often have a powerful sense, as we have already seen, of the world's injustices and catastrophes. This awareness can include a sense of pending doom. Our daughter, Rache, approaching 18 at the time, heard of the leak of radioactivity from Chernobyl and, thinking back to the recent raid on Libya by the United States and the seemingly endless sequence of terrorist attacks worldwide, said wistfully: 'What nasty thing is going to happen in the world next? I'm sure there'll be a Big Bang and we'll all be killed.'

It is perspectives like these, often coupled with a sense of personal need and a desire to put things right, that compel young people towards new loyalties – perhaps to a political party, to campaigning for some just cause, to a faith in God. Ideally, these options fuse into one. There are few more

formidable in zeal and winsomeness than a young man or
woman whose commitment to the Lord is lived out fer-
vently in seeking to bring his righteousness and compassion
to the issues of the day. Lorna is a clergyman's daughter in
her mid- to late teens who became a Christian at the age of
12 while at a New Year's conference run by Scripture
Union. Attractive, alert, bright-eyed, wearing large, dangling earrings and sporting Christian CND and Greenpeace
badges, she insisted that her conversion to Christ was *while
away from home* and 'not because my father's a vicar'.[8]
Here is an independence of spirit and a largeness of vision
that echo the words of Ecclesiastes 12:1, with which this
chapter is headed:

> Remember your Creator
> in the days of your youth,
> before the days of trouble come
> and the years approach when you will say,
> 'I find no pleasure in them'

It is of the essence of youth that loyalty to the Lord God is
often marked by an enthusiasm and single-mindedness
which puts to shame the jaded and cynical views of those
older people who no longer 'find pleasure' within the
advancing years. Let us consider, then, in the closing pages
of *Understanding Adolescence*, something of the inspi-
ration seen among those who 'remember their Creator in
the days of their youth'. Let us look at this under the
headings of *service* and *unity*.

Service

The story of Taizé is a remarkable tale of loving service in
the name of Christ which has inspired thousands of young
people over the last twenty years or so. Brother Roger, who
founded the community in a poor district in Eastern
France, began his own Christian pilgrimage in his teen
years through his landlady, of whom he has said, 'She left

an indelible mark on me; she was the living expression of
the Gospel's sovereign freedom.'[9] Helping Jewish refugees
escape to Switzerland during the Second World War and
caring for orphaned children locally after the war, Roger
and his fellow Christians have always seen Taizé as a centre
for both contemplation and action, for prayer and service.
Since the 1950s, small groups of brothers have dispersed
from France to spend a few months or years in some of the
neediest corners of the world, only to return for varying
periods to Taizé for refreshment and fellowship. Recent
years have seen these 'fraternities' serving the Lord in the
slums of the Mathare Valley, Kenya, among Puerto Ricans
in downtown New York, with the poor in North-east
Brazil and alongside Mother Teresa's Brothers of Charity
in Calcutta.[10]

From Easter 1970 onwards, young people of all nations,
linked with Taizé, have picked up Brother Roger's vision
for Christian service worldwide. This service, though, has
not been an arrogant 'do-gooding' by those with privilege,
condescending to reach out to those with none. It has been,
rather, a desire to learn as well as teach, to receive as well
as give. One group of young members, following a time
of living among the poor of Calcutta and Bangladesh,
expressed themselves like this:

> Both in Calcutta and Chittagong, our home has been
> in very poor neighbourhoods. There, every day has
> been filled with innumerable encounters with those
> living around us, in their homes and in ours. We have
> been very much struck by their ability to share and by
> the warmth of their welcome . . . All day long we have
> children around us. Every morning we go out to work
> in company with many others, in the homes for the
> dying or abandoned children, or in the city's slums.[11]

Jesus himself is the model for this radical form of service.
James and John were like most of us in their desire for
recognition (Matt. 20:20–8). They sought the places of

honour through someone else – in their case, their mother. We too might, in effect, nudge others forward to make our claims for us. It is somehow less vulgar when a friend or relative raises the query in a get-together or, say, a committee meeting: 'Come on now, you must put our Kevin in for the football team – he's got what it takes you know!' or 'Jan should definitely be chairperson – she's got all the right qualities.' It is not that the Lord is against the likes of Kevin and Jan using God-given talents for his glory, so much that attitudes of self-seeking so often spoil responses to the call to service. Jesus challenges our deep desire to be 'centre stage':

> . . . whoever wants to become great among you must be your servant, and whoever wants to be first must be your slave – just as the Son of Man did not come to be served, but to serve, and to give his life as a ransom for many (Matt. 20:26–8).

One teenager, Michelle, demonstrates something of the liberating experience that finding God's daily presence can be in responding to his call to be a servant. Living in a district of Edinburgh that is notorious for its amount of drug abuse and frequency of AIDS, she was asked, 'Where is God in all this?' She replied, 'Everywhere! In all we do, helping the old, needy, and so on. God is always with us wherever we have to do these tasks. God is with me; I lose my fear of these so-called bad areas.'[12]

Adolescents like Michelle and the young people of Taizé show the way to a service which is freed from the individualism and competitiveness that stains the attitudes of so many in our acquisitive society. As Richard Foster writes:

> In the Discipline of service there is also great liberty. Service enables us to say 'no!' to the world's games of promotion and authority. It abolishes our need (and desire) for a 'pecking order'.[13]

Unity

As young people move from their mid-teens (the 'age of identity') to late adolescence (the 'age of coping'), the fragmentation of life into cliques tends to give way to a more outward-looking desire that wants to include others. Whereas at 15 a youngster might have built life around the fads and fashions of a particular pop subculture, at 19 he or she is likely to be reaching out to break down barriers. As we have seen, this reaching out may be an essentially selfish attempt to communicate and influence in order to feather one's own nest; it may, though, be a more altruistic longing to play one's part in bringing a measure of unity between the sexes, different ages, races, cultures, creeds, classes and people of varying ability and giftedness. This desire for oneness between often alienated sections of society is at its strongest, I suggest, among young people who, in their serving of the servant Lord, are drawn towards the answer to his high priestly prayer: 'Holy Father, protect them by the power of your name . . . so that they may be one as we are one' (John 17:11).

This unity that Jesus prays for can dismantle every division erected by our fallen human nature. For example, one of the deepest antipathies of history – between Jew and non-Jew – can be melted away by the reconciling work of Christ: 'For he himself is our peace, who has made the two one and has destroyed the barrier, the dividing wall of hostility' (Eph. 2:14). The antagonisms of race, culture, class and sex are challenged and overcome in the new society of Christ's lordship:

> There is neither Jew nor Greek, slave nor free, male nor female, for you are all one in Christ Jesus (Gal. 3:28).

Let us look briefly at three areas in which young people strive to break down barriers in the name of Jesus Christ: between the sexes, races and creeds.

Between the Sexes

The 'battle of the sexes' is written deeply into the history of humankind. We saw in chapter 2 how the legacy of this history has led to stereotypical views on boys and girls, and men and women generally, which can hamstring the growth to maturity of the young. The Biblical call to equality and mutual trust between the sexes has been undermined in a thousand and one ways by disturbed patterns of relating. We see this, for instance, in the award-winning novel *The Color Purple* by Alice Walker. Celie, a black adolescent living in the American deep south between the wars, has been raped by the man she calls father, has her two children taken from her and is forced into a destructive marriage. In the early pages of the book she has no one to turn to except God. She writes:

> Dear God,
>
> I am fourteen years old. I have always been a good girl. Maybe you can give me a sign letting me know what is happening to me.[14]

Understandably, much feminist writing has been 'anti-men' but there is a new emphasis emerging – particularly among Christians – which seeks to re-establish a mutual caring and respect between women and men, under the lordship of Christ. The London-based organisation, Men, Women & God, for example, aims to encourage nation-wide groups who will explore and live out this vision. Anne Atkins, in *Split Image*, challenges us with this call to unity:

> If the church were truly faithful, we would out-feminist the feminists. If we were really loving our neighbours we would be more genuinely concerned for sexual justice than the most militant of feminine extremists. If we were the body of believers we ought to be, there would be more sexual liberation in our ranks than anywhere else in the world.[15]

Between the Races

Just as sexism rests on clichés about sex and gender so racism is supported by stereotypical views on race and culture. Paul Harrison defines racial prejudice as 'the application to all members of certain races of unfavourable stereotypes derived from myth or limited acquaintance.'[16] In point of fact, the myths between one people and another are fed and watered by this 'limited acquaintance' – whether between the British and the Irish, English and Welsh, French and Germans, Russians and Poles, Turks and Greeks, white Americans and Puerto Ricans, Indians and Pakistanis, Chinese and Tibetans, white Australians and Aborigines. Dismissive images and nationalistic jokes work best when alien peoples are kept at a distance.

In the BBC 2 programme 'Girls Apart', shown in November 1987, two South African 16-year-olds were interviewed separately. Sisca, white, open-faced and confident, with grey-green eyes, was from a reasonably well-off Afrikaner family living in Johannesburg. Sylvia, black, sturdy, caring and committed to change, lived in Soweto. Sisca, who hoped to become a doctor or join the Army, declared, 'There is no apartheid now' and added, 'I wouldn't change South Africa for any other country in the world.' She declared, 'I've never been to Soweto . . . I imagine it's like any other suburb of Johannesburg.'

In contrast, Sylvia, who had been interrogated and tortured by the police, said, 'Soweto is a very dangerous place to live. We have many thugs . . . because of the oppression.' Here we see an example of 'myth' and 'limited acquaintance' which, I should hope, could at least be partly dispelled if, by some miracle, Sylvia and Sisca could actually meet and be left together for a day or two to listen to each other.

In reality, racism and classism often go together. In Britain, for example, although there are clear links between being black and poor housing, inadequate education and a high conviction rate for crime, it is also true that

Afro-Caribbeans and Asians are over-represented in areas of deprivation. As Paul Harrison puts it:

> . . . institutional racialism [sic] is none other than institutional class-ism, as seen from one particular standpoint. It crushes poor working-class whites as well as blacks, and divides them against each other into the bargain.[17]

It is where God is honoured that this division of one group against another can begin to be broken down. In this process it is worth white, Anglo-Saxon protestants (WASPs) recalling that Jesus, often depicted as a blue-eyed Aryan, was, in fact, of Middle-Eastern, Semitic stock.

When, in the 1950s and 1960s, half a million or so West Indians arrived in Britain they brought with them a very high commitment to church attendance. Many settled in inner-city areas where as few as 1 per cent of local white people worshipped regularly.[18] Black Christians met, on the one hand, white apathy to all things God-centred and, on the other hand, a cold formalism and a chilling lack of welcome in many British churches. It is small wonder that great numbers of Afro-Caribbeans have gravitated into what are, in effect, all-black congregations. Even so, such fellowships experience an ecstatic vitality which can shame the staid gatherings of many Anglo-Saxon worshippers. John Rex, writing of West Indian and Asian youth in Britain, comments on the warmth and vibrancy often found in the Pentecostalist and Holiness churches of the immigrant population:

> There is a simple atmosphere of faith, a joy in communion and community, an unaffected enjoyment of singing and worship and a belief, above all, in the spontaneous and immediate action of the Holy Spirit rather than in a sacramental grace dispensed solely by ordained priests.[19]

It is surely good news that, from both black and white perspectives, there is a new, if tentative, coming together of multiracial groups among God's people. Philip Mohabir, a Guyanese Indian converted from Hinduism to Christianity, is a man who is deeply concerned to help answer Jesus's prayer to the Father 'that they may be one.' Instrumental in founding the West Indian Evangelical Alliance in April 1984 and committed to closer links between the black churches and mainstream denominations, he voices a 'real need for partnership between black and white Christians.'[20] Further, there are many attempts in a number of urban areas to reach out in the power of the unifying Spirit to gather together young and old, black and white, deprived and privileged. The work of Jim Wallis in Washington, DC, of Raymond Bakke in Chicago and John Wimber in Pasadena in the United States, of Roger Sainsbury in Walsall, Chris Brain in Sheffield, Laurie Green in Birmingham and Peter Stow in East London are just a few examples of a ground-swell of obedient outreach among the powerless in the name of Christ.[21]

Such enterprises include a response to the call to bring streetwise young people to faith in God. This work often entails the dismantling of old, familiar and secure structures and, under the Spirit's leading, the use of newer ways of communicating and worshipping. The Gospel has always been for the people and, though unchanging in its central message of God's reconciling love, has constantly needed expression within the rich variety of human culture. Peter Stow, writing of the venture of 'Freedom Gate' among the adolescents of Hackney, indicates the realities of Christian work with the disadvantaged young:

> We seemed to attract mainly West Indian teenagers at first, but it has gradually become more multiracial. Whereas with the old youth service the problem often was in keeping order, now the biggest problem is getting the kids to stop smoking marijuana in the middle of prayers.[22]

Between the Creeds

The third, and final, area we shall consider, within which the power and love of Christ can break down divisions, is that of belief. It is a long-running sore in the history of the Church that personal and corporate faith, which should be a source of unity, has often been a seedbed of dissent and schism. Many of us, of course, will be among the first to admit that what Christians believe is always under attack and needs, from time to time, clear statement and proclamation. Although the basic tenet of the lordship of Christ overall must always be held firm, there are bound to be disagreements between Christians over points of interpretation and emphasis. Sadly, difference of opinion has frequently hardened into a rigidly held dogma which is a far cry from the patience and loving tolerance urged on the body of believers by Paul:

> Be completely humble and gentle; be patient, bearing with one another in love. Make every effort to keep the unity of the Spirit through the bond of peace. There is one body and one Spirit – just as you were called to one hope when you were called – one Lord, one faith, one baptism; one God and Father of all, who is over all and through all and in all (Eph. 4:2–6).

We could take many examples where God's servants, often encouraged and inspired by the young in particular, have sought to live out this costly path of unity in the face of sectarian distrust. For many readers there are few more tragic and shameful situations of disunity than the continuing troubles in Northern Ireland. This is not to deny that there are political, economic and cultural factors behind the rifts, but rather to stress that religious differences have somehow fuelled and fanned the flames of dispute with, at times, fanatical vigour. In the last few pages of our book I want, then, to focus on the work of the Corrymeela Community and the story of Michael.

Corrymeela, meaning 'The Hill of Harmony', is a Christian community situated at Ballycastle on the North Antrim coast, 55 miles from Belfast. Founded in 1965 as a result of the obedient response of Ray Davey, the son of a Presbyterian minister, Corrymeela has always sought to be something of a protest group against 'the inflexibility, the institutionalism, the authoritarianism and the pietism of the churches.'[23] Seeking reconciliation between Roman Catholics and Protestants, it declares a simple, but potentially unifying, creed:

> We believe in God as revealed in Jesus Christ and in the continuing work of the Holy Spirit. We are called together as a Community to be an instrument of God's peace, to serve our society and to share in the life of the Church.[24]

Michael Healey is a young man to whose life God's reconciling love has been mediated, at least partly, through the Corrymeela Community. I met him for the first time just a couple of months ago while lecturing at Trinity College, Bristol – for Michael is now an ordinand, training for full-time work as an Anglican minister. Brought up in a Catholic family in one of Belfast's housing estates, Michael, an epileptic, was the third of four boys. On August 9th, 1971, Desmond, aged 14 and one of Michael's older, twin brothers, was shot dead by British troops during a day of rioting and bloodshed, following a round-up of suspected terrorists.[25] A few months after this death, Michael's father also died – at the age of 42. Following the killing of Desmond, Michael, then aged 12, experienced a dramatic worsening of his epilepsy – one 'grand mal' seizure succeeding another in rapid sequence. His mother, Peg Healey, described how Michael 'went wild' with fury and wanted to 'kill all around him'. About a year after Desmond's death, the twice-bereaved family was sent to Corrymeela for a spell. It was here, at 'The Hill of Harmony', that the first faint glimmerings of hope came to Michael's bitter situation. Mrs Healey put it this way:

> It helped Michael. He really showed his brother's death. He was ready to knife the soldiers, throw stones and everything else. I didn't know what was going to happen to him. I was afraid to let him through the front door. He had this thing about Protestants, they were as bad as the Army. He would not trust anybody but Catholics. But Corrymeela did help him.

In due course this young teenager was sent to a Roman Catholic school in England. His hatred for the nation which killed his brother was hardly helped by the discovery that quite a few of his classmates had fathers who were in the army. Further, coming to terms with his angry emotions was not fostered by the nuns at the school, some of whom told him that he would be judged by God for his rage towards the English. This God had other ideas about Michael. Two new sisters came to the school from Ireland and brought with them the compassion of Jesus for this anguished teenager. For the first time since Corrymeela, Michael began to hear that God is a God of love. His resistance to giving up his burning feelings of enmity towards the 'Brits' was gradually melted by the sisters' words. They told him that Jesus loved him whether he accepted him or not; and added that, if he rejected Christ, the Lord would love him no less and, if he responded, that same Lord would love him no more. Michael, having nursed revenge for so long, capitulated to the God of love and unity. It was the sisters' final thoughts that broke through to him: 'Words are cheap . . . we will say no more words to you. It's up to you.'

Conclusion

As we finish this journey of trying to understand adolescence, it is worth recalling once more that young and old need one another. Relationships between parent and child, teacher and teenager, youth worker and young people, are often fraught, as we have seen throughout, with misunderstanding and conflict. And yet, where God is at work, the so-called 'generation gap' can be narrowed – and even closed. For Michael Healey, besides his grieving mother, the community at Corrymeela and the gallant sisters, there was one other adult who played an important part in bringing reconciliation. In February 1985, at a selection board for ordination, Michael met a tutor – a complete stranger – who said to him, 'I know about you, Michael. Haven't I read about you in Alf McCreary's book *Corrymeela*? I've prayed daily for a lad called Michael Healey for eight years – and here you are, obeying God's call!'

Lionel Blue, the well-known Jewish broadcaster and writer, recalled a fellow rabbi's words to God, 'I don't want your heaven and I'm not scared of your hell. I only want you.' And it is where adolescents, like Michael and many others we have met in this book, 'remember their Creator in the days of their youth', wanting only God, that they can show the way forward for us all. As Derek Kidner puts it, in his commentary on Ecclesiastes 12:1, this remembering is 'a matter of passionate fidelity' towards God – and 'youth and the whole span of life are not too much to pour into it.'[26] Let that 'passionate fidelity' be our resolve as we face the remaining span of our lives, telling God, 'we, young and old, only want you.'

NOTES

Preface

1. J. L. G. Balado, *The Story of Taizé* (London: Mowbray 1980) p. 21.

Chapter One

1. J. D. R. McConnell in *Eton – How it Works*, quoted in Ronald Gibson 'The Satchel and the Shining Morning Face', *British Medical Journal*, 1971, **2**, 551.
2. John C. Coleman, *The Nature of Adolescence* (London: Methuen 1980) p. 23f. I am indebted to Coleman's work for many of this book's insights.
3. J. M. Tanner, quoted in John Conger, *Adolescence: generation under pressure* (London: Harper & Row 1979) p. 19.
4. Coleman, op. cit. pp. 18–19.
5. Ibid. pp. 19–22.
6. Margaret Mead, *Male and Female* (Harmondsworth: Penguin 1950) pp. 172–3.
7. Jack Dominian, *Marriage, Faith & Love* (London: Darton, Longman & Todd 1981) pp. 30–1.

Chapter Two

1. Dick Keyes, *Beyond Identity: finding yourself in the image and character of God* (London: Hodder & Stoughton 1986) pp. 5, 8.
2. Ogden Nash, 'The Octopus' from *Family Reunion* (Dent 1951).
3. I am indebted to J. A. Hadfield, *Childhood and Adolescence* (Harmondsworth: Penguin 1962) chapters 3 and 4 for some of the detail in this section.
4. Psychologists use the term 'ego ideal' to cover the child's emerging conception of how he or she wishes to be as a person.

5. Frances Hodgson Burnett, *The Secret Garden* (Penguin 1951) p. 75.

6. Erik Erikson, quoted in John C. Coleman, *The Nature of Adolescence* (Methuen 1980) p. 51.

7. John C. Coleman, *The Nature of Adolescence* (London: Methuen 1980) p. 56; see pp. 51–6 for recent thinking and research on 'identity crises' in young people.

8. David Elkind, 'Egocentrism in Adolescence', *Child Development* (1967) **38** pp. 1025–1034, discussed in Coleman, op. cit. pp. 31–2.

9. *The Diary of Anne Frank* (London: Pan Books 1954) p. 114.

10. Sue Townsend, *The Secret Diary of Adrian Mole Aged 13¾* (Methuen 1983) p. 50.

11. Interview by Ron Eyre in 'Seven Days', *BBC2*, September 28th 1987.

12. Elaine Storkey, *What's Right With Feminism* (London: SPCK 1985) p. 101.

13. For books which, on the whole, argue liberation for women *and* men and have useful sections on 'sex and gender', see: Anne Atkins, *Split Image: male and female after God's likeness* (Hodder & Stoughton 1987); Kathy Keay (ed.), *Men, Women & God* (Basingstoke: Marshall Pickering 1987); Mary Hayter *The New Eve in Christ: the use and abuse of the Bible in the debate about women in the Church* (SPCK 1987); Elaine Storkey, op. cit.

14. For some of the material in this section on sexual identity in children and adolescents, see John Nicholson, *Men & Women: how different are they?* (Oxford: Oxford University Press 1984) pp. 16–26.

15. Ibid., p. 26.

16. See Paul K. Jewett, *Man as Male and Female* (Grand Rapids: Eerdmans 1975) pp. 142–7. I do not want to oversimplify the current debate in the Church on women and men. My own views are given more fully in Roger F. Hurding 'Restoring the Image – Is Wholeness Possible?' in Kathy Keay (ed.), op. cit.

17. Jules Feiffer, caption to drawing in *Observer*, February 3rd, 1974, in J. M. & M. J. Cohen, *The Penguin Dictionary of Modern Quotations* (1980).

18. Erik H. Erikson, *Childhood and Society* (Penguin 1965) p. 253.

19. Erikson, *Identity: youth and crisis* (London: Faber & Faber 1968) p. 40.

20. Keyes, op. cit., p. 76.
21. We meet the same singularity in the 'I am' sayings of Jesus recorded in John's Gospel. His claim to being God is at its starkest in the Garden of Gethsemane when, confronted by Judas and a detachment of soldiers, he replies to the request for 'Jesus of Nazareth' with the words, "I am he". We read, 'When Jesus said, 'I am he', they drew back and fell to the ground.' (John 18:6).
22. Kenneth Grahame, *The Wind in the Willows* (Methuen 1961) pp. 113–14.
23. For further images of treasure see: Prov. 2:3–5; Isa. 33:6; Matt. 13:44–6; 19:21; 2 Cor. 4:7; Col. 2:3; 1 Tim. 6; 18,19.
24. Keyes, op. cit., p. 13.
25. Ibid., p. 14.
26. Jim Wallis, *The Call to Conversion* (Lion 1986) p. 145.

Chapter Three

1. Marshall McLuhan & Quentin Fiore, *The Medium is the Message: an inventory of effects* (Harmondsworth: Penguin 1967) p. 114.
2. Broadcast in 'Screen Two', BBC2, January 10th, 1988.
3. All quoted in Martin Large, *Who's Bringing Them Up?; television and child development* (Gloucester: Martin Large for TV Action Group 1980) introductory pages.
4. Quoted in Large, op. cit., p. 80.
5. Ibid., pp. 114–15.
6. Christopher Dunkley, *Television Today and Tomorrow: wall-to-wall Dallas?* (Harmondsworth: Penguin 1985) p. 14.
7. See, for example, Large, p. 25, and *Social Trends 1987* (London: HMSO) p. 164.
8. *Young people in the 80s: a survey* (HMSO: Dept. of Education and Science 1983) p. 74.
9. Dunkley, op. cit., pp. 25–6.
10. *Social Trends 1987*, p. 111.
11. Geoffrey Barlow & Alison Hill (eds), *Video Violence and Children* (London: Hodder & Stoughton 1985) p. 41.
12. Ibid., p. 33.
13. Quoted in David Barrat, *Media Sociology* (London: Tavistock Publications 1986) p. 21.
14. Ibid., pp. 16–20.
15. Graham Melville-Thomas, 'Television Violence and Children' in Barlow & Hill, op. cit., p. 20; see also pp. 8–23. For a

recent discussion on the issues, see the seminar papers in *Violence and the Media* (London: British Broadcasting Corporation 1988).

16. Barlow & Hill p. 147.
17. Christina Preston, 'Children and the nasties', *New Society*, November 22nd, 1985 pp. 325–7.
18. David Porter, *Children at Risk* (Eastbourne: Kingsway Publications 1986) p. 102.
19. See, for example, the section on horror comics in Porter, op. cit., pp. 123–7.
20. Comment in 'Drink and Young People', *Panorama*, BBC1, October 12th, 1987.
21. Joanna Bogle (ed.), *The Seductive Sell: a look at today's teenage magazines* (Milton Keynes: The Responsible Society Research & Education Trust 1986).
22. Ibid., p. 8.

Chapter Four

1. John Street *Rebel Rock: the politics of popular music* (Oxford: Basil Blackwell 1986) pp. 4–5.
2. Ibid., p. 5.
3. Ibid., p. 3.
4. Johan Huizinga *Homo Ludens* (Paladin 1970) p. 21.
5. Quoted in Street, op. cit., p. 176.
6. Leland Ryken, *Triumphs of the Imagination: literature in Christian perspective* (Downers Grove: Illinois IVP 1979) pp. 57–9.
7. Lynden Barber, *Melody Maker* February 6th, 1982.
8. Eamon Dunphy, *Unforgettable Fire: the story of U2* (London: Viking 1987) p. 305.
9. Steve Turner, *Hungry For Heaven: rock and roll and the search for redemption* (London: W. H. Allen and Eastbourne: Kingsway 1988) p. 27.
10. Tony Jasper, *Rock Solid: beyond the music, what really matters* (Milton Keynes: Word Publishing 1986) pp. 13–14.
11. Martin Wroe, 'Bruce Cockburn', *Third Way* (August 1987) Vol. 10, No. 8, p. 19.
12. Nik Cohn *Awopbopaloobop Alopbamboom* (London: Paladin 1970) p. 161.
13. David Porter, 'Bob Dylan – Infidels', *Third Way* (February 1984) Vol. 7, No. 2, p. 26.

14. Wroe, op. cit., p. 20.
15. Dunphy, op. cit., p. 255.
16. See Isaiah 44:28–45:1.
17. Peter Everett, *You'll Never Be 16 Again: an illustrated history of the British teenager* (BBC Publications 1986) p. 129.
18. Everett, op. cit., p. 128.
19. E. Ellis Cashmore, *No Future: youth and society* (London: Heinemann 1984) pp. 44–5.
20. Quoted in Everett, op. cit., p. 138.
21. Quoted in Everett, op. cit.
22. Toby Young, 'The Teen age', *New Society* November 1st, 1985, p. 185ff.
23. Everett, op. cit., p. 158.
24. Andrew Thornton, *Youth Music and the Church* (Edinburgh: The Handsel Press 1985) p. 10.

Chapter Five

1. Quoted in Ronald Gibson, 'The Satchel and the Shining Morning Face', *British Medical Journal*, June 5th, 1971.
2. I am indebted to John C. Coleman, *The Nature of Adolescence* (London: Methuen 1980) pp. 65–75, and Martin Herbert, *Living with Teenagers* (Oxford: Basil Blackwell 1987) pp. 26–30, for much of the insight in this section.
3. D. Baumrind, 'Authoritarian versus authoritative parental control', *Adolescence* (1968) **3** pp. 255–72, quoted in Coleman, op. cit., p. 74.
4. See Leslie J. Francis, *Young and Unemployed* (Guildford: Costello 1984) pp. 129–33.
5. Comment on *Tuesday Call*, Radio 4, February, 1986.
6. Baumrind, op. cit., in Coleman, p. 74.
7. Roger F. Hurding, *As Trees Walking* (Exeter: The Paternoster Press 1982) p. 178.
8. For more detailed guidelines on this issue, see Herbert, op. cit., pp. 33–5.
9. Ibid., pp. 24–5.
10. Ibid., p. 33.
11. Coleman, op. cit., p. 76.
12. David Stafford-Clark, *Prejudice in the Community* (London: National Committee for Commonwealth Immigrants 1965) p. 15. I am grateful to John Smith, Head of Student Services at Bristol Polytechnic, for this reference.

13. C. E. Bowerman and S. J. Bahr, 'Conjugal power and adolescent identification with parents' *Sociometry* (1973) **36** pp. 366–77, quoted in Coleman, op. cit., p. 74.
14. Paul Tournier, *The Gift of Feeling* (London: SCM Press 1981) pp. 2–3.
15. Ibid., p. 3.
16. Tournier, *Creative Suffering* (SCM: 1982) p. 24.
17. Ibid., p. 32.
18. Ibid., p. 3.
19. Edersheim, *Sketches on Jewish Social Life in the days of Christ* (London: Religious Tract Society 1876) p. 147. For comments on the autocracy of Roman fathers, see William Barclay quoted in John R. W. Stott, *God's New Society: the message of Ephesians* (Leicester: IVP 1979) p. 245.
20. For natural and revealed law in these verses, see Stott, op. cit., pp. 238–40.
21. See, for example, 1 Timothy 5:3,4.
22. For a full and scholarly discussion on masculine and feminine imagery and the Godhead, see Mary Hayter, *The New Eve in Christ: the use and abuse of the Bible in the debate about women in the Church* (London: SPCK 1987) pp. 7–44.
23. John White, *Parents in Pain* (IVP 1980) p. 211.
24. M. Rutter *et al.*, 'Adolescence turmoils: fact or fiction?' *Journal of Child Psychology and Psychiatry* (1976) **17** pp. 35 –56, quoted in Coleman, op. cit., pp. 67–8.
25. Coleman, op. cit., p. 70.
26. Jean Vanier, *Man And Woman He Made Them* (London: Darton, Longman & Todd) p. 24.

Chapter Six

1. See, for example, Lewis Way, *Alfred Adler: an introduction to his psychology* (Harmondsworth: Penguin 1956) pp. 72–6.
2. E. Douvan and J. Adelson, *The Adolescent Experience* (New York: John Wiley 1966) in John C. Coleman, *The Nature of Adolescence* (London: Methuen 1980) pp. 97–8.
3. Quoted in *The Concise Oxford Dictionary of Quotations* (Oxford: OUP 1981) p. 96.
4. John C. Coleman, *The Nature of Adolescence* (London: Methuen 1980) p. 91.
5. Peter Everett, *You'll Never Be 16 Again* (BBC 1986) p. 129.

6. *Young People in the 80s: a survey* (HMSO/Dept. of Education and Science 1983) pp. 11–12.

7. N. Feshbach and G. Sones, 'Sex differences in adolescent reactions towards newcomers', *Developmental Psychology* **4** pp. 381–6 in Coleman, op. cit., p. 95. For this section generally, see Coleman, pp. 94–6.

8. Chaim Potok, *The Chosen* (Penguin 1970) p. 230.

9. See, for example, Mark 5:37; 9:2; 13:3; 14:33; Luke 22:8 (Peter, James and John) and Matt 21:17; Mark 11:11; Luke 10:38,39; John 11:1–3; 12:1–3 (Mary, Martha and Lazarus).

10. Quoted in *The Penguin Dictionary of Modern Quotations* (Penguin 1980) pp. 229–30.

11. Carson McCullers, *The Member of the Wedding* (Penguin 1962) pp. 17–18.

12. Roger Scruton, *Sexual Desire* (London: Weidenfeld and Nicolson 1986) p. 160.

13. Roy Kerridge, 'Young hearts that pump to the "bhangra" beat', *The Independent*, February 15th, 1988.

14. Quoted in Coleman, op. cit., p. 143.

15. Woody Allen in the film *Annie Hall*.

16. Cited in Richard J. Foster, *Money, Sex & Power: the challenge to the disciplined life* (London: Hodder & Stoughton 1985) pp. 123–4.

17. John Conger, *Adolescence: generation under pressure* (London: Harper & Row 1979) p. 57.

18. Thomas Szasz, 'Sex' in *The Second Sin*, quoted in *Modern Quotations*, op. cit., p. 323.

19. For helpful writing on masturbation, see Foster, op. cit., pp. 123–7, Joyce Huggett, *Just Good Friends? growing in relationships* (Leicester: IVP 1985) pp. 156–72 and John White, *Eros Defiled* (IVP 1978) pp. 34–42. I am grateful to Foster's book for the broad perspectives here.

20. Many young people who are Christians, or on the margins of faith in Christ, become convinced that they have committed the 'sin against the Holy Spirit'. It is important to understand that this sin is essentially one of accusing Jesus of serving the devil, of calling good evil, and of generally turning God's perspectives upside down (see Matt 12:22–37).

21. White, op. cit., pp. 34ff.

22. Foster, op. cit., p. 125.

23. Ibid.

24. See, for example: Foster op. cit. p. 110 and Martin Herbert

Living with Teenagers (Oxford: Basil Blackwell 1987) p. 110.

25. Alfred C. Kinsey *et al.*, *Sexual Behaviour in the Human Male* (1949); *Sexual Behaviour in the Human Female* (1953). See Foster, op. cit., pp. 109–110.
26. See Gen. 19:1–8; Lev. 18:22; 20:13; Judges 19:22–3; Rom. 1:26–7; 1 Cor. 6:9–11; 1 Tim. 1:8–11. For a full and helpful discussion of these verses, see D. J. Atkinson, *Homosexuals in the Christian Fellowship* (Oxford: Latimer House 1979) pp. 79–92.
27. John 8:1–11.
28. Elizabeth R. Moberly, *Homosexuality: a new Christian ethic* (Cambridge: James Clarke & Co. 1983) pp. 21–2.
29. Ibid., p. 22.
30. Ibid., p. 52.
31. C. Farrell, *My Mother Said* (London: Routledge & Kegan Paul 1978), quoted in Coleman, op. cit., p. 125.
32. Coleman, op. cit., p. 126.
33. See, for example, Coleman, op. cit., pp. 123–8; A. C. Kinsey *et al.*, *Sexual Behaviour in the Human Male* (Philadelphia: W. B. Saunders 1948) and *Sexual Behaviour in the Human Female* (Saunders 1953); and Michael Schofield, *The Sexual Behaviour of Young People* (Penguin 1968).
34. Herbert, op. cit., pp. 99–100.
35. Deut. 22:13–21.
36. Deut. 22:28–9.
37. I would especially commend Lewis Smedes, *Sex in the Real World* (Tring: Lion Publishing 1979) pp. 101–28 for his discussion on premarital sex; I follow the gist of his argument here.
38. H. Reisser in Colin Brown (ed.), *The New International Dictionary of New Testament Theology* (Exeter: The Paternoster Press) Vol. 1, p. 497.
39. Smedes, op. cit., p. 124.

Chapter Seven

1. C. Farrell, *My Mother Said* (London: Routledge and Kegan Paul 1978), in Coleman, op. cit., p. 129.
2. David J. Hill in letter to *The Guardian*, July 30th, 1983.
3. *Social Trends 1988* (HMSO) p. 47.
4. Ibid., p. 49.

5. E. L. Mascall in J. H. Channer (ed.), *Abortion & the Sanctity of Human Life* (Exeter: The Paternoster Press 1985) pp. 8–9.
6. L. W. Sumner quoted in ibid., p. 113.
7. For this section, see J. W. Rogerson, ibid., pp. 89–91.
8. R. F. R. Gardner, *Abortion: the personal dilemma* (The Paternoster Press 1972) p. 173.
9. Ibid., p. 244.
10. Donald M. MacKay, 'The Beginnings of Personal Life' in *In the Service of Medicine*, Vol. 30:2, No. 118, April 1984, p. 10.
11. For those who would like to pursue the discussion, see Gordon M. Stirrat, *Legalised Abortion – the continuing dilemma* (London: Christian Medical Fellowship 1979), and Gordon Wenham & Richard Winter, *Abortion: the biblical and medical challenge* (London: Care Trust 1983), as well as the books already cited.
12. See Gardner, op. cit., pp. 207–8.
13. R. Nicol Thin & David Barlow in *Medicine International*, Vol. 2, No. 30, June 1986, p. 1217.
14. See Michael Schofield, *The Sexual Behaviour of Young Adults* (London: Allen Lane 1973) p. 75.
15. Caroline Bradbeer, 'AIDS – epidemiology and screening' in *Medicine International*, op. cit., p. 1246.
16. *Report: AIDS – monitoring response of the public education campaign* (HMSO 1987), quoted in *The Independent*, October 1st, 1987.
17. Figures cited in Caroline Collier, *The 20th Century Plague* (Tring: Lion Publishing 1987) p. 39.
18. *Social Trends 1988*, p. 117.
19. Quoted in Collier, op. cit., p. 56.

Chapter Eight

1. G. Stanley Hall and Anna Freud, both quoted in John C. Coleman, *The Nature of Adolescence* (London: Methuen 1980) p. 147.
2. Coleman, op. cit., pp. 162–3.
3. Jill Welbourne & Joan Purgold, *The Eating Sickness: anorexia, bulimia and the myth of suicide by slimming* (Brighton: The Harvester Press 1984) p. 2.
4. Marilyn Lawrence, *The Anorexia Experience* (London: The Women's Press 1984) p. 32.
5. Ibid., p. 51.

6. Christopher P. Freeman, 'Eating Disorders' in *Medicine International*, Vol. 2, No. 45, September 1987, p. 1846.
7. Sheila MacLeod, *The Art of Starvation* (London: Virago 1981) p. 32.
8. Ibid., pp. 62–3.
9. Hilde Bruch, *Eating Disorders* (London: Routledge and Kegan Paul 1974), cited in Lawrence, op. cit., pp. 63–4.
10. Welbourne & Purgold, op. cit., p. 56.
11. Ibid., p. 148.
12. Helena Wilkinson, *Puppet on a String* (London: Hodder & Stoughton 1984) p. 190.
13. I am grateful here to Andrew Sims, *Neurosis in Society* (London: The Macmillan Press 1983) pp. 74–6 for an analysis of stress.
14. Sims, op. cit., p. 3.
15. For a helpful, accessible book on phobic states, see Joy Melville, *Phobias* (London: Unwin 1979).
16. M. Rutter *et al.*, cited in Coleman, op. cit., p. 151.
17. Roger Hurding, *Coping with Illness* (Hodder & Stoughton 1988) pp. 45–54.
18. Quoted in Ross Mitchell, *Depression* (Harmondsworth: Penguin Books 1975) p. 93.
19. Coleman, op. cit., p. 176.
20. Ibid., p. 159.
21. For this section, see John S. Wodarski & Pamela Harris, 'Adolescent Suicide: a review of influences and the means for prevention', *Social Work*, Vol. 32, No. 6, Nov.–Dec. 1987, pp. 447–84.
22. See Coleman, op. cit., p. 161.

Chapter Nine

1. See the report, *Grave Crimes . . . Grave Doubts* (London: National Association for the Care and Resettlement of Offenders 1988) p. 10.
2. See the report, *The Route from Care to Custody* (London: Prison Reform Trust 1988) p. 4.
3. See Martin Herbert, *Living with Teenagers* (Oxford: Basil Blackwell 1987) pp. 79–81.
4. See John Coleman, *The Nature of Adolescence* (London: Methuen 1980) p. 156.

5. E. Ellis Cashmore, *No Future: youth and society* (London: Heinemann 1984) p. 98.

6. Ibid., p. 100.

7. Morris Fraser, *Children in Conflict* (Penguin Books 1974) p. 23.

8. Ibid., p. 136.

9. Featured in 'Seeking the Jack-pot', *40 Minutes* BBC2, January 21st, 1988.

10. Quoted in Annas Dixon, *Dealing with Drugs* (London: BBC Books 1987) p. 10.

11. Quoted by Larry Harrison in 'Tobacco Battered' in *The Saturday Feature*, Radio 4, and printed in *Radio Times*, January 16th, 1988.

12. Quoted in *Pulse*, April 16th, 1988, p. 40.

13. Quoted in *The Independent*, April 20th, 1988.

14. John Balding, *Young People in 1986* (University of Exeter: HEA Schools Health Education Unit 1987) p. 93.

15. Quoted in *The Independent*, March 9th, 1988.

16. Reported in *Social Trends 1988*, pp. 119–20.

17. Cited in Herbert, op. cit., p. 130.

18. *Social Trends 1988*, p. 120.

19. Dixon, op. cit., p. 27.

20. Described by David F. Peck & Martin A. Plant in 'Unemployment and illegal drug use' in Tom Heller, Marjorie Gott & Carole Jeffery, *Drug Use & Misuse: a reader* (Chichester: John Wiley & Sons, with The Open University 1987) pp. 63–7.

21. See Dixon, op. cit., p. 37.

22. Ibid., p. 120.

23. Richard Hartnoll, Emmanuelle Daviaud & Robert Power, 'Patterns of drug taking in Britain' in Heller *et al.* (eds), op. cit., p. 16.

24. Sarah Helm, 'Lost Generation in Smack City', *The Independent*, May 6th, 1988, p. 17.

25. Hartnoll *et al.*, in Heller, op. cit., p. 13.

26. Dixon, op. cit., p. 16.

27. Cited in *General Practitioner*, April 15th, 1988, p. 24.

28. See Floyd McClung Jr, *Just Off Chicken Street* (New Jersey: Fleming H. Revell Company 1975); Jackie Pullinger, *Chasing the Dragon* (Hodder & Stoughton 1980); and David Wilkerson, *The Cross and the Switchblade* (London: Marshall Pickering 1967).

29. Kenneth Leech, *Pastoral Care and the Drug Scene* (London: SPCK 1970) p. 96.

Chapter Ten

1. John Halliburton, *Educating Rachel: growing up as a Christian* (London: SPCK 1987) pp. 27–8.
2. Peter Stow with Mike Fearon, *Youth in the City: the Church's response to the challenge of youth work* (London: Hodder & Stoughton 1987) pp. 175–6.
3. I am grateful for much in this section to John Rex, 'West Indian and Asian Youth' in Ernest Cashmore & Barry Troyna (eds), *Black Youth in Crisis* (London: George Allen & Unwin 1982) pp. 59–71.
4. Quoted in David Sheppard, *Bias to the Poor* (Hodder & Stoughton 1983) p. 84.
5. Ernest Cashmore, 'Black Youth for Whites' in Cashmore & Troyna (eds), op. cit., p. 12.
6. Mary Fuller, 'Young, Female and Black' in Cashmore & Troyna, op. cit., p. 93.
7. *Social Trends 1988* (HMSO) p. 134.
8. Paul Harrison, *Inside the Inner City: life under the cutting edge* (Harmondsworth: Penguin Books 1985) p. 188.
9. Stow, op. cit., p. 118.
10. Ibid., pp. 122–5.
11. See Luke 2:1–7; Matthew 2:13–23.
12. Henri J. M. Nouwen, *In the House of the Lord: the journey from fear to love* (London: Darton, Longman & Todd 1986) p. 21.
13. Quoted in Udo Middelmann, *Pro-Existence: the place of man in the circle of reality* (Hodder & Stoughton 1975) p. 21.
14. Michael Moynagh, *Making Unemployment Work* (Tring: Lion Publishing 1985) p. 96.
15. *Social Trends 1988*, p. 77.
16. Moynagh, op. cit., p. 39.
17. Erik H. Erikson, *Childhood and Society* (Penguin Books 1965) p. 253.
18. Leslie J. Francis, *Young and Unemployed* (Costello 1984) pp. 120–1.
19. 'England and Wales Youth Cohort Study, 1984–1986', in *Social Trends 1988*, pp. 55–6.
20. Moynagh, op. cit., p. 41.

21. See ibid., pp. 169–174, where Moynagh cites R. Nathan & M. Syrett, *How to Survive Unemployment* (Institute of Personnel Management 1981) and gives other practical tips for the unemployed.
22. Quoted in *The Independent*, November 25th, 1987.
23. Moynagh, op. cit., p. 179.

Chapter Eleven

1. Fyodor Dostoyevsky, *The Idiot* (Penguin Books 1955) p. 494.
2. Gustavo Gutierrez, *We Drink from Our Own Wells: the spiritual journey of a people* (London: SCM Press 1984) p. 108.
3. *Youth Lifestyles* (London: Mintel 1988) reported on in *The Independent*, May 11th, 1988.
4. Ibid.
5. Quoted by Alastair Cook in *Letter from America*, Radio 4, June 1987.
6. I would particularly recommend two books by Joyce Huggett on the growth of love between young people: *Growth into Love* (Leicester: IVP 1982) and *Just Good Friends?: growing in relationships* (IVP 1985).
7. Jean Vanier, *Men and Women He Made Them* (Darton, Longman & Todd 1985) p. 24.
8. Interviewed on *Songs of Praise*, BBC 1, January 17th, 1988.
9. Quoted in J. L. G. Balado, *The Story of Taizé* (London: Mowbray & Co 1980) p. 26.
10. Ibid., pp. 47–9.
11. Ibid., p. 87.
12. Interviewed on *Songs of Praise*, BBC 1, December 13th, 1987.
13. Richard J. Foster, *Celebration of Discipline: the path to spiritual growth* (Hodder & Stoughton 1980) pp. 110–11.
14. Alice Walker, *The Color Purple* (London: The Women's Press 1983) p. 3.
15. Anne Atkins, *Split Image: male and female after God's likeness* (Hodder & Stoughton 1987) p. 239.
16. Paul Harrison, *Inside the Inner City: life under the cutting edge* (Harmondsworth: Penguin Books 1985) p. 373.
17. Ibid., p. 387.
18. Peter Stow with Mike Fearon, *Youth in the City: the Church's*

response to the challenge of youth work (London: Hodder & Stoughton 1987) p. 159.

19. John Rex in E. Ellis Cashmore & Troyna, *No Future: youth and society* (London: Heinemann 1984) p. 98.

20. See report by Andrew Brown, 'Revival in the churches born of rejection' in *The Independent*, May 23rd 1988. Philip Mohabir tells his memorable story in *Building Bridges* (London: Hodder & Stoughton 1988).

21. See accounts in, for example, Raymond Bakke, *The Urban Christian* (Marc Europe 1987); Laurie Green, *Power to the Powerless: theology brought to life* (Basingstoke: Marshall Pickering 1987); Peter Stow, op. cit.; and Jim Wallis, *The Call to Conversion* (Lion Publishing 1986).

22. Stow, op. cit., p. 53.

23. Alf McCreary, *Corrymeela: the search for peace* (Belfast: Christian Journals 1975) p. 92.

24. Ibid., p. 103.

25. See ibid., pp. 10–13, for the Healeys' story.

26. Derek Kidner, *A time to mourn and a time to dance: Ecclesiastes and the way of the world* (IVP 1976) p. 101.

SUGGESTED READING

(*a specifically Christian view)

General

John C. Coleman, *The Nature of Adolescence* (Methuen 1980).
* James Dobson, *Preparing for Adolescence* (Kingsway 1982).
* John Halliburton, *Educating Rachel* (SPCK 1987).
Martin Herbert, *Living with Teenagers* (Basil Blackwell 1987).
* John White, *Parents in Pain* (IVP 1980).

The Media

* Geoffrey Barlow & Alison Hill (eds), *Video Violence and Children* (Hodder & Stoughton 1985).
Joanna Bogle (ed.), *The Seductive Sell: a look at today's teenage magazines* (The Responsible Society 1986).
Christopher Dunkley, *Television Today and Tomorrow* (Penguin 1985).
Martin Large, *Who's Bringing Them Up?* (TV Action Group 1980).
* David Porter, *Children at Risk* (Kingsway 1986).
* David Porter, *User's Guide to the Media* (IVP 1988).

Pop and Rock

Peter Everett, *You'll Never Be 16 Again* (BBC 1986).
* Tony Jasper, *Rock Solid* (Word 1986).
John Street, *Rebel Rock* (Blackwell 1986).
* Andrew Thornton, *Youth Music and the Church* (Handsel Press 1985).
* Steve Turner, *Hungry for Heaven* (W. H. Allen & Kingsway 1988).

Sex and Friendship

* Anne Atkins, *Split Image* (Hodder & Stoughton 1987). A good overview on the Bible and sex and gender.

* Richard J. Foster, *Money, Sex & Power* (Hodder & Stoughton 1985).
* Joyce Huggett, *Growth into Love* (IVP 1982).
* Joyce Huggett, *Just Good Friends?* (IVP 1985).
* Joyce Huggett, *Life in a Sex-Mad Society* (IVP 1988).
* Michael Lawson & David Skipp, *Sex 'n That – What's it all About?* (Lion Publishing 1987).
* Elizabeth R. Moberly, *Homosexuality* (James Clarke 1983).
* Lance Pierson, *Sex and Young People* (Kingsway 1987).
* Elaine Storkey, *What's Right with Feminism* (SPCK 1985).
* Lewis Smedes, *Sex in the Real World* (Lion 1979).
* John White, *Eros Defiled* (IVP 1978).

Ethical Issues

* J. H. Channer (ed.), *Abortion & the Sanctity of Human Life* (Paternoster 1985).
* Caroline Collier, *The 20th Century Plague* (Lion 1987). A useful overview on AIDS.
* R. F. R. Gardner, *Abortion: the personal dilemma* (Paternoster 1972).
* Gordon Wenham & Richard Winter, *Abortion: the biblical and medical challenge* (Care Trust 1983).

Stress

* Gaius Davies, *Stress* (Kingsway 1988).

Moses Laufer, *Adolescent Disturbance and Breakdown* (Penguin 1975).

Marilyn Lawrence, *The Anorexia Experience* (Women's Press 1984).

* Michael Lawson, *Facing Anxiety and Stress* (Hodder & Stoughton 1986).
* Michael Lawson, *Facing Depression* (Hodder & Stoughton 1989).

Sheila MacLeod, *The Art of Starvation* (Virago 1981). The author's personal story of battling with anorexia nervosa.

Jill Welbourne & Joan Purgold, *The Eating Sickness* (Harvester 1984).

* Richard Winter, *The Roots of Sorrow* (Marshalls 1985).

Drug Abuse

Drug Abuse: a basic briefing (DHSS 1985).

Annas Dixon, *Dealing with Drugs* (BBC 1987).

*Michael Hastings, *Addiction* (Scripture Union 1988).

Tom Heller, Marjorie Gott & Carole Jeffery, *Drug Use & Misuse* (John Wiley & Son, with The Open University 1987).

*George & Meg Patterson, *The Power Factor: the Key to Conquering Addiction* (Word Books 1986).

*Jackie Pullinger, *Chasing the Dragon* (Hodder & Stoughton 1980).

*M. T. Rall, *Escape to Reality* (Marshall Pickering 1985).

Social Issues

E. Ellis Cashmore, *No Future: youth and society* (Heinemann 1984).

Ernest Cashmore & Barry Troyna (eds), *Black Youth in Crisis* (George Allen & Unwin 1982).

*Leslie J. Francis, *Teenagers and the Church: a profile of church-going youth in the 1980s* (Collins 1984).

*Leslie J. Francis, *Young and Unemployed* (Costello 1984). A survey of unemployed youngsters in London.

*Michael Moynagh, *Making Unemployment Work* (Lion 1985).

*Peter Stow with Mike Fearon, *Youth in the City* (Hodder & Stoughton 1987). A graphic account of Christian outreach in London's East End.

SOME USEFUL ADDRESSES

General

Citizens' Advice Bureaux. The local branch of CAB is a valuable first 'port of call' for queries.

The Girl Guides Association, 17–19 Buckingham Palace Road, London, SW1 0PT (01-834 6242).

National Association of Youth Clubs, PO Box 1, Nuneaton, Warwickshire, CV11 4DB (0203-61921/22).

National Council for Voluntary Youth Services, Wellington House, 29 Albion Street, Leicester, LE1 6GD (0533-471400).

National Youth Bureau, 17–23 Albion Street, Leicester, LE1 6GD (0533-471200). Excellent for information on all social aspects.

The Scout Association, Baden Powell House, Queens Gate, London, SW7 5JS (01-584 7030).

Young Men's Christian Association, 640 Forest Road, London, E17 3DZ (01-520 5599). International organisation for young people of both sexes.

Young Women's Christian Association, Clarendon House, 52 Cornmarket Street, Oxford, OX1 3EJ (0865-726110). Accommodation, meeting social needs, help for unemployed young people.

Social Needs

Centrepoint Night Shelter, 65a Shaftesbury Avenue, London (01-434 2861). For homeless young people, aged 16 to 19.

Catholic Social Services, 150 Brownlow Hill, Liverpool, L3 5RF.

Christian Action, St Peter's house, 308 Kennington Lane, London, SE11 5HY (01-735 2372). Race relations in inner city.

The Christian Alliance, Exton Street, London, SE1 8UE (01-633 0533). Evangelical work, including residential hostels for young people.

Church Action on Poverty, 27 Blackfriars Road, Salford, Greater Manchester, M3 7AQ.

Church Army, Independents Road, Blackheath, London, SE3 9LS (01-318 1226).

Evangelical Christians for Racial Justice, 12 Bell Barn Shopping Centre, Cregoe Street, Birmingham, B15 2D2 (021-622 5799).

Homes for Homeless People (formerly National Cyrenians) 4th Floor, Smithfield House, Digbeth, Birmingham, B5 6BS.

Frontier Youth Trust, Scripture Union House, 130 City Road, London, EC1 2NJ (01-250 1966). Also based in Glasgow. Committed to sharing Christ's love with disadvantaged young people.

Methodist Church Division of Social Responsibility, Central Buildings, Westminster, London, SW1H 9NH (01-222 8010).

National Association for the Care and Resettlement of Offenders, 169 Clapham Road, London, SW9 0PU.

Prison Reform Trust, 59 Caledonian Road, London, N1 9BU (01-276 9815). Includes working for juvenile justice.

Project Fullemploy Ltd., 102 Park Village East, London, NW1 3SP. A multi-ethnic organisation for inner city problems.

Runnymede Trust, 178 North Gower Street, London, NW1 2NB (01-387 8943). Christian organisation for education and research on race and racism.

Salvation Army, Social Services Headquarters, 280 Mare Street, London, E8 1HG (01-985 1181). Christian work includes tracing missing young people.

Shelter, 157 Waterloo Road, London, SE1 8UU.

Personal Needs

The Terrence Higgins Trust, BM AIDS, 53–54 Grays Inn Road, London, WC1 (01-278 3047).

Anorexic Aid, The Priory Centre, 11 Priory Road, High Wycombe, Buckinghamshire. Can advise on local contacts.

Deo Gloria Outreach, 7 London Road, Bromley, Kent, BR1 1BY (01-460 8411: 24-hr service.) Christian ministry arranging counselling in areas of the cults and occult.

Incest Crisis Line, PO Box 32, Northolt, Middlesex, UB5 4JC (01-422 5100).

London Rape Crisis Centre, PO Box 69, London, WC1X 9NJ (01-837 1600).

Men, Women & God, c/o St Peter's Church, Vere Street, London W1M 9HP, plan to appoint a sexual abuse worker by late 1988.

National Association of Victim's Support Schemes, Cranmer House, 39 Brixton Road, London SW9 6DZ (01-735 9166).

The Richmond Fellowship, 8 Addison Road, London, W14 8DL (01-603 6373/4/5). Community mental health, including prevention and after-care. For adolescents: Bristol; Exeter; Liverpool: Belsize Park, London. For students: Manchester; Oxford.

St Christopher's Fellowship, 53 Warwick Road, London, SW5 9HD (01-370 2522/1083). Provision for young people, both in and out of care.

The Samaritans. Local branches for befriending for the suicidal and despairing.

Pregnancy Advice

British Agencies for Adoption and Fostering, 11 Southwark Street, London, SE1 1RO (01-407 8800).

CARE Trust, 21a Down Street, London, W1Y 7DN (01-499 5949). Runs a 'Home Programme', a nationwide network of Christian families who offer accommodation to pregnant teenagers.

The Catholic Child Welfare Council, 1a Steet Street, Abingdon, Oxfordshire, OX14 3JE (0235–21812).

The Church Adoption Society, 282 Vauxhall Bridge Road, London, SW1V 1AJ (01-828 6443/7).

LIFE, 118–120 Warwick Street, Leamington Spa, Warwickshire, CV32 4DG (0926-21587/311667).

National Council for One Parent Families, 255 Kentish Town Road, London, NW5 2LX (01-267 1361).

Society for the Protection of the Unborn Child, 7 Tufton Street, London, SW1P 3QN (01-222 5845).

Alcohol and Drugs

Alcoholics Anonymous, PO Box 1, Stonebow House, Stonebow, York, YO1 2NJ (0904-644026); London enquiries (01-352 3001). Local branches.

Alcohol Concern, 3 Grosvenor Crescent, London, SW1 6LD (01-235 4182).

The Churches Council on Alcohol and Drugs, 4 Southampton Row, London, WC1B 1AA (01-242 6511).

The Coke Hole Trust, 70 Junction Road, Andover, Hants, SP10 3QX (0264 61745). Christian centre for rehabilitation.

Families Anonymous, 310 Finchley Road, London, NW3 7AG (01-731 8060). Self-help groups for families or friends of drug abusers.

Information and Resource Unit on Addiction, 82 West Regent Street, Glasgow, G2 (041-332 0062).

Institute for the Study of Drug Dependence, 1 Hatton Place, London, EC1N 8ND (01-430 1991). Valuable for information.

Life for the World Trust, 24 Boulevard, Weston-Super-Mare, Avon, BS23 1NQ (0934 418083). Christian residential centres for rehabilitation in Bristol, Telford and Norwich.

Narcotics Anonymous, PO Box 417, London, SW10 0RF (01-351 6794). Self-help groups to aid individuals in recovery from *any* form of drug addiction.

Teen Challenge UK, Daldorch House, Catrine, Mauchline, Ayrshire, KA5 6NA (0290 51205). Christian counselling and rehabilitation of young people with drug and other problems.

Other Christian Links

L'Abri Fellowship, Manor House, Greatham, Liss, Hants, GU33 6HF (042 07 436). Residential study centre.

British Youth for Christ, Cleobury Place, Cleobury Mortimer, Kidderminster, Worcs, DY14 8JG (0299 270260). Evangelism and training.

Boy's Brigade (and Girl's Brigade), The Brigade House, Parsons Green, London, SW6 4TH (01-736 8481). Interdenominational, international, uniformed organisations for young people.

Careforce, 130 City Road, London, EC1V 2NJ (01-250 1966). To help evangelical work through young Christian volunteer workers.

Catholic Youth Services, 41 Cromwell Road, London, SW7 2DH (01-589 7550).

Church Youth Fellowships (CYFA and Pathfinders), CPAS Mission at Home, Falcon Court, 32 Fleet Street, London, EC4Y 1DB (01-353 0751). Aiding the Church in evangelism and teaching of young people.

The Corrymeela Community, 8 Upper Crescent, Belfast, BT7 1NT (0232 225008). Christian community of reconciliation.

The Corrymeela Link, PO Box 118, Reading, Berks, RG1 1CL (0734 589800). Support throughout Britain for 'waging peace in Northern Ireland'.